Fodor's 2000
Pocket
San
Francisco

D0685391

Excerpted from *Fodor's San Francisco 2000*

Fodor's Travel Publications, Inc.
New York • Toronto • London • Sydney • Auckland
www.fodors.com/sanfrancisco

Fodor's Pocket San Francisco

EDITOR: Melisse Gelula and Jennifer Levitsky Kasoff

Contributors: Lotus Abrams, Chris Baty, Lisa Hamilton, Denise M. Leto, Daniel Mangin, Amy McConnell, Andy Moore, Marty Olmstead, Sharon Silva

Editorial Production: Brian Vitunic

Maps: David Lindroth, *cartographer;* Bob Blake, Rebecca Baer, *map editors*

Design: Fabrizio La Rocca, *creative director;* Lyndell Brookhouse-Gil, *cover design;* Jolie Novak, *photo editor*

Production/Manufacturing: Mike Costa

Database Production: Martin Walsh

Cover Photo (Golden Gate Bridge): Phil Schermeister/Photographers/Aspen

Copyright

Special Sales

Fodor's Travel Publications are available at special discounts for bulk purchases for sales promotions or premiums. Special editions, including personalized covers, excerpts of existing guides, and corporate imprints, can be created in large quantities for special needs. For more information, contact your local bookseller or write to Special Markets, Fodor's Travel Publications, 201 East 50th Street, New York, NY 10022. Inquiries from Canada should be directed to your local Canadian bookseller or sent to Random House of Canada, Ltd., Marketing Department, 2775 Matheson Boulevard East, Mississauga, Ontario L4W 4P7. Inquiries from the United Kingdom should be sent to Fodor's Travel Publications, 20 Vauxhall Bridge Road, London SW1V 2SA, England.PRINTED IN THE UNITED STATES OF AMERICA

10 9 8 7 6 5 4 3 2 1

Important Tip

Although all prices, opening times, and other details in this book are based on information supplied to us at press time, changes occur all the time in the travel world, and Fodor's cannot accept responsibility for facts that become outdated or for inadvertent errors or omissions. So **always confirm information when it matters,** especially if you're making a detour to visit a specific place.

CONTENTS

On the Road with Fodor's   *v*

Don't Forget to Write *v*

Smart Travel Tips   *ix*

1 **Destination: San Francisco**   *1*

2 **Exploring San Francisco**   *8*

Union Square Area *10*
South of Market (SoMa) and the Embarcadero *15*
The Heart of the Barbary Coast *20*
Chinatown *24*
North Beach and Telegraph Hill *27*
Nob Hill and Russian Hill *30*
Pacific Heights *34*
Civic Center *36*
Mission District *39*
The Castro *41*
The Haight *43*
The Northern Waterfront *46*
The Marina and the Presidio *51*
Golden Gate Park *54*

3 **Dining**   *62*

4 **Lodging**   *90*

5 **Nightlife and the Arts**   *114*

6 **Outdoor Activities and Sports**   *139*

7 **Shopping**   *146*

Index   *170*

Maps

San Francisco *vi–vii*

The Bay Area *viii*

Downtown San Francisco *12–13*

The Castro and the Haight *40*

Northern Waterfront/ Marina and the Presidio *48–49*

Golden Gate Park *57*

Downtown San Francisco Dining *64–65*

Downtown San Francisco Lodging *94–95*

ON THE ROAD WITH FODOR'S

EVERY Y2K TRIP is a significant trip. So if there was ever a time you needed excellent travel information, it's now. Acutely aware of that fact, we've pulled out all stops in preparing *Fodor's Pocket San Francisco 2000.* To direct you to the places that are truly worth your time and money in this important year, we've rallied the team of endearingly picky know-it-alls we're pleased to call our writers. Having seen all corners of San Francisco, they're real experts on the subjects they cover for us.

Smart Travel Tips updater **Chris Baty** lives on the tranquil shores of Oakland's Lake Merritt. A contributor to numerous Fodor's guides, he also writes for the *East Bay Express,* the *San Francisco Weekly,* and his own zine, *Frolic.*

Nightlife, Shopping, and Outdoors updater **Denise M. Leto** is a Berkeley-based writer. In addition to writing and editing books in Fodor's now-defunct budget-travel series, The Berkeley Guides, her work has appeared in the *San Francisco Bay Guardian.* She is the San Francisco editor of a Web site for business travelers.

Daniel Mangin, who wrote the Exploring section, returned to San Francisco in 1998 after a three-year stint in New York as a senior editor for Fodor's. The former arts editor of the *Bay Area Reporter,* he co-wrote Fodor's *Sundays in San Francisco* and edited *Where Do We Take the Kids? California* and Fodor's *California '94–'99.*

Lodging updater **Andy Moore** is a native southern Californian who has lived in San Francisco for more than 20 years. He enjoyed staying at so many hotels in his own home town, though he fears he wore out his white gloves in the line of duty. He is a frequent Fodor's contributor and also an independent filmmaker.

Dining updater **Sharon Silva** has been dining and writing her way through the San Francisco Bay Area for more than 20 years. She is a contributor to *San Francisco* magazine and Microsoft's *sidewalk.com* on-line city service.

Don't Forget to Write

Keeping a travel guide fresh and up-to-date is a big job. So we love your feedback and follow up on all suggestions. Contact the San Fransisco editor at editors@fodors.com or c/o Fodor's, 201 East 50th Street, New York, NY 10022. Have a wonderful trip!

Karen Cure

Karen Cure
Editorial Director

San Francisco

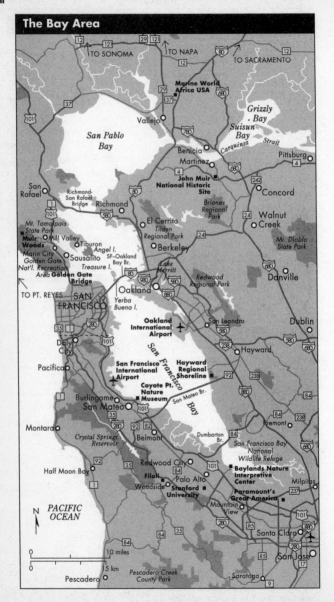

The Bay Area

SMART TRAVEL TIPS

Basic Information on Traveling in San Francisco, Savvy Tips to Make Your Trip a Breeze, and Companies and Organizations to Contact

AIR TRAVEL

BOOKING YOUR FLIGHT
When you book **look for nonstop flights** and **remember that "direct" flights stop at least once.** Try to avoid connecting flights, which require a change of plane.

CARRIERS
➤ MAJOR AIRLINES: **America West** (☎ 800/235–9292) to Oakland, San Francisco. **American** (☎ 800/433–7300) to Oakland, San Francisco. **Continental** (☎ 800/523–3273) to Oakland, San Francisco. **Delta** (☎ 800/221–1212) to Oakland, San Francisco. **Northwest** (☎ 800/225–2525) to San Francisco. **Southwest** (☎ 800/435–9792) to Oakland, San Francisco. **TWA** (☎ 800/892–4141) to San Francisco. **United** (☎ 800/241–6522) to Oakland, San Francisco. **US Airways** (☎ 800/428–4322) to San Francisco.

➤ SMALLER AIRLINES: **Midwest Express** (☎ 800/452–2022) to San Francisco. **Reno Air** (☎ 800/736–6247) to San Francisco.

➤ FROM THE U.K.: **British Airways** (☎ 0345/222–111). **United** (☎ 0845/844–4777). **Virgin Atlantic** (☎ 01293/747–747). **TWA** (☎ 020/8815–0707). **American** (☎ 0345/789–789) flies via New York, Boston, or Chicago, and **Delta** (☎ 0800/414–767) flies via Atlanta or Cincinnati.

CHECK-IN & BOARDING
Assuming that not everyone with a ticket will show up, airlines routinely overbook planes. When that happens, airlines ask for volunteers to give up their seats. In return these volunteers usually get a certificate for a free flight and are rebooked on the next flight out. If there are not enough volunteers, the airline must choose who will be denied boarding. The first to get bumped are passengers who checked in late and those flying on discounted tickets, so **get to the gate and check in as early as possible,** especially during peak periods.

Always **bring a government-issued photo ID to the airport.** You may be asked to show it before you are allowed to check in.

CUTTING COSTS
The least-expensive airfares to San Francisco must usually be purchased in advance and are nonrefundable. It's smart to **call a number of airlines, and when you**

are quoted a good price, book it
on the spot—the same fare may
not be available the next day. Always **check different routings** and
look into using different airports.
Travel agents, especially low-fare
specialists (☞ Discounts & Deals,
below), are helpful.

Consolidators are another good
source. They buy tickets for scheduled international flights at reduced rates from the airlines, then
sell them at prices that beat the
best fare available directly from
the airlines, usually without re-
strictions. Sometimes you can even
get your money back if you need
to return the ticket. Carefully read
the fine print detailing penalties
for changes and cancellations, and
**confirm your consolidator reserva-
tion with the airline.**

When you **fly as a courier** you
trade your checked-luggage space
for a ticket deeply subsidized by a
courier service. There are restric-
tions on when you can book and
how long you can stay.

➤ CONSOLIDATORS: **Cheap Tickets**
(☎ 800/377–1000). **Up & Away
Travel** (☎ 212/889–2345). **Discount Airline Ticket Service** (☎
800/576–1600). **Unitravel** (☎
800/325–2222). **World Travel
Network** (☎ 800/409–6753).

ENJOYING THE FLIGHT
For more legroom **request an
emergency-aisle seat.** Don't sit in
the row in front of the emergency
aisle or in front of a bulkhead,

where seats may not recline. If you
have dietary concerns, **ask for special meals when booking.** These
can be vegetarian, low-cholesterol,
or kosher, for example. On long
flights, try to maintain a normal
routine, to help fight jet lag. At
night **get some sleep.** By day **eat
light meals, drink water** (not alcohol), and **move around the cabin**
to stretch your legs.

FLYING TIMES
Flying time is 6 hours from New
York, 10 hours from London, and
15 hours from Sydney.

HOW TO COMPLAIN
If your baggage goes astray or
your flight goes awry, complain
right away. Most carriers require
that you **file a claim immediately.**

➤ AIRLINE COMPLAINTS: U.S. Department of Transportation **Aviation Consumer Protection
Division** (✉ C-75, Room 4107,
Washington, DC 20590, ☎ 202/
366–2220). **Federal Aviation Administration Consumer Hotline**
(☎ 800/322–7873).

AIRPORTS & TRANSFERS
The major gateway to San Francisco is **San Francisco International Airport (SFO),** just south
of the city, off U.S. 101. Several
domestic airlines serve **Oakland
Airport (OAK),** which is across
the bay but not much farther
from downtown San Francisco
(via I–880 and I–80). Several
domestic airlines serve **San Jose**

International Airport (SJC), which is about 40 mi south of San Francisco. Heavy fog is infamous for causing chronic delays in and out of San Francisco.

➤ AIRPORT INFORMATION: **San Francisco International Airport** (☎ 650/761–0800). **Oakland International Airport** (☎ 510/577–4000). **San Jose International Airport** (☎ 408/277–4759).

TRANSFERS FROM SAN FRANCISCO INTERNATIONAL AIRPORT

A taxi ride from SFO to downtown costs about $30. Airport shuttles are inexpensive and efficient: the SFO Airporter ($10) picks up passengers at baggage claim (lower level) and serves selected downtown hotels. Super-Shuttle ($10 to $12) stops at the upper-level SFO traffic islands and takes you anywhere within the San Francisco city limits. Shuttles to the East Bay (among them Bayporter Express; $20) also depart from SFO's upper-level traffic islands. The cheapest way to get from the airport to San Francisco is via SamTrans Bus 7B (55 minutes; $2.20) and 7F (35 minutes; $3; only one small carry-on bag permitted) to San Francisco or Bus 3X to the Colma BART train station (☞ BART, *below*). Board the SamTrans buses on the upper (departures) level.

To get to downtown San Francisco from the airport, take U.S. 101 north to the Civic Center (9th Street), 7th Street, or 4th Street exit. If you're headed to the Embarcadero or Fisherman's Wharf, take I–280 north (the exit is to the right, just past 3Com Park) and get off at the 4th Street/King Street exit. King Street becomes the Embarcadero a few blocks east of the exit. The Embarcadero winds around the waterfront to Fisherman's Wharf.

TRANSFERS FROM OAKLAND INTERNATIONAL AIRPORT

A taxi from Oakland's airport to downtown San Francisco costs between $30 and $35. America's Shuttle, Bayporter Express, and other shuttles serve major hotels and provide door-to-door service to the East Bay and San Francisco. Marin Door to Door serves Marin County for a flat $50 fee. The best way to get to San Francisco via public transit is to take the AIR BART bus ($2) to the Coliseum/Oakland International Airport BART station (BART fares vary depending on where you're going; the ride to downtown San Francisco costs $2.75).

If you're driving from Oakland International Airport, take Hegenberger Road east to I–880 north to I–80 west.

TRANSFERS FROM SAN JOSE INTERNATIONAL AIRPORT

A taxi from San Jose's airport to downtown San Jose costs about $12 (a taxi to San Francisco costs about $100). South & East Bay Airport Shuttle to downtown San Jose costs $15. VIP Shuttle provides service from the airport in San Jose to downtown San Francisco for $69.

To get to downtown San Jose from the airport, take Airport Boulevard east to Highway 87 south. To get to San Francisco from the airport, take Airport Boulevard east to Highway 87 south to I–280 north.

➤ TAXIS & SHUTTLES: **America's Shuttle** (☎ 510/841–0272). **Bayporter Express** (☎ 415/467–1800). **Marin Door to Door** (☎ 800/540–4815). **SFO Airporter** (☎ 415/495–8404). **South & East Bay Airport Shuttle** (☎ 408/559–9477). **SuperShuttle** (☎ 415/558–8500). **VIP Airport Shuttle** (☎ 408/885–1800 or 800/235–8847).

BART
You can use Bay Area Rapid Transit (BART) trains for city travel and to reach Oakland, Berkeley, and beyond. Trains also travel south from San Francisco as far as Daly City and Colma. Fares range from $1.10 to $4.45; trains run until midnight.

➤ BART: **Bay Area Rapid Transit** (☎ 650/992–2278).

BOAT & FERRY TRAVEL
Several ferry lines run out of San Francisco. Blue and Gold Fleet operates a number of lines, including a Golden Gate cruise, service to Alcatraz and Angel Island, and ferries to Sausalito and Tiburon; tickets can be purchased at Pier 39 and Pier 41. Golden Gate Ferry runs seven days a week to and from Sausalito and Larkspur, leaving from behind the San Francisco Ferry Building on the Embarcadero. The Oakland/Alameda Ferry operates seven days a week between Alameda's Main Street Ferry Building and San Francisco's Pier 39 and the Ferry Building; tickets may be purchased onboard.

➤ FERRY LINES: **Golden Gate Ferry** (☎ 415/923–2000). **Blue and Gold Fleet** (☎ 415/705–5555). **Oakland/Alameda Ferry** (☎ 510/522–3300).

BUS TRAVEL
In San Francisco, San Francisco Municipal Railway, or Muni, operates light rail vehicles, the F Market historic streetcar line, trolley buses, and the world-famous cable cars. Muni has 24-hour service. AC Transit serves the East Bay, and Golden Gate Transit serves Marin County.

On San Francisco buses and streetcars, the fare is $1. Exact change is required, and dollar bills are accepted in the fare boxes. For all Muni vehicles other than cable cars, 90-minute transfers, valid for a single ride, are issued free upon request when you pay your fare. Cable car fares are $2 for a one-way trip. The conductors can make change for up to $20; transfers are neither issued nor accepted.

CUTTING COSTS

A $6 all-day unlimited-travel pass can be purchased on the cable cars. Also, one-day ($6), three-day ($10), or seven-day ($15) Passports can be purchased at several outlets, including the cable car ticket booth at Powell and Market streets and the Visitors Information Center downstairs in Hallidie Plaza. The Passports are also good for discounts, including the museums in Golden Gate Park.

➤ BUS INFORMATION: **AC Transit** (☎ 510/839–2882). **Golden Gate Transit** (☎ 415/923–2000). **San Francisco Municipal Railway System (Muni)** (☎ 415/673–6864).

CABLE CARS

Don't miss traversing some of San Francisco's steepest hills in a small, open-air, clanging cable car. The fare (for one direction) is $2. You can buy tickets onboard (exact change is preferred) or at the cable-car kiosks at Hyde and Beach streets and Powell and Market streets.

CALTRAIN

CalTrain connects San Francisco to Palo Alto, San Jose, and Santa Clara. Trains leave the city at 4th and Townsend streets. One-way fares run $3.75–$5.25. Trips last 1–1½ hours.

➤ CALTRAIN: **CalTrain** (☎ 800/ 660–4287).

CAR RENTAL

Unless you plan on making excursions into Marin County, the East Bay, the South Bay, or the Wine Country, **avoid renting a car.** Let the efficient public transportation system maneuver you through the city's traffic and hills.

Rates in San Francisco begin at $36 a day and $123 a week for an economy car with air-conditioning, an automatic transmission, and unlimited mileage. This does not include tax on car rentals, which is 8.25%. For budget cars, stick to companies like Reliable. If you're looking to rent a BMW, Corvette, or Ford Explorer, try Sunbelt. Major hotels charge as much as $28 per day for parking.

➤ MAJOR AGENCIES: **Alamo** (☎ 800/327–9633; 020/8759–6200 in the U.K.). **Avis** (☎ 800/331–1212; 800/879–2847 in Canada; 02/ 9353–9000 in Australia; 09/525– 1982 in New Zealand). **Budget** (☎ 800/527–0700; 0144/227– 6266 in the U.K.). **Dollar** (☎ 800/ 800–4000; 020/8897–0811 in the U.K., where it is known as Eurodollar; 02/9223–1444 in Australia). **Hertz** (☎ 800/654–3131; 800/263–0600 in Canada; 020/ 8897–2072 in the U.K.; 02/9669– 2444 in Australia; 03/358–6777 in New Zealand). **National InterRent** (☎ 800/227–7368; 0345/222525 in the U.K., where it is known as Europcar Inter-Rent).

CUTTING COSTS

To get the best deal **book through a travel agent who will shop around.** Also **price local car-rental companies,** although the service and maintenance may not be as good as those of a major player. Remember to ask about required deposits, cancellation penalties, and drop-off charges if you're planning to pick up the car in one city and leave it in another. If you're traveling during a holiday period, also make sure that a confirmed reservation guarantees you a car.

➤ LOCAL AGENCIES: **Reliable** (☎ 415/928–4414). **Sunbelt** (☎ 415/ 772–1919).

INSURANCE

When driving a rented car you are generally responsible for any damage to or loss of the vehicle as well as for any property damage or personal injury that you may cause. Before you rent see what coverage your personal auto-insurance policy and credit cards already provide.

For about $15 to $20 per day, rental companies sell protection, known as a collision- or loss-damage waiver (CDW or LDW), that eliminates your liability for damage to the car. Some states, including California, have capped the price of the CDW and LDW. In most states you don't need a CDW if you have personal auto insurance or other liability insurance. However, **make sure you**
have enough coverage to pay for the car. If you do not have auto insurance or an umbrella policy that covers damage to third parties, purchasing liability insurance and a CDW or LDW is highly recommended.

REQUIREMENTS & RESTRICTIONS

In San Francisco you must be 21 to rent a car, and rates may be higher if you're under 25. You'll pay extra for child seats (about $3 per day), which are compulsory for children under five, and for additional drivers (about $2 per day). Non-U.S. residents will need a reservation voucher, a passport, a driver's license, and a travel policy that covers each driver, in order to pick up a car.

SURCHARGES

Before you pick up a car in one city and leave it in another **ask about drop-off charges or one-way service fees,** which can be substantial. Note, too, that some rental agencies charge extra if you return the car before the time specified in your contract. To avoid a hefty refueling fee **fill the tank just before you turn in the car,** but be aware that gas stations near the rental outlet may overcharge.

CAR TRAVEL

Driving in San Francisco can be a challenge because of the hills, one-way streets, and traffic. Take it easy, remember to **curb your**

wheels when parking on hills, and **use public transportation** or **cab it** whenever possible.

Rush hour takes places from 7 to 10 in the morning and 4:30 to 6:30 in the evening. Bridge traffic is erratic but generally remains fairly congested during the day and on weekends.

PARKING

This is a great city for walking and a terrible city for parking. On certain streets, parking is forbidden during rush hours. **Look for the warning signs**; illegally parked cars are towed. Downtown parking lots are often full and most are expensive. (The city-owned Sutter-Stockton, Ellis-O'-Farrell, and 5th and Mission garages have the most reasonable rates in the downtown area.) Finding a spot in North Beach at night can be exceedingly difficult; try the five-level 766 Vallejo Garage.

ROAD MAPS

The detailed Thomas Bros. Maps are sold at most city bookstores. If you're an American Automobile Association or Canadian Automobile Association member, you can pick up maps at the California State Automobile Association. The San Francisco Convention and Visitors Bureau storefront on the lower level of Hallidie Plaza also has maps.

➤ Maps: **California State Automobile Association** (⊠ 150 Van Ness Ave., at Hayes St., ☎ 415/565–2012). San Francisco Convention and Visitors Bureau (⊠ Hallidie Plaza, lower level, 5th and Powell Sts., ☎ 415/974–6900).

CONSUMER PROTECTION

Whenever shopping or buying travel services in San Francisco, **pay with a major credit card** so you can cancel payment or get reimbursed if there's a problem. If you're doing business with a particular company for the first time, **contact your local Better Business Bureau and the attorney general's offices** in your state and the company's home state, as well. Have any complaints been filed? Finally, if you're buying a package or tour, always **consider travel insurance** that includes default coverage (☞ Insurance, *below*).

➤ Local BBBs: **Council of Better Business Bureaus** (⊠ 4200 Wilson Blvd., Suite 800, Arlington, VA 22203, ☎ 703/276–0100, FAX 703/525–8277).

CUSTOMS & DUTIES

When shopping, **keep receipts** for all purchases. Upon reentering the country, **be ready to show customs officials what you've bought.** If you feel a duty is incorrect or object to the way your clearance was handled, note the inspector's badge number and ask to see a supervisor. If the problem isn't resolved, write to the appropriate authorities, beginning with the port director at your point of entry.

IN AUSTRALIA

Australian residents who are 18 or older may bring home $A400 worth of souvenirs and gifts (including jewelry), 250 cigarettes or 250 grams of tobacco, and 1,125 ml of alcohol (including wine, beer, and spirits). Residents under 18 may bring back $A200 worth of goods. Prohibited items include meat products. Seeds, plants, and fruits need to be declared upon arrival.

➤ INFORMATION: **Australian Customs Service** (Regional Director, ✉ Box 8, Sydney, NSW 2001, ☎ 02/9213–2000, FAX 02/9213–4000).

IN CANADA

Canadian residents who have been out of Canada for at least 7 days may bring home C$500 worth of goods duty-free. If you've been away less than 7 days but more than 48 hours, the duty-free allowance drops to C$200; if your trip lasts 24–48 hours, the allowance is C$50. You may not pool allowances with family members. Goods claimed under the C$500 exemption may follow you by mail; those claimed under the lesser exemptions must accompany you. Alcohol and tobacco products may be included in the 7-day and 48-hour exemptions but not in the 24-hour exemption. If you meet the age requirements of the province or territory through which you reenter Canada, you may bring in, duty-free, 1.14 liters (40 imperial ounces) of wine or liquor *or* 24 12-ounce cans or bottles of beer or ale. If you are 16 or older you may bring in, duty-free, 200 cigarettes and 50 cigars. Check ahead of time with Revenue Canada or the Department of Agriculture for policies regarding meat products, seeds, plants, and fruits.

You may send an unlimited number of gifts worth up to C$60 each duty-free to Canada. Label the package UNSOLICITED GIFT—VALUE UNDER $60. Alcohol and tobacco are excluded.

➤ INFORMATION: **Revenue Canada** (✉ 2265 St. Laurent Blvd. S, Ottawa, Ontario K1G 4K3, ☎ 613/993–0534; 800/461–9999 in Canada).

IN NEW ZEALAND

Homeward-bound residents 17 or older may bring back $700 worth of souvenirs and gifts. Your duty-free allowance also includes 4.5 liters of wine or beer; one 1,125-ml bottle of spirits; and either 200 cigarettes, 250 grams of tobacco, 50 cigars, or a combination of the three up to 250 grams. Prohibited items include meat products, seeds, plants, and fruits.

➤ INFORMATION: **New Zealand Customs** (Custom House, ✉ 50 Anzac Ave., Box 29, Auckland, ☎ 09/359–6655, FAX 09/359–6732).

IN THE U.K.

From countries outside the EU, you may bring home, duty-free, 200 cigarettes or 50 cigars; 1 liter of spirits or 2 liters of fortified or sparkling wine or liqueurs; 2 liters of still table wine; 60 ml of perfume; 250 ml of toilet water; plus £136 worth of other goods, including gifts and souvenirs. If returning from outside the EU, prohibited items include meat products, seeds, plants, and fruits.

➤ INFORMATION: **HM Customs and Excise** (⊠ Dorset House, Stamford St., Bromley Kent BR1 1XX, ☎ 020/7202–4227).

IN THE U.S.

Non-U.S. residents ages 21 and older may import into the United States 200 cigarettes or 50 cigars or 2 kilograms of tobacco, 1 liter of alcohol, and gifts worth $100. Meat products, seeds, plants, and fruits are prohibited.

➤ INFORMATION: **U.S. Customs Service** (inquiries, ⊠ 1300 Pennsylvania Ave. NW, Washington, DC 20229, ☎ 202/927–6724; complaints, ⊠ Office of Regulations and Rulings, 1300 Pennsylvania Ave. NW, Washington, DC 20229; registration of equipment, ⊠ Resource Management, 1300 Pennsylvania Ave. NW, Washington, DC 20229, ☎ 202/927–0540).

DINING

RESERVATIONS & DRESS

Reservations are always a good idea: we mention them only when they're essential or are not accepted. Book as far ahead as you can, and reconfirm as soon as you arrive. We mention dress only when men are required to wear a jacket or a jacket and tie.

DISCOUNTS & DEALS

Be a smart shopper and **compare all your options** before making decisions. A plane ticket bought with a promotional coupon from travel clubs, coupon books, and direct-mail offers may not be cheaper than the least expensive fare from a discount ticket agency. And always keep in mind that what you get is just as important as what you save.

DISCOUNT RESERVATIONS

To save money **look into discount-reservations services** with toll-free numbers, which use their buying power to get a better price on hotels, airline tickets, even car rentals. When booking a room, always **call the hotel's local toll-free number** (if one is available) rather than the central reservations number—you'll often get a better price. Always ask about special packages or corporate rates.

➤ AIRLINE TICKETS: ☎ 800/FLY-4–LESS. ☎ 800/FLY–ASAP.

➤ HOTEL ROOMS: **Accommodations Express** (☎ 800/444-7666). **Central Reservation Service (CRS)** (☎ 800/548–3311). **Hotel Reservations Network** (☎ 800/964–6835). **Players Express Vacations** (☎ 800/458-6161). **Quickbook**

(☎ 800/789–9887). **Room Finders USA** (☎ 800/473–7829). **RMC Travel** (☎ 800/245–5738). **Steigenberger Reservation Service** (☎ 800/223–5652).

PACKAGE DEALS

Don't confuse packages and guided tours. When you buy a package, you travel on your own, just as though you had planned the trip yourself. Fly/drive packages, which combine airfare and car rental, are often a good deal. In cities, ask the local visitor's bureau about hotel packages that include tickets to major museum exhibits or other special events.

EMERGENCIES

➤ DOCTORS & DENTISTS: **Davies Medical Center Physician Referral Service** (☎ 415/565–6333). **1-800-DENTIST** (☎ 800/336–8478). **St. Luke's Hospital Physician Referral Service** (☎ 415/821–3627). **San Francisco Dental Society Referral Service** (☎ 415/421–1435).

➤ EMERGENCY SERVICES: For **police, fire, or ambulance,** telephone ☎ 911.

➤ HOSPITALS: **San Francisco General Hospital** (⊠ 1001 Potrero Ave., ☎ 415/206–8000). **Medical Center at the University of California, San Francisco** (⊠ 505 Parnassus Ave., at 3rd Ave., near Golden Gate Park, ☎ 415/476–1000).

➤ 24-HOUR PHARMACIES: **Walgreens Drug Stores** (⊠ 498 Castro, at 18th St., ☎ 415/861–3136; ⊠ 25 Point Lobos, near 42nd Ave. and Geary St., ☎ 415/386–0736; ⊠ 3201 Divisadero St., at Lombard St., ☎ 415/931–6417).

GAY & LESBIAN TRAVEL

San Francisco's credentials as a gay-friendly destination are impeccable. The Castro District is ground zero for the lesbian and gay community, but gay-owned shops and nightlife are sprinkled throughout town.

➤ LOCAL RESOURCES: *Fodor's Gay Guide to the USA* (available in bookstores, or contact Fodor's Travel Publications, ☎ 800/533–6478; $20). The *Bay Area Reporter* (☎ 415/861–5019) is a weekly gay paper. Q San Francisco (www.qsanfrancisco.com/qsf/guide/contents.html) has entertainment listings, accommodation tips, and links to Bay Area organizations.

➤ GAY- AND LESBIAN-FRIENDLY TRAVEL AGENCIES: **Different Roads Travel** (⊠ 8383 Wilshire Blvd., Suite 902, Beverly Hills, CA 90211, ☎ 323/651–5557 or 800/429–8747, ℻ 323/651–3678). **Kennedy Travel** (⊠ 314 Jericho Turnpike, Floral Park, NY 11001, ☎ 516/352–4888 or 800/237–7433, ℻ 516/354–8849). **Now Voyager** (⊠ 4406 18th St., San Francisco, CA 94114, ☎ 415/626–1169 or 800/255–6951, ℻ 415/626–8626). **Yellowbrick Road** (⊠ 1500 W. Balmoral Ave., Chicago, IL 60640, ☎ 773/561–1800 or

800/642–2488, FAX 773/561–4497).
Skylink Travel and Tour (⊠ 1006
Mendocino Ave., Santa Rosa, CA
95401, ☎ 707/546–9888 or 800/
225–5759, FAX 707/546–9891),
serving lesbian travelers.

HEALTH

DIVERS' ALERT
**Do not fly within 24 hours of
scuba diving.**

MEDICAL PLANS
No one plans to get sick while
traveling, but it happens, so **consider signing up with a medical-
assistance company.** Members
get doctor referrals, emergency
evacuation or repatriation, hot
lines for medical consultation,
cash for emergencies, and other
assistance.

INSURANCE
The most useful travel insurance
plan is a comprehensive policy
that includes coverage for trip
cancellation and interruption, default, trip delay, and medical ex-
penses (with a waiver for
preexisting conditions).

Without insurance you will
lose all or most of your money if
you cancel your trip, regardless of
the reason. Default insurance covers you if your tour operator, airline, or cruise line goes out of
business. Trip-delay covers ex-
penses that arise because of bad
weather or mechanical delays.
Study the fine print when compar-
ing policies.

Always **buy travel policies directly
from the insurance company;** if
you buy it from a cruise line, airline, or tour operator that goes
out of business you probably will
not be covered for the agency or
operator's default, a major risk.
Before you make any purchase **re-
view your existing health and
home-owner's policies** to find
what they cover away from home.

➤ TRAVEL INSURERS: In the U.S.
Access America (⊠ 6600 W.
Broad St., Richmond, VA 23230,
☎ 804/285–3300 or 800/284–
8300), **Travel Guard International**
(⊠ 1145 Clark St., Stevens Point,
WI 54481, ☎ 715/345–0505 or
800/826–1300). In Canada **Voyager Insurance** (⊠ 44 Peel Center
Dr., Brampton, Ontario L6T 4M8,
☎ 905/791–8700; 800/668–4342
in Canada).

➤ INSURANCE INFORMATION: In the
U.K. the **Association of British In-
surers** (⊠ 51–55 Gresham St.,
London EC2V 7HQ, ☎ 020/
7600–3333, FAX 020/7696–8999).
In Australia the **Insurance Council
of Australia** (☎ 03/9614–1077,
FAX 03/9614–7924).

LODGING
The lodgings we list are the cream
of the crop in each price category.
We always list the facilities that
are available—but we don't specify whether they cost extra. When
pricing accommodations, always
ask what's included and what
costs extra.

Properties indicated by an ✕🏠 are lodging establishments whose restaurant warrants a special trip.

Assume that hotels operate on the European Plan (EP, with no meals) unless we specify that they use the Continental Plan (CP, with a Continental breakfast daily), Modified American Plan (MAP, with breakfast and dinner daily), or the Full American Plan (FAP, with all meals).

APARTMENT RENTALS

If you want a home base that's roomy enough for a family and comes with cooking facilities **consider a furnished rental.** These can save you money, especially if you're traveling with a group. Home-exchange directories sometimes list rentals as well as exchanges.

➤ INTERNATIONAL AGENTS: **Europa-Let/Tropical Inn-Let** (✉ 92 N. Main St., Ashland, OR 97520, ☎ 541/482–5806 or 800/462–4486, FAX 541/482–0660). **Hometours International** (✉ Box 11503, Knoxville, TN 37939, ☎ 423/690–8484 or 800/367–4668). **Interhome** (✉ 1990 N.E. 163rd St., Suite 110, Miami Beach, FL 33162, ☎ 305/940–2299 or 800/882–6864, FAX 305/940–2911). **Rent-a-Home International** (✉ 7200 34th Ave. NW, Seattle, WA 98117, ☎ 206/789–9377, FAX 206/789–9379). **Vacation Home Rentals Worldwide** (✉ 235 Kensington Ave., Norwood, NJ 07648,

☎ 201/767–9393 or 800/633–3284, FAX 201/767–5510). **Hideaways International** (✉ 767 Islington St., Portsmouth, NH 03801, ☎ 603/430–4433 or 800/843–4433, FAX 603/430–4444; membership $99).

B&BS

San Francisco's bed-and-breakfast inns are quite good, and run the gamut from noteworthy Victorians to funky Haight-Ashbury digs.

➤ RESERVATION SERVICES: **Bed and Breakfast California** (☎ 650/696–1690 or 800/872–4500). **Bed and Breakfast San Francisco** (☎ 415/479–1913 or 800/452–8249).

HOME EXCHANGES

If you would like to exchange your home for someone else's **join a home-exchange organization,** which will send you its updated listings of available exchanges for a year and will include your own listing in at least one of them. It's up to you to make specific arrangements.

➤ EXCHANGE CLUBS: **HomeLink International** (✉ Box 650, Key West, FL 33041, ☎ 305/294–7766 or 800/638–3841, FAX 305/294–1448; $88 per year). **Intervac U.S.** (✉ Box 590504, San Francisco, CA 94159, ☎ 800/756–4663, FAX 415/435–7440; $83 per year).

HOSTELS

No matter what your age you can **save on lodging costs by staying**

at hostels. In some 5,000 locations in more than 70 countries around the world, Hostelling International (HI), the umbrella group for a number of national youth-hostel associations, offers single-sex, dorm-style beds and, at many hostels, couples rooms and family accommodations. Membership in any HI national hostel association, open to travelers of all ages, allows you to stay in HI-affiliated hostels at member rates (one-year membership is about $25 for adults; hostels run about $10–$25 per night). Members also have priority if the hostel is full; they're eligible for discounts around the world, even on rail and bus travel in some countries.

➤ ORGANIZATIONS: **Australian Youth Hostel Association** (✉ 10 Mallett St., Camperdown, NSW 2050, ☎ 02/9565–1699, FAX 02/9565–1325). **Hostelling International—American Youth Hostels** (✉ 733 15th St. NW, Suite 840, Washington, DC 20005, ☎ 202/783–6161, FAX 202/783–6171). **Hostelling International—Canada** (✉ 400–205 Catherine St., Ottawa, Ontario K2P 1C3, ☎ 613/237–7884, FAX 613/237–7868). **Youth Hostel Association of England and Wales** (✉ Trevelyan House, 8 St. Stephen's Hill, St. Albans, Hertfordshire AL1 2DY, ☎ 01727/855215 or 01727/845047, FAX 01727/844126). **Youth Hostels Association of New Zealand** (✉ Box 436, Christchurch, ☎ 03/379–9970, FAX 03/365–4476). Membership in the U.S. $25, in Canada C$26.75, in the U.K. £9.30, in Australia $44, in New Zealand $24.

HOTELS

Most of the major chains have properties in or near San Francisco. All hotels listed have private bath unless otherwise noted.

➤ TOLL-FREE NUMBERS: **Adam's Mark** (☎ 800/444–2326). **Baymont Inns** (☎ 800/428–3438). **Best Western** (☎ 800/528–1234). **Choice** (☎ 800/221–2222). **Clarion** (☎ 800/252–7466). **Colony** (☎ 800/777–1700). **Comfort** (☎ 800/228–5150). **Days Inn** (☎ 800/325–2525). **Doubletree and Red Lion Hotels** (☎ 800/222–8733). **Embassy Suites** (☎ 800/362–2779). **Fairfield Inn** (☎ 800/228–2800). **Forte** (☎ 800/225–5843). **Four Seasons** (☎ 800/332–3442). **Hilton** (☎ 800/445–8667). **Holiday Inn** (☎ 800/465–4329). **Howard Johnson** (☎ 800/654–4656). **Hyatt Hotels & Resorts** (☎ 800/233–1234). **Inter-Continental** (☎ 800/327–0200). **La Quinta** (☎ 800/531–5900). **Le Meridien** (☎ 800/543–4300). **Marriott** (☎ 800/228–9290). **Nikko Hotels International** (☎ 800/645–5687). **Omni** (☎ 800/843–6664). **Quality Inn** (☎ 800/228–5151). **Radisson** (☎ 800/333–3333). **Ramada** (☎ 800/228–2828). **Renaissance Hotels & Resorts** (☎ 800/468–3571). **Ritz-Carlton** (☎ 800/341–3333). **ITT**

Sheraton (☎ 800/325–3535).
Sleep Inn (☎ 800/753–3746).
Westin Hotels & Resorts (☎ 800/
228–3000). Wyndham Hotels &
Resorts (☎ 800/822–4200).

MONEY MATTERS

Prices throughout this guide are
given for adults. Substantially reduced fees are almost always
available for children, students,
and senior citizens. For information on taxes, *see* Taxes, *below.*

ATMS

ATMs are widely available all
throughout San Francisco.

➤ ATM LOCATIONS: **Cirrus** (☎
800/424–7787). **Plus** (☎ 800/
843–7587) for locations in the
U.S. and Canada, or visit your
local bank.

CREDIT CARDS

Throughout this guide, the follow-
ing abbreviations are used: **AE,**
American Express; **D,** Discover;
DC, Diner's Club; **MC,** Master-
Card; and **V,** Visa.

➤ REPORTING LOST CARDS: To report lost or stolen credit cards,
call the following toll-free numbers: **American Express** (☎ 800/
327–2177); **Discover Card** (☎
800/347–2683); **Diners Club** (☎
800/234–6377); **MasterCard** (☎
800/307–7309); and **Visa** (☎ 800/
847–2911).

NATIONAL PARKS

Look into discount passes to save
money on park entrance fees. The

Golden Eagle Pass ($50) gets you
and your companions free admission to all parks for one year.
(Camping and parking are extra.)
Both the Golden Age Passport
($10), for those 62 and older, and
the Golden Access Passport (free),
for travelers with disabilities, enti-
tle holders to free entry to all national parks, plus 50% off fees for
the use of many park facilities and
services. You must show proof of
age and of U.S. citizenship or permanent residency (such as a U.S.
passport, driver's license, or birth
certificate) and, if requesting
Golden Access, proof of disability.
All three passes are available at all
national park entrances where entrance fees are charged. Golden
Eagle and Golden Access passes
are also available by mail.

➤ PASSES BY MAIL: **National Park
Service** (✉ National Capitol Area
Office, 1100 Ohio Dr. SW, Washington, DC 20242, ☎ 202/208–
4747).

PACKING

When packing for a trip here, **prepare for temperature variations.**
Take along sweaters, jackets, and
clothes for layering, bearing in
mind that **the city can be chilly at
any time of the year,** especially
during the summer, when the fog
is apt to descend and stay, and
after dusk. Also bring a raincoat
or umbrella.

Although casual dressing is a hall-
mark of the California lifestyle,

men will need a jacket and tie for many good restaurants in the evening, and women will be more comfortable in something dressier than regulation sightseeing garb.

In your carry-on luggage **bring an extra pair of eyeglasses or contact lenses** and **enough of any medication you take** to last the entire trip. You may also want your doctor to write a spare prescription using the drug's generic name, since brand names may vary from country to country. In luggage to be checked, **never pack prescription drugs or valuables.** To avoid customs delays, carry medications in their original packaging. And don't forget to copy down and carry addresses of offices that handle refunds of lost traveler's checks.

CHECKING LUGGAGE

How many carry-on bags you can bring with you is up to the airline. Most allow two, but not always, so make sure that everything you carry aboard will fit under your seat, and get to the gate early. Note that if you have a seat at the back of the plane, you'll probably board first, while the overhead bins are still empty.

If you are flying internationally, note that baggage allowances may be determined not by piece but by weight—generally 88 pounds (40 kilograms) in first class, 66 pounds (30 kilograms) in business class, and 44 pounds (20 kilograms) in economy.

Airline liability for baggage is limited to $1,250 per person on flights within the United States. On international flights it amounts to $9.07 per pound or $20 per kilogram for checked baggage (roughly $640 per 70-pound bag) and $400 per passenger for unchecked baggage. You can buy additional coverage at check-in for about $10 per $1,000 of coverage, but it excludes a rather extensive list of items, shown on your airline ticket.

Before departure **itemize your bags' contents** and their worth, and label the bags with your name, address, and phone number. (If you use your home address, cover it so that potential thieves can't see it readily.) Inside each bag **pack a copy of your itinerary.** At check-in **make sure that each bag is correctly tagged** with the destination airport's three-letter code. If your bags arrive damaged or fail to arrive at all, file a written report with the airline before leaving the airport.

PASSPORTS & VISAS

➤ U.K. CITIZENS: **U.S. Embassy Visa Information Line** (☎ 01891/200–290; calls cost 49p per minute, 39p per minute cheap rate) for U.S. visa information. **U.S. Embassy Visa Branch** (✉ 5 Upper Grosvenor Sq., London W1A 1AE) for U.S. visa information; send a self-addressed, stamped envelope. Write the **U.S. Consulate General** (✉ Queen's

House, Queen St., Belfast BTI 6EO) if you live in Northern Ireland. Write the **Office of Australia Affairs** (✉ 59th fl., MLC Centre, 19-29 Martin Pl., Sydney NSW 2000) if you live in Australia. Write the **Office of New Zealand Affairs** (✉ 29 Fitzherbert Terr., Thorndon, Wellington) if you live in New Zealand.

PASSPORT OFFICES

The best time to apply for a passport or to renew is during the fall and winter. Before any trip, check your passport's expiration date, and, if necessary, renew it as soon as possible.

➤ AUSTRALIAN CITIZENS: **Australian Passport Office** (☎ 131–232).

➤ CANADIAN CITIZENS: **Passport Office** (☎ 819/994–3500 or 800/567–6868).

➤ NEW ZEALAND CITIZENS: **New Zealand Passport Office** (☎ 04/494–0700 for information on how to apply; 04/474–8000 or 0800/225–050 in New Zealand for information on applications already submitted).

➤ U.K. CITIZENS: **London Passport Office** (☎ 0990/210–410) for fees and documentation requirements and to request an emergency passport.

SAFETY

Those flying with a laptop computer should **be on the lookout for scam artists at the airport.** The ruse typically involves a pair who wait until your computer case is on the X-ray belt, then step through the portal and set off an alarm. While security checks that person for contraband—forcing you to wait—their partner walks off with your computer.

Be wary of solicitations at the airport. Recently, airline travelers have complained of harassment by solicitors, including some who pose as airport officials asking unsuspecting foreign passengers for "airport taxes," which don't exist. Officials have begun cracking down on all charities—some of which are legitimate—by allowing them to accept only checks or credit cards.

Like many cities on the West Coast, San Francisco is a magnet for the down and out. Be prepared to hear some hard luck stories. While most are no threat to the traveler, some street people are more aggressive than others and can persist in their pleas for cash until it feels like harassment. If you feel uncomfortable, don't reach for your wallet.

Use common sense and **avoid certain neighborhoods late at night**— the Tenderloin, Civic Center plaza, parts of the Mission (around 14th Street, for example, or south of 24th to Army Street), and the Lower Haight—especially if you're walking alone.

SIGHTSEEING TOURS

Most tour companies have city tours and excursions to various destinations such as Marin County and the Wine Country, as well as farther-flung areas such as Monterey and Yosemite. City tours generally last 3½ hours and cost $25–$30. Golden Gate Tours offers bay cruises ($38) as well as standard city bus tours. Gray Line has bay cruises and city tours in motorized cable cars ($16–$32); Great Pacific Tours conducts their city tours (starting at $32).

➤ TOUR COMPANIES: **Golden Gate Tours** (☎ 415/788–5775). **Gray Line Tours** (☎ 415/558–9400). **Great Pacific Tour** (☎ 415/626–4499). **Tower Tours** (☎ 415/434–8687).

WALKING TOURS

Tours of San Francisco neighborhoods generally cost $15–$35. Trevor Hailey leads a popular "Cruising the Castro" tour focusing on the history and development of the city's gay and lesbian community. Cookbook author Shirley Fong-Torres and her team lead a tour through Chinatown—"Chinatown with the Wok Wiz," with stops at Chinese herbal markets and art studios. The Chinese Culture Center leads a Chinatown heritage walk and a culinary walk for groups of four or more. City Guides, a free service sponsored by the San Francisco Public Library, has the greatest variety of walks, including historic Market Street, the Palace Hotel, and downtown roof gardens and atriums. Schedules are available at the San Francisco Visitors Center at Powell and Market streets and at library branches. Javawalk explores San Francisco's historic ties to coffee while visiting a few of San Francisco's more than 300 cafés. Victorian Home Walk is a low-impact amble through Pacific Heights and Cow Hollow.

➤ TOUR OPERATORS: **Chinatown with the "Wok Wiz"** (☎ 415/981–8989). **Chinese Culture Center** (☎ 415/986–1822). **City Guides** (☎ 415/557–4266). **Javawalk** (☎ 415/673–9255). **Trevor Hailey** (☎ 415/550–8110). **Victorian Home Walk** (☎ 415/252–9485).

SMOKING

In 1998 the California state legislature passed a law banning smoking in all indoor public spaces, including bars and nightclubs. Smoking is also prohibited in all restaurants and many other public places.

TAXES

The sales tax in San Francisco is 8.5%. The tax on hotel rooms is 14%.

TAXIS

It can be difficult to hail a cab, but you can always duck into the nearest bar or restaurant to call one.

➤ TAXI COMPANIES: **City Wide Cab** (☎ 415/920–0700; San Francisco).

Yellow Cab (☎ 415/626–2345; San Francisco).

TELEPHONES

AREA CODES

The 415 area code is used in San Francisco and Marin County. San Jose and other South Bay cities use 408. Oakland and Berkeley use 510, and a new 925 area code covers the area east of the Oakland Hills. The area code in the Wine Country is 707.

COUNTRY CODES

The country code for the United States is 1.

DIRECTORY & OPERATOR INFORMATION

Dial 411 for information in the 415 area code. Dial 1, the area code, and 555–1212 for information outside the city.

INTERNATIONAL CALLS

Dial 011+country code+city code+number. The country code for Australia is 61; New Zealand, 64; and the United Kingdom, 44. To reach Canada, dial 1+area code+number.

LOCAL CALLS

Dial only the seven-digit phone number (and not the area code) for all local calls.

LONG-DISTANCE CALLS

Competitive long-distance carriers make calling within the United States relatively convenient and let you avoid hotel surcharges. By dialing an 800 number, you can get connected to the long-distance company of your choice.

➤ LONG-DISTANCE CARRIERS: **AT&T** (☎ 800/225–5288). **MCI** (☎ 800/888–8000). **Sprint** (☎ 800/366–2255).

TIPPING

At restaurants a 15% to 20% tip is customary, and the latter is expected at more expensive establishments. The same goes for taxi drivers and bartenders. Tip $1 per bag for bellhops and hotel maids in upscale hotels should get about $1 per day of your stay.

TOURS & PACKAGES

On a prepackaged tour or independent vacation everything is prearranged so you'll spend less time planning—and often get it all at a good price.

BOOKING WITH AN AGENT

Travel agents are excellent resources. But it's a good idea to collect brochures from several agencies because some agents' suggestions may be influenced by relationships with tour and package firms that reward them for volume sales. If you have a special interest **find an agent with expertise in that area**; ASTA (☞ Travel Agencies, *below*) has a database of specialists worldwide.

Make sure your travel agent knows the accommodations and other services of the place they're recommending. Ask about the hotel's location, room size, beds, and whether it has a pool, room service, or programs for children, if you care about these. Has your agent been there in person or sent others whom you can contact?

Do some homework on your own, too: Local tourism boards can provide information about lesser-known and small-niche operators, some of which may sell only direct.

BUYER BEWARE

Each year consumers are stranded or lose their money when tour operators—even large ones with excellent reputations—go out of business. So **check out the operator.** Ask several travel agents about its reputation, and try to **book with a company that has a consumer-protection program.** (Look for information in the company's brochure.) In the United States, members of the National Tour Association and United States Tour Operators Association are required to set aside funds to cover your payments and travel arrangements in case the company defaults. It's also a good idea to choose a company that participates in the American Society of Travel Agent's Tour Operator Program (TOP); ASTA will act as mediator in any disputes between you and your tour operator.

Remember that the more your package or tour includes the better you can predict the ultimate cost of your vacation. Make sure you know exactly what is covered, and **beware of hidden costs.** Are taxes, tips, and transfers included? Entertainment and excursions? These can add up.

➤ TOUR-OPERATOR RECOMMENDATIONS: **American Society of Travel Agents** (☞ Travel Agencies, *below*). **National Tour Association** (NTA, ✉ 546 E. Main St., Lexington, KY 40508, ☎ 606/226–4444 or 800/682–8886). **United States Tour Operators Association** (USTOA, ✉ 342 Madison Ave., Suite 1522, New York, NY 10173, ☎ 212/599–6599 or 800/468–7862, FAX 212/599–6744).

TRAVEL AGENCIES

A good travel agent puts your needs first. Look for an agency that has been in business at least five years, emphasizes customer service, and has someone on staff who specializes in your destination. In addition **make sure the agency belongs to a professional trade organization.** The American Society of Travel Agents (ASTA), with 27,000 agents in some 170 countries, is the largest and most influential in the field. Operating under the motto "Integrity in Travel," it maintains and enforces a strict code of ethics and will step in to help mediate any agent-client disputes if necessary. ASTA also maintains a Web site that includes a directory of agents. Note that if a travel agency is also acting as your tour operator, *see* Buyer Beware *in* Tours & Packages, *above*.

➤ LOCAL AGENT REFERRALS:
American Society of Travel Agents
(ASTA, ☎ 800/965–2782 24-hr
hot line, ☒ 703/684–8319,
www.astanet.com). **Association of
British Travel Agents** (☒ 55–57
Newman St., London W1P 4AH,
☎ 020/7637–2444, ☒ 020/7637–
0713). **Association of Canadian
Travel Agents** (☒ 1729 Bank St.,
Suite 201, Ottawa, Ontario K1V
7Z5, ☎ 613/521–0474, ☒ 613/
521–0805). **Australian Federation
of Travel Agents** (☒ Level 3, 309
Pitt St., Sydney 2000, ☎ 02/
9264–3299, ☒ 02/9264–1085).
**Travel Agents' Association of
New Zealand** (☒ Box 1888,
Wellington 10033, ☎ 04/499–
0104, ☒ 04/499–0786).

VISITOR INFORMATION

The San Francisco Convention and
Visitors Bureau can mail you
brochures, maps, and festivals and
events listings; or try the bureau's
24-hour fax-on-demand service.
For information about the Wine
Country, redwood groves, and
northwestern California, contact
the Redwood Empire Association
Visitor Information Center. For $3
they'll send you a visitors guide; or
pick one up at the center for $1.

➤ CITY: **San Francisco Convention
and Visitors Bureau** (☒ Box
429097, San Francisco 94142-
9097, or lower level of Hallidie
Plaza at Powell Street cable car

turn-around, ☎ 415/974–6900,
☒ 800/220–5747).

➤ WINE COUNTRY: **Redwood Empire Association Visitor Information Center** (☒ 2801 Leavenworth
St., 94133, ☎ 800/200–8334, ☒
415/394–5994).

WEB SITES

**Do check out the World Wide Web
when you're planning.** You'll find
everything from up-to-date
weather forecasts to virtual tours
of famous cities. Fodor's Web site,
www.fodors.com, is a great place
to start your on-line travels.

➤ NEWS AND LISTINGS: **The Gate**
(www.sfgate.com). *The Guardian*
(www.sfbg.com). *SF Weekly*
(www.sfweekly.com).

➤ OFFICIAL SITES: **California Division of Tourism** (gocalif.ca.gov).
National Park Service
(www.nps.gov). **San Francisco
Convention and Visitors Bureau**
(www.sfvisitor.org).

WHEN TO GO

You can comfortably **visit San
Francisco any time of year.** The
climate here always feels Mediterranean and moderate—with a
foggy, sometimes chilly twist. The
temperature rarely drops lower
than 40°F, and anything warmer
than 80°F is considered a heat
wave. Be prepared for rain in winter, especially December and January. Winds off the ocean can add
to the chill factor, so pack warm
clothing. North, east, and south of

the city, summers are warmer. Shirtsleeves and thin cottons are usually fine for the Wine Country.

Peak visiting season in San Francisco runs from May to October. Fall is the busiest time. Plan on calling at least several weeks ahead for weekend dining and lodging reservations.

CLIMATE

➤ FORECASTS: **Weather Channel Connection** (☎ 900/932–8437), 95¢ per minute from a Touch-Tone phone.

The following chart lists the average daily maximum and minimum temperatures for San Francisco.

Jan.	56F	13C	May	64F	17C	Sept.	70F	21C
	46F	8C		51F	10C		56F	13C
Feb.	60F	15C	June	66F	19C	Oct.	69F	20C
	48F	9C		53F	11C		55F	13C
Mar.	61F	16C	July	66F	19C	Nov.	64F	18C
	49F	9C		54F	12C		51F	10C
Apr.	63F	17C	Aug.	66F	19C	Dec.	57F	14C
	50F	10C		54F	12C		47F	8C

FESTIVALS AND SEASONAL EVENTS

➤ JAN.: The **Shrine East-West All-Star Football Classic** takes place at Stanford Stadium (☎ 415/661–0291), 25 mi south of San Francisco in Palo Alto.

➤ JAN.–APR.: **Whale-watching** season peaks during winter, when hundreds of gray whales migrate along the Pacific coast. Contact the **San Francisco Convention and Visitor Information Center** (☎ 415/391–2000).

➤ FEB.: The **Chinese New Year** celebration in San Francisco's Chinese community, North America's largest, lasts for two weeks, culminating with the Golden Dragon Parade. Contact the **Chinese Chamber of Commerce** (☎ 415/982–3071).

➤ MAR.: On the Sunday closest to March 17, San Francisco's **St. Patrick's Day** celebration includes snake races and a parade through downtown.

➤ APR.: The **Cherry Blossom Festival** (☎ 415/563–2313), an elaborate presentation of Japanese culture and customs, winds up with a colorful parade through San Francisco's Japantown.

➤ MAY: Thousands sign up to run the *San Francisco Examiner* **Bay to Breakers Race** (☎ 415/777–7770), a 7½-mi route from bay side to ocean side that's a hallowed San Francisco tradition.

➤ MAY: The **San Francisco International Film Festival** (☎ 415/931–3456) draws scads of film buffs, eager to catch the premieres the festival brings to theaters across town.

➤ MAY–JUNE: **Carnaval** (☎ 415/826–1401), held in the Mission District, includes a parade and street festival.

➤ JUNE: The **North Beach Festival** (☎ 415/989–2220), held every Father's Day weekend, transforms Washington Square Park and Grant Avenue into an Italian marketplace, with food, music, and entertainment.

➤ JUNE: **The Lesbian, Gay, Bisexual, and Transgendered Pride Parade and Celebration** (☎ 415/864–3733) winds its way from the Embarcadero to the Civic Center on the third or fourth Sunday of the month.

➤ JULY: The **Fourth of July** celebration, at Crissy Field in the Presidio, begins in mid-afternoon and has a fireworks display at 9.

➤ JULY: The **Cable Car Bell-Ringing Championship** (☎ 415/673–6864) is on the third Thursday of July at noon in Union Square.

➤ SEPT.: **A La Carte A La Park** (☎ 415/383–9378) is an opportunity

to sample the food of the city's best restaurants in the lush environs of Golden Gate Park.

➤ SEPT.: **Opera in the Park** (☎ 415/864–3330) takes place in Golden Gate Park on the Sunday after Labor Day.

➤ SEPT.: The **San Francisco Blues Festival** (☎ 415/979–5588), on the Great Meadow at Fort Mason, is held on the third weekend of September.

➤ OCT.: Beginning the second weekend of the month, **Fleet Week** celebrates the navy's first day in the port of San Francisco with a Blue Angels air show over the bay.

➤ OCT.: On the Sunday closest to Columbus Day, a parade through North Beach kicks off the **Columbus Day** celebration (☎ 415/434–1492).

➤ DEC.: The San Francisco Ballet's rendition of *The Nutcracker* (☎ 415/703–9400) is an elaborate, memorable production.

➤ DEC.: The annual **Sing-It-Yourself Messiah** (☎ 415/759–3410) takes place at St. Ignatius Church during the second week of the month.

1 Destination: San Francisco

SPLENDOR IN THE FOG

THAT VISITORS WILL ENVY San Franciscans is a given—at least, so say Bay Area residents, who tend to pity anyone who did not have the foresight to settle here. (There's probably never been a time when the majority of the population was native born.) Their self-satisfaction may surprise some, considering how the city has been battered by fires and earthquakes from the 1840s onward, most notably in the 1906 conflagration and again in 1989, when the Loma Prieta earthquake rocked the city's foundations and caused serious damage to the Marina District as well as to numerous local freeways. Since its earliest days San Francisco has been a phoenix, the mythical bird that periodically dies in flame to be reborn in greater grandeur.

Its latest rebirth has occurred in SoMa, the neighborhood south of Market Street, where the Yerba Buena Gardens development has taken shape with the world-class SFMOMA (San Francisco Museum of Modern Art) at its heart—transforming a formerly seedy neighborhood into a magnet of culture. As a peninsula city, surrounded on three sides by water, San Francisco grows from the inside out. Its blighted areas are improved, not abandoned. The museum development's instant success—measured by a huge influx of residents, suburban commuters, and international visitors—perfectly exemplifies this tradition.

In its first life San Francisco was little more than a small, well-situated settlement. Founded by Spaniards in 1776, it was prized for its natural harbor, so commodious that "all the navies of the world might fit inside it," as one visitor wrote. Around 1849 the discovery of gold at John Sutter's sawmill in the nearby Sierra foothills transformed the sleepy little settlement into a city of 30,000. Millions of dollars' worth of gold was panned and blasted out of the hills, the impetus for the development of a western Wall Street. Fueled by the 1859 discovery of a fabulously rich vein of silver in Virginia City, Nevada, San Francisco became the West Coast's cultural fulcrum and major transportation hub, and its population soared to 342,000. In 1869 the transcontinental railway was completed, linking the once-isolated western capital to the East. San Francisco had become a major city of the United States. Of course the boom was not without its price. Gambling and violent crime were rampant, destructive fires flared up on an almost daily basis, and immigrant railroad workers suffered cruelly under multifarious anti-Chinese laws.

San Francisco has long been a bastion of what it likes to refer to as "progressive politics." The Sierra Club, founded here in 1892 by John Muir, has its national headquarters on Polk Street. The turn-of-the-century "yellow journalism" of William Randolph Hearst's *San Francisco Examiner* gave way to such leftish publications as *Mother Jones* magazine and today's left-of-center weekly newspapers. Political contentiousness has sometimes led to violence, most notably in 1978 when the city's liberal mayor, George Moscone, and its first gay supervisor, Harvey Milk, were assassinated by a vindictive right-wing ex-supervisor.

However, despite a boomtown tendency toward raucousness and a sad history of anti-Asian discrimination, the city today prides itself on its tolerance. Consider the makeup of the city's chief administrative body, the 11-member Board of Supervisors. Chinese, Hispanics, gays, blacks, and women have all been representatives. The mix, everybody knows, is what makes San Francisco.

Loose, tolerant, and even licentious are words that are used to describe San Francisco. Bohemian communities thrive here. As early as the 1860s the Barbary Coast—a collection of taverns, whorehouses, and gambling joints along Pacific Avenue close to the waterfront—was famous, or infamous. North Beach, the city's Little Italy, became the home of the beat movement in the 1950s (Herb Caen, the city's best-known columnist, coined the term beatnik). Lawrence Ferlinghetti's City Lights, a bookstore and publishing house that still stands on Columbus Avenue, brought out, among other titles, Allen Ginsberg's *Howl* and *Kaddish*. Across Broadway a plaque identifies the Condor as the site of the nation's first topless and bottomless performances. In the '60s the Free Speech Movement began at the University of California at Berkeley, and Stanford's David Harris, who went to prison for defying the draft, numbered among the nation's most famous student leaders. In October 1965 Allen Ginsberg introduced the term *flower power,* and the Haight-Ashbury district became synonymous with hippiedom, giving rise to such legendary bands as Jefferson Airplane and the Grateful Dead. Thirty years later the Haight's history and its name still draw neo-hippies, as well as new wavers with black lips and blue hair, and some rather menacing skinheads. Transients make panhandling one of Haight Street's major business activities, and the potential for crime and violence after dark has turned many of the liberal residents into unlikely law-and-order advocates. Still, most remain committed to keeping the Haight the Haight.

SOUTHWEST OF THE Haight is the onetime Irish neighborhood known as the Castro, which during the 1970s became identified with gay and lesbian liberation. Castro Street is dominated by the elaborate Castro Theatre, a 1922 vision in Spanish baroque style, which presents first-run art and independent films with occasional revivals of Hollywood film classics. (The grand old pipe organ still plays during intermissions, breaking into "San Francisco" just before the feature begins.) There's been much talk, most of it exaggerated, about how AIDS has "chastened" and "matured" the Castro. The disease *has* spawned the creation of AIDS education, treatment, and care-giving networks, such as Shanti and Project Open Hand, models for the rest of the nation. The Castro is still an effervescent neighborhood, and—as housing everywhere has become more and more scarce—an increasingly mixed one. At the same time, gays, like Asians, are moving out of the ghetto and into neighborhoods all around the city.

In terms of both geography and culture, San Francisco is about as close as you can get to Asia in the continental United States. The first great wave of Chinese immigrants came as railroad laborers. Chinese workers quickly became the target of race hatred and discrimina-

tory laws. Chinatown—which began when the Chinese moved into old buildings that white businesses seeking more fashionable locations had abandoned—developed as a refuge, as much as anything else. It is still a fascinating place to wander and a good bet for late-night food, but it's not the whole story by any means. The Asian community, which now accounts for a fifth of San Francisco's population, reaches into every San Francisco neighborhood and particularly into the Sunset and Richmond districts, west toward the ocean. There was heavy Japanese immigration earlier in this century, but most of it went to southern California, where organized labor had less of a foothold and where there were greater opportunities for Asian workers. Still, San Francisco has its Japantown, with the Japan Center complex and a handful of shops and restaurants. Working hard to establish themselves over the decades, today Asian-Americans of every persuasion are at the highest levels of the city's elected and appointed government and in leadership positions in San Francisco's business, medical, and educational communities.

Geographically, San Francisco is the thumbnail on a 40-mi thumb of land, the San Francisco Peninsula, which stretches northward between the Pacific Ocean and San Francisco Bay. Hemmed in on three sides by water, its land area (less than 50 square mi) is relatively small. The population, at about 750,000, is small, too. Technically speaking, it's only California's fourth-largest city, behind Los Angeles, San Diego, and nearby San Jose. But that statistic is misleading: The Bay Area, extending from the bedroom communities north of Oakland and Berkeley south through the peninsula and the San Jose area, is really one continuous megacity, with San Francisco as its heart.

Not so many centuries ago the area that was to become San Francisco was a windswept, virtually treeless, and, above all, sandy wasteland. Sand even covered the hills. The sand is still there, but—except along the ocean—it's well hidden. City Hall is built on 80 ft of it. The westerly section of the city seems flat only because sand has filled in the contours of the hills.

The hills that remain are spectacular. They provide vistas all over the city. Nothing is more common than to find yourself staring out toward Angel Island or Alcatraz, or across the bay at Berkeley and Oakland. The hills also made cable cars a necessity early on. The city's two bridges, which are almost as majestic as their surroundings, had their 50th birthdays in 1986 and 1987. The Golden Gate Bridge, which crosses to Marin County, got a bigger party, but the San Francisco–Oakland Bay Bridge got a better present: a neck-lace of lights along its spans. They were supposed to be temporary, but the locals were so taken with the glimmer that bridge boosters started a drive to make them permanent. Radio DJs and newspaper columnists put out daily appeals, drivers gave extra quarters to the toll takers, various corporations put up shares, and now—nearly one million dollars later—the lights on the Bay Bridge shine nightly.

First-time visitors to San Francisco sometimes arrive with ideas about its weather gleaned from movie images of sunny California or from a misinformed 1967 song that celebrated "a warm San Franciscan night." Sunny, perhaps. Warm—not likely. That's *southern* California. (A perennially popular T-shirt quotes Mark Twain's alleged remark: "The coldest winter I ever spent was a summer in San Francisco.") Still, it almost never freezes here, and heat waves are equally rare. Most San Franciscans come to love the climate, which is genuinely temperate—sufficiently welcoming for the imposing row of palms down the median of Dolores Street but seldom warm enough for just a T-shirt at night. The coastal stretch of ocean may look inviting, but the surfers you sometimes see along Ocean Beach are wearing wet suits (though the beach can be fine for sunning). And, of course, there's the famous fog—something that tourists tend to find more delightful than do the residents. It's largely a summer phenomenon: San Francisco's real summer begins in September, when the fog lifts and the air warms up for a while. November brings on the rains.

Victorian architecture is as integral to the city as fog and cable cars. Bay-windowed, ornately decorated Victorian houses—the ahistorical, multicolor paint jobs that have become popular make them seem even more ornate—are the city's most distinguishing architectural feature. They date mainly from the latter part of Queen Victoria's reign, 1870 to the turn of the century. In those three decades San Francisco more than doubled in population (from 150,000 to 342,000); the transcontinental railway, linking the once-isolated western capital to the East, had been completed in 1869. That may explain the exuberant confidence of the architecture.

Another measure of the city's exuberance is its many festivals and celebrations. The Lesbian, Gay, Bisexual, and Transgendered Pride Parade and Celebration held each June, vies with the Chinese New Year's Parade, an annual February event, as the city's most elaborate. They both get competition from Japantown's Cherry Blossom Festival, in April; the Columbus Day and St. Patrick's Day parades; Carnaval, held in the Hispanic Mission District in May;

and the May Day march, a labor celebration in a labor town. The mix of ethnic, economic, social, and sexual groups can be bewildering, but the city's residents—whatever their origin—face it with aplomb and even gratitude. Nearly everyone smiles on the fortunate day they arrived on this windy, foggy patch of peninsula.

QUICK TOURS

If you're here for just a short period you need to plan carefully so you don't miss the must-see sights. The following itineraries will help you structure your visit efficiently. See the neighborhood exploring listings in Chapter 2 for more information about individual sights.

Tour One

Start your day downtown at **Union Square.** Explore tiny Maiden Lane (east of the square) before walking north on Grant Avenue through the **Chinatown** gate. From Chinatown continue into **North Beach;** walking north on Columbus Avenue or Grant Avenue you'll pass any number of San Francisco landmarks from the beat era. From Washington Square in North Beach, walk or take Muni Bus 39 to **Coit Tower** atop Telegraph Hill for a fabulous view of the entire bay.

Tour Two

Make reservations for a **boat ride to Alcatraz** (call at least a week in advance during the summer); boats leave from the Fisherman's Wharf area. If you have time after the boat ride, walk west along Beach Street to Hyde Street, where you can either take a ride on the **Powell-Hyde cable car** or explore the historic vessels anchored at the **Hyde Street Pier.**

Tour Three

Explore the eastern half of **Golden Gate Park.** Begin at the **Conservatory of Flowers** and walk west on John F. Kennedy Drive to Tea Garden Drive. Stop into the **M. H. de Young Museum,** which has a very fine collection of American art. The **Asian Art Museum** is part of the de Young complex. After visiting the museums, stop at the **Japanese Tea Garden,** adjacent to the Asian Art Museum, for a soothing cup of tea. If you've still got time, head south across the Music Concourse to the **California Academy of Sciences.**

Tour Four

Begin South of Market (**SoMa**) at **Yerba Buena Gardens.** Across the street is the **San Francisco Museum of Contemporary Art.** From the museum walk up 3rd Street to Market Street and then walk west on Market to the **cable-car terminus** at Powell Street, where you can catch wither the Powell-Hyde or the Powell-Mason cable car to **Nob Hill.** If you walk to Nob Hill, it's about eight blocks, four of which are fairly steep. At the intersection of Powell and California streets walk west one block on California Street. After exploring Nob Hill, slip into the **Tonga Room** (☞ San Francisco's Favorite Bars *in* Chapter 5) at the Fairmont Hotel for a tropical cocktail (if it's earlier than 5 PM, head across California Street to the Top of the Mark at the Mark Hopkins Inter-Continental hotel).

2 Exploring San Francisco

Revised by
Daniel
Mangin

YOU COULD LIVE IN SAN FRANCISCO a
month and ask no greater entertainment
than walking through it," wrote Inez
Hayes Irwin, the author of *The Californiacs,* an effusive 1921
homage to the state of California and the City by the Bay.
Her claim remains true today: As in the '20s, touring on
foot is the best way to experience this diverse metropolis.

The avowedly radical Bound Together Anarchist Book Collective at 1369 Haight Street has been "fighting the good
fight" against capitalism for decades. Whatever your political persuasion, you may find the collection of political
literature intriguing. For a 1960s flashback, head across the
street to Pipedreams, at Number 1376. This head shop keeps
the hippie era alive with merchandise like hookahs, bongs,
and water pipes.

The flashbacks continue as you cross Masonic Avenue. You
can't miss the brightly colored building on the southwest
corner of Haight and Masonic that houses Positively Haight
Street. Here you can purchase tie-dye T-shirts, dresses, and
scarves, along with Grateful Dead paraphernalia.

San Francisco is a relatively small city. About 750,000 residents live on a 46.6-square-mi tip of land between San Francisco Bay and the Pacific Ocean. San Franciscans cherish the
city's colorful past; many older buildings have been spared
from demolition and nostalgically converted into modern offices and shops. Longtime locals rue the sites that got away—
railroad and mining boom–era residences lost in the 1906
earthquake, the baroque Fox Theater, and Playland at the
Beach. Despite acts of God, the indifference of developers,
and the mixed record of the city's planning commission, much
of the architectural and historical interest remains. Bernard
Maybeck, Julia Morgan, Willis Polk, and Arthur Brown Jr.
are among the noteworthy architects whose designs remain.

San Francisco's charms are great and small. First-time vis-
itors won't want to miss Golden Gate Park, the Palace of
Fine Arts, the Golden Gate Bridge, or a cable car ride over
Nob Hill. But a walk down the Filbert Steps or through
Macondray Lane, or a peaceful hour gazing east from Ina
Coolbrith Park can be equally inspiring.

The neighborhoods of San Francisco retain strong cultural, political, and ethnic identities. Locals know this pluralism is the real life of the city. Experiencing San Francisco means visiting the neighborhoods: the colorful Mission District, the gay Castro, countercultural Haight Street, swank Pacific Heights, exotic Chinatown, and still-bohemian North Beach.

Exploring involves navigating a maze of one-way streets and restricted parking zones. San Francisco's famed 40-plus hills can be a problem for drivers who are new to the terrain. Cable cars, buses, and trolleys can take you to or near many attractions.

Union Square Area

Much of San Francisco may feel like a collection of small towns strung together, but the Union Square area bristles with big-city bravado. The city's finest department stores do business here, along with exclusive emporiums like Tiffany & Co. and big-name franchises like Niketown, Planet Hollywood, Borders Books and Music, and the Virgin Megastore. Several dozen hotels within a three-block walk of the square cater to visitors. The downtown theater district and many fine arts galleries are nearby.

Numbers in the margin correspond to numbers on the Downtown San Francisco map.

Sights to See

① Cable car terminus. San Francisco's cable cars were declared National Landmarks (the only ones that move) in 1964. Two of the three operating lines begin and end their runs here. The Powell–Mason line climbs up Nob Hill, then winds through North Beach to Fisherman's Wharf. The Powell–Hyde line also crosses Nob Hill but then continues up Russian Hill and down Hyde Street to Victorian Park, across from the Buena Vista Café and near Ghirardelli Square. Buy your ticket ($2 one-way) on board, at nearby hotels, or at the police/information booth near the turnaround.

Depending on your disposition, you'll find the panhandlers, street preachers, and other regulars at the Powell and Market terminus daunting or diverting. Either way you'll wait

longer here to board a cable car than at any other stop in
the system. If it's just the experience of riding a cable car
you're after, board the less-busy California line at Van Ness
Avenue and ride it down to the Hyatt Regency Hotel. ⊠
Powell and Market Sts.

6 **450 Sutter Street.** Handsome Mayan-inspired designs adorn
the exterior and interior surfaces of this 1928 Art Deco
skyscraper, a masterpiece of terra-cotta and other detailing. ⊠ *Between Stockton and Powell Sts.*

7 **Hallidie Building.** Named for cable car inventor Andrew S.
Hallidie, this 1918 structure is best viewed from across the
street. Willis Polk's revolutionary glass-curtain wall—be-
lieved to be the world's first such facade—hangs a foot beyond the reinforced concrete of the frame. The reflecting
glass, decorative exterior fire escapes that appear to be
metal balconies, and Venetian Gothic cornice are worth not-
ing. Ornamental bands of birds at feeders stretch across the
building on several stories. ⊠ *130 Sutter St., between
Kearny and Montgomery Sts.*

5 **Maiden Lane.** Known as Morton Street in the raffish Barbary Coast era (☞ The Heart of the Barbary Coast, *below*),
this former red-light district reported at least one murder
a week during the late 19th century. After the 1906 fire destroyed the brothels, the street emerged as Maiden Lane,
and it has since become a semi-chic pedestrian mall stretching two blocks, between Stockton and Kearny streets. Traffic is prohibited most days between 11 and 5, when the lane
becomes a patchwork of umbrella-shaded tables. Masses
of daffodils and balloons lend a carnival mood during the
annual spring festival, when throngs of street musicians,
arts-and-crafts vendors, and spectators emerge.

With its circular interior ramp and skylights, the handsome
brick 1948 structure at **140 Maiden Lane,** the only Frank
Lloyd Wright building in San Francisco, is said to have been
his model for the Guggenheim Museum in New York. The
Folk Art International/Boretti Amber/Xanadu (☎ 415/
392–9999) galleries, showcases for Baltic, Latin-American, and African folk art, occupy the space. ⊠ *Between
Stockton and Kearny Sts.*

Downtown San Francisco

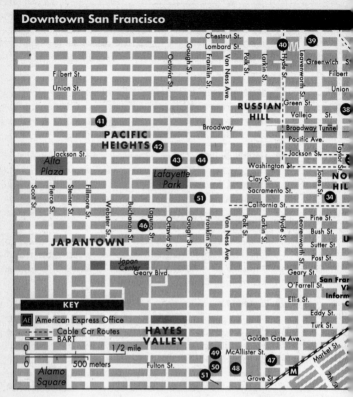

Filbert St.
Union St.
Chestnut St.
Lombard St.
40 **39**
Greenwich St
Filbert
Union

Gough St.
Octavia St.
Franklin St.
Van Ness Ave.
Polk St.
Larkin St.
Hyde St.
Leavenworth St.

41
**PACIFIC
HEIGHTS** **42**
Jackson St.
Alta
Plaza
43 **44**
*Lafayette
Park*
51

Scott St.
Pierce St.
Steiner St.
Fillmore St.
Webster St.
Buchanan St.
Laguna St.
Octavia St.
Gough St.
Franklin St.
Van Ness Ave.
Polk St.
Larkin St.
Hyde St.
Leavenworth St.

JAPANTOWN
46
Japan
Center
Geary Blvd.

**RUSSIAN
HILL**
Broadway
Green St.
Vallejo St.
Broadway Tunnel
Pacific Ave.
Jackson St.
Washington St.
Clay St.
Sacramento St.
California St.
Pine St.
Bush St.
Sutter St.
Post St.

Taylor St.
Jones St.
38
NOI
HIL
34

Geary St.
O'Farrell St.
Ellis St.
Eddy St.
Turk St.

San Fran
V
Inform
C

KEY
AE American Express Office
- - - - Cable Car Routes
BART
0   1/2 mile
0   500 meters

**HAYES
VALLEY**
Golden Gate Ave.
49 McAllister St.
50   **48**
Fulton St.
Alamo
Square
51   Grove St.

47
M
Market St.
7th St.

Ansel Adams Center for Photography, **12**	Center for the Arts, **9**	450 Sutter Street, **6**	Jackson Square, **21**
Broadway and Webster street estates, **47**	Chinatown Gate, **23**	Franklin Street buildings, **45**	Jewish Museum, **16**
Cable Car Museum, **37**	Chinese Culture Center, **24**	Golden Gate Fortune Cookies Co., **26**	Julius' Castle, **33**
Cable car terminus, **1**	City Hall, **48**	Grace Cathedral, **34**	Kong Chow Temple, **27**
California Historical Society, **11**	City Lights Bookstore, **29**	Haas-Lilienthal House, **44**	Lombard Street, **40**
Cartoon Art Museum, **13**	Coit Tower, **32**	Hallidie Building, **7**	Louise M. Davies Symphony Hall, **51**
	Embarcadero Center, **18**	Ina Coolbrith Park, **38**	Maiden Lane, **5**
	Fairmont Hotel, **36**		Mark Hopkins Inter-Continental Hotel, **35**

San Francisco Bay

Noteworthy
Victorians, **46**

Old Chinese
Telephone
Exchange, **28**

Pacific Stock
Exchange, **17**

Palace Hotel, **14**

Portsmouth
Square, **25**

Rincon Center, **15**

Saints Peter and
Paul Catholic
Church, **30**

San Francisco
Art Institute, **39**

San Francisco
Brewing Co., **22**

San Francisco
Museum of
Modern Art
(SFMOMA), **8**

San Francisco
Public Library, **47**

Spreckels
Mansion, **43**

Telegraph Hill, **31**

TIX Bay Area, **4**

Transamerica
Pyramid, **30**

Union Square, **3**

Veterans
Building, **49**

War Memorial
Opera House, **50**

Washington
Square, **28**

Wells Fargo Bank
History
Museum, **19**

Westin St.
Francis Hotel, **2**

Whittier
Mansion, **42**

Yerba Buena
Gardens, **10**

San Francisco Visitors Information Center. A multilingual staff operates this facility below the cable car terminus. Staff members answer questions and provide maps and pamphlets. You can also pick up discount coupons—the savings can be significant, especially for families—and hotel brochures here. ⊠ *Hallidie Plaza, lower level, Powell and Market Sts.,* ☎ *415/391–2000.* ☉ *Weekdays 9–5:30, Sat. 9–3, Sun. 10–2.*

❹ **TIX Bay Area.** This excellent service provides half-price day-of-performance tickets (cash or traveler's checks only) to all types of performing arts events, as well as regular full-price box office services for concerts, clubs, and sporting events (credit cards accepted). Telephone reservations are not accepted for half-price tickets. Half-price tickets for Sunday and Monday events are sold on Saturday. Also sold at the booth is the **Golden Gate Park Explorer Pass** ($14; good for discount admission to the main attractions in Golden Gate Park) and Muni Passports and adult Fast Passes for use on the transit system. ⊠ *Union Square,* ☎ *415/433–7827.* ☉ *Tues.–Thurs. 11–6, Fri.–Sat. 11–7.*

❸ **Union Square.** The heart of San Francisco's downtown since 1850, the 2.6-acre square takes its name from the violent pro-union demonstrations staged here prior to the Civil War. At center stage, the *Victory Monument,* by Robert Ingersoll Aitken, commemorates Commodore George Dewey's victory over the Spanish fleet at Manila in 1898. The 97-ft Corinthian column, topped by a bronze figure symbolizing naval conquest, was dedicated by Theodore Roosevelt in 1903 and withstood the 1906 earthquake. After the earthquake and fire of 1906, the square was dubbed "Little St. Francis" because of the temporary shelter erected for residents of the St. Francis Hotel. Actor John Barrymore, the grandfather of actress Drew Barrymore and a notorious carouser, was among the guests pressed into volunteering to stack bricks in the square. His uncle, thespian John Drew, remarked, "It took an act of God to get John out of bed and the United States army to get him to work."

Once the jewel of downtown, the square looks rather dowdy in the late 20th century, but it is scheduled for a makeover during 2000, so you may find portions of it closed. After the renovations the same kaleidoscope of characters will likely return: office workers sunning and brown-bagging, street musicians, the occasional preacher, and a fair share of homeless people. The square often hosts public events such as fashion shows, free noontime concerts, and noisy demonstrations. Union Square covers a convenient but costly four-level underground garage. For cheaper parking try the nearby Sutter-Stockton Garage. ⊠ *Between Powell, Stockton, Post, and Geary Sts.*

❷ **Westin St. Francis Hotel.** The second-oldest hotel in the city, established in 1904, was conceived by railroad baron and financier Charles Crocker and his associates as a hostelry for their millionaire friends. Swift service and sumptuous surroundings—glass chandeliers, a gilt ceiling, and marble columns—have always been hallmarks of the property. After the hotel was ravaged by the 1906 fire, a larger, more luxurious Italian Renaissance–style residence was opened in 1907 to attract loyal clients from among the world's rich and powerful. The hotel's checkered past includes the ill-fated 1921 bash in the suite of the silent-film comedian Fatty Arbuckle, at which a woman became ill and later died. Arbuckle endured three sensational trials for rape and murder before being acquitted, by which time his career was kaput. In 1975 Sara Jane Moore, standing among a crowd outside the hotel, attempted to shoot then-president Gerald R. Ford. As might be imagined, no plaques commemorate these events in the lobby. The ever-helpful staff will, however, direct you to tea (daily from 3 to 5) or champagne and caviar in the **Compass Rose** (☎ 415/774–0167) lounge. Elaborate Chinese screens, secluded seating alcoves, and soothing background music make this an ideal rest stop after frantic shopping or sightseeing. Reservations are not required, but walk-ins should expect a wait during December and on weekends. ⊠ *335 Powell St., at Geary St.,* ☎ *415/397–7000.*

South of Market (SoMa) and the Embarcadero

Key players in San Francisco's arts scene migrated to the area south of Market Street along the waterfront and west to the Mission District in the 1990s. At the heart of the action in this area, known as SoMa, are the San Francisco Museum of Modern Art (SFMOMA) and the Center for the Arts at Yerba Buena Gardens.

SoMa's emergence as a focal point of San Francisco's cultural life was more than three decades in the making. Huge sections of this former industrial neighborhood were razed in the 1960s to make way for an ambitious multiuse redevelopment project, but squabbling over zoning and other issues delayed construction well into the 1970s. In the meantime, alternative artists and the gay leather crowd set up shop. A dozen bars frequented by the latter group existed alongside warehouses, small factories, and art studios. Although many artists moved farther southwest within SoMa or to the Mission District when urban renewal began in earnest, they still show their work at the Center for the Arts at Yerba Buena Gardens and other galleries. ⊠

SoMa was once known as South of the Slot, in reference to the cable car slot that ran up Market Street. Beginning with tents set up in 1848 by Gold Rush miners, SoMa has played a major role in housing immigrants to the city; except for a brief flowering of elegance during the mid-19th century, these streets were reserved for newcomers who couldn't yet afford to move to another neighborhood. Industry took over most of the area when the 1906 earthquake collapsed most of the homes into their quicksand bases.

Today the mood is upscale industrial. The gentrifying South Park area is where the cybercrowd from *Wired* magazine and other new media tank up on lattes and toasted baguettes. Even with the influx of money, the neighborhood still has an edge that keeps it interesting.

Numbers in the margin correspond to numbers on the Downtown San Francisco map.

Sights to See

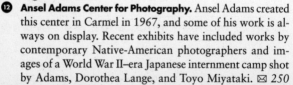

⑫ Ansel Adams Center for Photography. Ansel Adams created this center in Carmel in 1967, and some of his work is always on display. Recent exhibits have included works by contemporary Native-American photographers and images of a World War II–era Japanese internment camp shot by Adams, Dorothea Lange, and Toyo Miyataki. ⊠ *250*

4th St., ☎ *415/495–7000.* 🎫 *$5.* ⊘ *Daily 11–5, 1st Thurs. of month 11–8.*

⓫ **California Historical Society.** The society, founded in 1871, administers a vast repository of Californiana—500,000 photographs, 150,000 manuscripts, thousands of books, periodicals, and paintings as well as Gold Rush paraphernalia. The airy sky-lit space has a central gallery, two adjacent galleries, the North Baker Research Library (accessible by appointment only), and a well-stocked bookstore. ✉ *678 Mission St.,* ☎ *415/357–1848.* 🎫 *$2; free 1st Tues. of month.* ⊘ *Tues.–Sat. 11–5 (galleries close between exhibitions).*

⓭ **Cartoon Art Museum.** Krazy Kat, Zippy the Pinhead, Batman, and other colorful cartoon icons greet you as you walk in the door to the Cartoon Art Museum. In addition to a 12,000-piece permanent collection, a 3,000-volume library, and a CD-ROM gallery, changing exhibits examine everything from the impact of underground comics to the output of women and African-American cartoonists. The museum store carries a wide range of books on popular and underground strips and animated movies. ✉ *814 Mission St., 2nd Floor,* ☎ *415/227–8666.* 🎫 *$5 (pay what you wish 1st Wed. of month).* ⊘ *Wed.–Fri. 11–5, Sat. 10–5, Sun. 1–5.*

❾ **Center for the Arts.** The dance, music, theater, visual arts, films, and videos presented at this facility in Yerba Buena Gardens range from the community-based to the international. At the outdoor performance stage there's often music at midday between April and October. ✉ *701 Mission St.,* ☎ *415/978–2787.* 🎫 *Galleries $5; free 1st Thurs. of month 6 pm–8 pm.* ⊘ *Galleries and box office: Tues.–Sun. 11–6 (until 8 pm 1st Thurs. of month).*

⓲ **Embarcadero Center.** John Portman designed this five-block complex built during the 1970s and early 1980s. Shops and restaurants abound on the first three levels; there's ample office space on the floors above. Louise Nevelson's 54-ft-high black-steel sculpture, *Sky Tree,* stands guard over Building 3 and is among 20-plus artworks throughout the center. The indoor–outdoor **SkyDeck** atop Embarcadero 1 (buy tickets on the ground floor and take the mezzanine-level elevator) provides an enticing 360-degree view of the city and interactive multimedia presentations about San Francisco history and culture. Tickets ($6) to the deck, which is open daily 9:30–9, sometimes sell out days in advance for certain hours; call the hot line for information. ⊠ *Clay St. between Battery St. (Embarcadero 1) and the Embarcadero (Embarcadero 5),* ☎ *800/733–6318 for Embarcadero Center information; 888/737–5933 for SkyDeck hot line; 415/772–0591 for SkyDeck ticket booth.*

Ferry Building. The beacon of the port area, erected in 1896, has a 230-ft clock tower modeled after the campanile of the cathedral in Seville, Spain. On April 18, 1906, the four great clock faces on the tower, powered by the swinging of a 14-ft pendulum, stopped at 5:17—the moment the great earthquake struck—and stayed still for 12 months. The Ferry Building contains the offices of the Port Commission and the World Trade Center, though plans surface periodically for more high-profile uses of this prime real estate. A waterfront promenade that extends from the piers on the north side of the Ferry Building south to the Bay Bridge is great for jogging, in-line skating, watching sailboats on the bay, or enjoying a picnic. Ferries behind the building sail to Sausalito, Larkspur, Tiburon, and the East Bay. ⊠ *The Embarcadero at the foot of Market St.*

⑯ **The Jewish Museum.** The exhibits at this small museum survey Jewish art, history, and culture. The museum was open only sporadically in 1999, but its operators expect to resume regular hours in 2000. ⊠ *121 Steuart St.,* ☎ *415/543–8880.* ☞ *$5; free 1st Mon. of month.* ⊘ *Mon.–Wed. noon–6, Thurs. noon–8, Sun. 11–6. Hrs may vary.*

⑭ **Palace Hotel.** The city's oldest hotel, a Sheraton property, opened in 1875. Fire destroyed the original Palace following the 1906 earthquake despite the hotel's 28,000-gallon reservoir fed by four artesian wells; the current building dates from 1909. President Warren Harding died at the Palace while still in office in 1923, and the body of King Kalakaua of Hawaii spent a night chilling here after he died in San Francisco in 1891. The managers play up this ghoulish past with talk of a haunted guest room. Free **guided tours** (☎ 415/557–4266) of the hotel's grand interior take in the glass-dome Garden Court restaurant, mosaic-tile floors in Oriental-rug designs, and Maxfield Parrish's wall-size painting,

The Pied Piper, the centerpiece of the Pied Piper Bar. Glass cases off the main lobby contain memorabilia of the hotel's glory days. ⊠ *2 New Montgomery St.,* ☎ *415/512–1111.* ☉ *Tours Tues. and Sat. 10:30 am, Thurs. 2 pm.*

⑮ Rincon Center. A sheer five-story column of water resembling a mini-rainstorm stands out as the centerpiece of the indoor arcade at this mostly modern office-retail complex. The lobby of the Streamline Moderne–style former post office on the Mission Street side contains a Works Project Administration **mural by Anton Refregier.** The 27 panels depict California life from the days when Native Americans were the state's sole inhabitants through World War I. Completion of this significant work was interrupted by World War II and political infighting. The latter led to some alteration in Refregier's "radical" historical interpretations; they exuded too much populist sentiment for some of the politicians who opposed the artist. A permanent exhibit below the murals contains photographs and artifacts of life in the Rincon area in the 1800s. ⊠ *Between Steuart, Spear, Mission, and Howard Sts.*

★ ⑧ San Francisco Museum of Modern Art (SFMOMA). Mario Botta designed the striking SFMOMA facility, completed in early 1995, which consists of a sienna brick facade and a central tower of alternating bands of black and white stone. Inside, natural light from the tower floods the central atrium and some of the museum's galleries. A black-and-gray stone staircase leads from the atrium to four floors of galleries. Works by Matisse, Picasso, O'Keeffe, Kahlo, Pollock, and Warhol form the heart of the diverse permanent collection. The photography holdings are also strong. The adventurous programming includes traveling exhibits and multimedia installations. The café, accessible from the street, provides a comfortable, reasonably priced refuge for drinks and light meals. ⊠ *151 3rd St.,* ☎ *415/357–4000.* ⊡ *$8; free 1st Tues. of each month; ½-price entry Thurs. 6–9.* ☉ *Memorial Day–Labor Day, Fri.–Tues. 10–6, Thurs. 10–9; Labor Day–Memorial Day, Fri.–Tues. 11–6, Thurs. 11–9.*

★ ⑩ Yerba Buena Gardens. The centerpiece of the SoMa redevelopment area is the two blocks that encompass the Center for the Arts, Moscone Center, Metreon, and the Rooftop@Yerba Buena Gardens. A circular walkway lined with benches and sculptures surrounds the East Garden, a large patch of green amid this visually stunning complex. The waterfall memorial to Martin Luther King Jr. is the focal point of the East Garden. Powerful streams of water surge over large, jagged stone columns, mirroring the enduring force of King's words that are carved on the stone walls and on glass blocks behind the waterfall. Above the memorial are two restaurants and an overhead walkway to Moscone Convention Center's main entrance. ⊠ *Between 3rd, 4th, Mission, and Folsom Sts.* ◔ *Sunrise–10 pm.*

The Heart of the Barbary Coast

"The slums of Singapore at their foulest, the dens of Shanghai at their dirtiest, the waterfront of Port Said at its vicious worst—none of these backwaters of depravity and vice . . . achieved the depths of utter corruption that typified the 'Barbary Coast.'" So screamed the breathless dust jacket of Herbert Asbury's 1933 account of San Francisco's days as a brawling, extravagant upstart of a town in the latter half of the 19th century.

It was on Montgomery Street, in the Financial District, that Sam Brannan proclaimed the historic gold discovery that took place at Sutter's Mill on January 24, 1848. The Gold Rush brought streams of people from across America and Europe, transforming the onetime frontier town into a cosmopolitan city almost overnight. The population of San Francisco jumped from a mere 800 in 1848 to more than 25,000 in 1850, and to nearly 150,000 in 1870. Along with the prospectors came many other fortune seekers. Saloon keepers, gamblers, and prostitutes all flocked to the so-called Barbary Coast (now Jackson Square and the Financial District). Underground dance halls, casinos, bordellos, and palatial homes sprung up as the city grew into a world-class metropolis. Along with the quick money came a wave of violence. In 1852 the city suffered an average of two murders and one major fire each day. Diarists commented that hardly a day would pass without bloodshed in the city's estimated 500 bars and 1,000 gambling dens, and "houses of ill-repute" proliferated. As one Frenchman noted: "There are also some honest women in San Francisco, but not very many."

By 1917 the excesses of the Barbary Coast had fallen victim to the Red-Light Abatement Act and the ire of church leaders—the wild era was over, and the young city was forced to grow up. Since then the red-light establishments have edged upward to the Broadway strip of North Beach, and Jackson Square evolved into a sedate district of refurbished brick buildings decades ago. Only one remnant of the era remains. Below Montgomery Street between California Street and Broadway, underlying many building foundations along the former waterfront area (long since filled in), lay at least 100 ships abandoned by frantic crews and passengers caught up in gold fever.

Numbers in the margin correspond to numbers on the Downtown San Francisco map.

Sights to See

㉑   **Jackson Square.** Here was the heart of the Barbary Coast of the Gay '90s. Though most of the red-light district was destroyed in the 1906 fire, old redbrick buildings and narrow alleys recall the romance and rowdiness of the early days. Some of the city's earliest business buildings, survivors of the 1906 quake, still stand in Jackson Square, between Montgomery and Sansome streets.

By the end of World War II most of the 19th-century brick structures had fallen on hard times. But in 1951 a group of preservation-minded designers and furniture wholesale dealers selected the area for their showrooms, turning Jackson Square into the interior design center of the West. In 1972 the city officially designated the area—bordered by Columbus Avenue on the west, Broadway and Pacific Avenue on the north, Washington Street on the south, and Sansome Street on the east—San Francisco's first historic district. When property values soared, many of the fabric and furniture outlets fled to Potrero Hill. Advertising agencies, attorneys, and antiques dealers now occupy the Jackson Square area structures.

Restored 19th-century brick buildings line Hotaling Place, which connects Washington and Jackson streets. The lane is named for the head of the **A. P. Hotaling Company whiskey distillery** (✉ 451 Jackson St., at Hotaling Pl.), which was the largest liquor repository on the West Coast in its day. The Italianate Hotaling building reveals little of its infamous past, but a plaque on the side of the structure repeats a famous query about its surviving the quake: IF, AS THEY SAY, GOD SPANKED THE TOWN FOR BEING OVER FRISKY, WHY DID HE BURN THE CHURCHES DOWN AND SAVE HOTALING'S WHISKEY?

The **Ghirardelli Chocolate Factory** once occupied 415 Jackson Street. It was quite common for the upper floors of these buildings to be used as flats by owners and tenants; Domenico Ghirardelli moved his growing business and his family into this property in 1857. By 1894 the enterprise had become large enough to necessitate the creation of what's now **Ghirardelli Square** (☞ The Northern Waterfront, *below*), near Fisherman's Wharf.

With the gentrification, it takes a bit of conjuring to evoke the Barbary Coast days when viewing the Gold Rush–era buildings in the **700 block of Montgomery Street.** But much happened here. Writer Bret Harte wrote his novel *The Luck of Roaring Camp* at Number 730. He toiled as a typesetter for the spunky *Golden Era* newspaper, which occupied Number 732 (now part of the building at Number 744). The late ambulance-chaser extraordinaire, lawyer Melvin Belli, had offices in Numbers 722–728. The lawyer's headquarters were in the former Melodeon Theater at Number 722, where Lotta Crabtree—she of Lotta's Fountain fame—performed. ⊠ *Jackson Square district: Between Broadway and Washington and Montgomery and Sansome Sts.*

⑰ Pacific Stock Exchange. Ralph Stackpole's monumental 1930 granite sculptural groups, *Earth's Fruitfulness* and *Man's Inventive Genius,* flank this imposing structure, which dates from 1915. The Stock Exchange Tower, around the corner at 155 Sansome Street, is a 1930 modern classic by architects Miller and Pfleuger, with an Art Deco gold ceiling and a black marble wall entry. ⊠ *301 Pine St. (tower around corner at 155 Sansome St.).*

㉒ San Francisco Brewing Company. Built in 1907, this pub looks like a museum piece from the Barbary Coast days. An old upright piano sits in the corner under the original stained-glass windows. Take a seat at the mahogany bar and look down at the white-tile spittoon. In an adjacent room look for the handmade copper brewing kettle used to produce a dozen beers—with names like Pony Express—by means of old-fashioned gravity-flow methods. ⊠ *155 Columbus Ave.,* ☏ *415/434–3344.*

㉒ Transamerica Pyramid. The city's most photographed high-rise is the 853-ft Transamerica Pyramid. Designed by William Pereira and Associates in 1972, the initially controversial icon has become more acceptable to most locals over time. A fragrant redwood grove along the east side of the building, replete with benches and a cheerful fountain, is a placid patch in which to unwind. ⊠ *600 Montgomery St.*

㉑ Wells Fargo Bank History Museum. There were no formal banks in San Francisco during the early years of the Gold Rush, and miners often entrusted their gold dust to saloon keepers. In 1852 Wells Fargo opened its first bank in the city, and the company established banking offices in the mother-lode camps, using stagecoaches and pony express riders to service the burgeoning state. (California's population boomed from 15,000 to 200,000 between 1848 and 1852.) The museum displays samples of nuggets and gold dust from mines, a mural-size map of the Mother Lode, original art by western artists Charles M. Russell and Maynard Dixon, mementos of the poet bandit Black Bart ("Po8," as he signed his poems), and an old telegraph machine on which you can practice sending codes. The showpiece is the red Concord stagecoach, the likes of which carried passengers from St. Joseph, Missouri, to San Francisco in three weeks during the 1850s. ⊠ *420 Montgomery St.,* ☏ *415/396–2619.* ▩ *Free.* ☉ *Weekdays 9–5.*

OFF THE
BEATEN
PATH

BANK OF AMERICA BUILDING – This 52-story polished red granite-and-marble building takes up nearly an entire downtown block. A massive, abstract black-granite sculpture designed by the Japanese artist Masayuki commands the corner of the complex at Kearny and California streets. The work has been dubbed the "Banker's Heart" by local wags. On top of the building is the **Carnelian Room** (☏ 415/433–7500), a chic cocktail lounge and restaurant—open daily from 3 to 11 and for Sunday brunch from 10 to 1:30—with a view of the city and the bay. This is a perfect spot for a sunset drink; until mid-afternoon the room is the exclusive Banker's Club, open only to members or by invitation. ✉ *Between California, Pine, Montgomery, and Kearny Sts.*

....

Chinatown

Prepare to have your senses assaulted in Chinatown. Pungent smells waft out of restaurants, fish markets, and produce stands. Good-luck banners of crimson and gold hang beside dragon-entwined lampposts, pagoda roofs, and street signs with Chinese calligraphy. Honking cars chime in with shoppers bargaining loudly in Cantonese or Mandarin. Add to this the visual assault of millions of Chinese-theme goods spilling out of the numerous shops lining Grant Avenue, and you get an idea of what Chinatown is all about.

Bordered roughly by Bush, Kearny, and Powell streets and Broadway, Chinatown is home to one of the largest Chinese communities outside Asia. The area is tightly packed, mostly because housing discrimination in the past kept residents from moving outside Chinatown. There was nowhere to go but up and down—thus the many basement establishments in Chinatown. The two main drags of Chinatown are Grant Avenue, jammed with kitschy tourist shops, and Stockton Street, where the locals do their business.

Many of Chinatown's earliest residents came from southern China, and they brought their cuisine with them. Nowadays Cantonese cooking exists alongside spicier Szechuan, Hunan, and Mandarin specialties. In the windows of markets on Stockton Street and Grant Avenue you can see roast ducks hanging, fish and shellfish swimming in tanks, and strips of Chinese-style barbecued pork shining in pink glaze.

Merely strolling through Chinatown and its many bazaars, restaurants, and curio shops yields endless pleasures, but you'll have a better chance of experiencing an authentic bit of one of the world's oldest cultures by venturing off the beaten track. You needn't be shy about stepping into a temple or an herb shop: Chinatown has been a tourist stop for more than 100 years, and most of its residents welcome guests.

You may find the noisy stretches of Grant Avenue and Stockton Street difficult to navigate, especially by car. Park outside the area, as a spot here is extremely hard to find and traffic is impossible.

Numbers in the margin correspond to numbers on the Downtown San Francisco map.

Sights to See

㉓ Chinatown Gate. Stone lions flank the base of this pagoda-top gate, the official entrance to Chinatown and a symbolic and literal transition from the generic downtown atmosphere to what sometimes seems like another country altogether. The male lion's right front paw rests playfully on a ball; the female's left front paw tickles a cub lying on its back. The lions and the glazed clay dragons atop the largest of the gate's three pagodas symbolize, among other things, wealth and prosperity. The fish whose mouths wrap tightly around the crest of this pagoda symbolize prosperity. The four Chinese characters immediately beneath the pagoda represent the philosophy of Sun Yat-sen (1866–1925), the leader who unified China in the early 20th century. Sun Yat-sen, who lived in exile in San Francisco for a few years, promoted the notion of friendship and peace among all nations based on equality, justice, and goodwill. The vertical characters under the left pagoda read "peace" and "trust," the ones under the right pagoda read "respect" and "love." ⊠ *Bush St. and Grant Ave.*

㉔ Chinese Culture Center. The San Francisco Redevelopment Commission agreed to let Holiday Inn build in Chinatown if the chain provided room for a Chinese culture center. Inside the center are the works of Chinese and Chinese-American artists as well as traveling exhibits relating to Chinese culture. Walking tours ($15; make reservations one week ahead) of historic points in Chinatown take place on most days at 10:30 AM and on Saturday at 2 PM. ⊠ *Holiday Inn, 750 Kearny St., 3rd Floor,* ☎ *415/986–1822.* ⌨ *Free.* ☻ *Tues.–Sun. 10–4.*

㉖ Golden Gate Fortune Cookies Co. The workers at this small factory sit at circular motorized griddles. A dollop of batter drops onto a tiny metal plate, which rotates into an oven. A few moments later out comes a cookie that's pliable and ready for folding. It's easy to peek in for a moment here. A bagful of cookies (with mildly racy "adult" fortunes or more benign ones) costs $2 or $3. ⊠ *56 Ross Alley (north of and parallel to Grant Ave., between Washington and Jackson Sts.),* ☎ *415/781–3956.* ☉ *Daily 10–7.*

㉗ Kong Chow Temple. The god to whom the members of this temple pray represents honesty and trust. You'll often see his image in Chinese stores and restaurants because he's thought to bring good luck in business. Chinese immigrants established the temple in 1851; its congregation moved to this new building in 1977. Take the elevator up to the fourth floor where incense fills the air. Your party can show its respect by placing a dollar or two in the donation box. Amid the statuary, flowers, orange offerings, and richly colored altars (red wards off evil spirits and signifies virility, green symbolizes longevity, and gold majesty) are a couple of plaques announcing that MRS. HARRY S. TRUMAN CAME TO THIS TEMPLE IN JUNE 1948 FOR A PREDICTION ON THE OUTCOME OF THE ELECTION . . . THIS FORTUNE CAME TRUE. The temple's balcony has a good view of Chinatown. ⊠ *855 Stockton St.,* ☎ *415/434–2513.* ▣ *Free.* ☉ *Mon.–Sat. 9–4.*

NEED A   Dim sum is the Chinese version of a smorgasbord. In most
BREAK?   dim sum restaurants women navigating stacked food-service
           carts patrol the premises. Customers choose dishes and the
           cost is stamped on the bill. Dim sum is served at the garishly
           fancy **New Asia** (⊠ 772 Pacific Ave., ☎ 415/391–6666)
           from 9 AM to 3 PM (no credit cards taken for dim sum). More
           down-to-earth and inexpensive, **Kay Cheung Seafood Restau-
           rant** (⊠ 615 Jackson St., ☎ 415/989–6838) serves dim
           sum from 9 to 2:30 (some credit cards taken). It's best to ar-
           rive at both restaurants before 1 PM for the best selection.

㉕ Portsmouth Square. Captain John B. Montgomery raised the American flag here in 1846, claiming the area from Mexico. The square—a former potato patch—was the plaza for Yerba Buena, the Mexican settlement that was renamed San Francisco. Robert Louis Stevenson, the author of *Treasure Island,* lived on the edge of Chinatown in the late 19th century and often visited this site, chatting up the sailors who hung out here. Some of the information he gleaned about life at sea found its way into his fiction. Bruce Porter designed the bronze galleon that sits on top of a 9-ft granite shaft in the northwestern corner of the square in the writer's memory. With its pagoda-shape structures, Portsmouth Square is a favorite spot for morning tai chi. By noon dozens of men huddle around Chinese chess tables, engaged in not-always-legal competition. Undercover police occasionally rush in to break things up, but this ritual, like tai chi, is an established way of life. Children scamper about two playgrounds within the square, which has rest room facilities. ⊠ *Bordered by Walter Lum Pl. and Kearny, Washington, and Clay Sts.*

North Beach and Telegraph Hill

Novelist and resident Herbert Gold calls North Beach "the longest-running, most glorious American bohemian operetta outside Greenwich Village." Indeed, to anyone who's spent some time in its eccentric old bars and cafés or wandered the neighborhood, North Beach evokes everything from the Barbary Coast days to the no-less-sedate beatnik era. Italian bakeries appear frozen in time, homages to Jack Kerouac and Allen Ginsberg pop up everywhere, and the modern equivalent of the Barbary Coast's "houses of ill-repute," strip joints, do business on Broadway.

More than 125,000 Italian-American residents once lived in North Beach, but now only about 2,000, most of them elderly, do. Much of the neighborhood is Chinese now. But walk down narrow Romolo Place (off Broadway east of Columbus) or Genoa Place (off Union west of Kearny) or Medau Place (off Filbert west of Grant) and you can feel the immigrant Italian roots of this neighborhood. North Beach is still the number one place for cappuccino and biscotti, after which you can pop into that icon of the beat era, the City Lights Bookstore (☞ *below*).

Like Chinatown, this is a neighborhood where eating is unavoidable. Several Italian restaurants specialize in family-style full-course meals at reasonable prices; other eateries serve pricey nuovo-Italian dishes. A local delicacy is focaccia—spongy, pizzalike bread slathered with olive oil and chives or tomato sauce—sold fresh from the oven at places like **Danilo Bakery** (✉ 516 Green St., near Grant Ave., ☎ 415/989–1806). Eaten warm or cold, focaccia is the perfect walking food. Many other aromas fill the air: coffee beans, deli meats and cheeses, Italian pastries, and—always—the pungent smell of garlic.

Numbers in the margin correspond to numbers on the Downtown San Francisco map.

Sights to See

★ ㉙ **City Lights Bookstore.** The hangout of beat-era writers—Allen Ginsberg and Lawrence Ferlinghetti among them—remains a vital part of San Francisco's literary scene. ✉ 261 Columbus Ave., ☎ 415/362–8193.

★ ㉜ **Coit Tower.** Among San Francisco's most distinctive skyline sights, the 210-ft-tall Coit Tower stands as a monument to the city's volunteer firefighters. During the early days of the Gold Rush, Lillie Hitchcock Coit (known as Miss Lil) was said to have deserted a wedding party and chased down the street after her favorite engine, Knickerbocker Number 5, while clad in her bridesmaid finery. She was soon made an honorary member of the Knickerbocker Company, and after that always signed her name as "Lillie Coit 5" in honor of her favorite fire engine. Lillie died in 1929 at the age of 86, leaving the city $125,000 to "expend in an appropriate manner . . . to the beauty of San Francisco."

Inside the tower, 19 Depression-era murals depict economic and political life in California. The government commissioned the murals, and the 25 artists who painted them were each paid $38 a week. Some were fresh from art school; others had found no market for art in the early 1930s. The radical Mexican painter Diego Rivera inspired the murals' socialist-realist style, with its biting cultural commentary, particularly about the exploitation of workers. At the time the murals were painted, clashes between management and labor along the waterfront and elsewhere in San Francisco were widespread.

Ride the elevator to the top of the tower to enjoy the view of the San Francisco–Oakland Bay Bridge and the Golden Gate Bridge; due north is famous Alcatraz Island. Artists are often at work in Pioneer Park, at the foot of the tower. For a modest price you can often pick up a small painting of the view you're witnessing. *Discoverer of America,* the impressive bronze statue of Christopher Columbus, was a gift from the local Italian community in 1957. ⊠ *Telegraph Hill Blvd., at Greenwich St. or Lombard St.,* ☏ *415/362–0808.* 🎟 *$3.75.* ⊙ *Daily 10–6.*

Grant Avenue. Originally called Calle de la Fundación, Grant Avenue is the oldest street in the city. Here you'll find dusty bars (the Saloon, Grant & Green Blues Club), odd curio shops, unusual import stores, atmospheric cafés, and authentic Italian delis. A June street fair celebrates the area's Italian culture. ⊠ *Between Columbus Ave. and Filbert St.*

③③ **Julius' Castle.** Every bit as romantic as its name implies, this contemporary Italian restaurant commands a regal view of the bay from its perch high up Telegraph Hill. An official historic landmark, whose founder, Julius Roz, had his craftsmen use materials left over from the 1915 Panama–Pacific International Exposition, the restaurant has a dark-paneled Victorian interior that befits the elegant setting. Ask for a table on the upper floor's outside terrace, where the views are especially dazzling. ⊠ *1541 Montgomery St.,* ☏ *415/392–2222.* ⊙ *Daily 5 pm–10 pm.*

③⓪ **Saints Peter and Paul Catholic Church.** Camera-toting tourists focus their lenses on the Romanesque splendor of what's often called the Italian Cathedral. Completed in 1924, the cathedral has Disney-esque stone-white towers that are local landmarks. On the first Sunday of October a mass followed by a parade to Fisherman's Wharf celebrates the Blessing of the Fleet. Another popular event is the Columbus Day pageant in North Beach. ⊠ *666 Filbert St., at Washington Square.*

③① **Telegraph Hill.** Telegraph Hill got its name from one of its earliest functions—in 1853 it became the location of the first Morse Code Signal Station. Hill residents command some of the best views in the city, as well as the most difficult ascents to their aeries (the flower-lined steps flanking the hill make the climb more than tolerable for visitors, though). The Hill rises from the east end of Lombard Street

to a height of 284 ft and is capped by Coit Tower (☞ *above*).
⊠ *Between Lombard, Filbert, Kearny, and Sansome Sts.*

㉘ Washington Square. Once the daytime social heart of Little Italy, this grassy patch has changed character numerous times over the years. The beats hung out in the 1950s, hippies camped out (sometimes literally) in the 1960s and early 1970s, and nowadays you're just as likely to see kids from Southeast Asia tossing a Frisbee as Italian men or women chatting about their children and the old country. In the morning elderly Asians perform the motions of tai chi, but by mid-morning groups of conservatively dressed Italian men in their 70s and 80s begin to arrive. Choose your line of sight carefully, and you might swear you've drifted back to the early 20th century. Lillie Hitchcock Coit, in another of her shows of affection for San Francisco's firefighters, donated the statue of two firemen with a child they've rescued. ⊠ *Bordered by Columbus Ave. and Stockton, Filbert, and Union Sts.*

Nob Hill and Russian Hill

Once called the Hill of Golden Promise, this area was officially dubbed Nob Hill during the 1870s when "the Big Four"—Charles Crocker, Leland Stanford, Mark Hopkins, and Collis Huntington, who were involved in the construction of the transcontinental railroad—built their hilltop estates. The lingo is thick from this era: Those on the hilltop were referred to as "nabobs" (originally meaning a provincial governor from India) and "swells," and the hill itself was called Snob Hill, a term that survives to this day. By 1882 so many estates had sprung up on Nob Hill that Robert Louis Stevenson called it "the hill of palaces." But the 1906 earthquake and fire destroyed all the palatial mansions, except for portions of the Flood brownstone. Though Nob Hill lacks the quirky flavor of other San Francisco neighborhoods, it exudes history.

Just nine blocks or so from downtown and a few blocks north of Nob Hill, Russian Hill has long been home to old San Francisco families, who were joined during the 1890s by bohemian artists and writers that included Charles Norris, George Sterling, and Maynard Dixon. Several stories explain the origin of Russian Hill's name, though none is known to be true. One legend has it that during San Francisco's early days, the steep hill (294 ft) was the site of a cemetery for unknown Russians; in another version Russian farmers raised vegetables here for Farallon Islands seal hunters; and a third attributes the name to a Russian sailor of prodigious drinking habits who drowned when he fell into a well on the hill. An astounding array of housing covers the hill: simple studios, spiffy pieds-à-terre, Victorian flats, Edwardian cottages, and boxlike condos. The bay views here are some of the city's best.

Numbers in the margin correspond to numbers on the Downtown San Francisco map.

Sights to See

★ ③⑦ **Cable Car Museum.** San Francisco once had more than a dozen cable car barns and powerhouses. The only survivor, this 1907 redbrick structure, an engaging stopover between Russian Hill and Nob Hill, contains photographs, old cable cars, signposts, ticketing machines, and other memorabilia dating from 1873. The massive powerhouse wheels that move the entire cable car system steal the show. The design is so simple it seems almost unreal. You can also go downstairs to the sheave room and check out the innards of the system. A 15-minute video describes how it all works—cables must be replaced every three to six months— or you can opt to read the detailed placards. The gift shop sells cable car paraphernalia. ⊠ *1201 Mason St., at Washington St.,* ☎ *415/474–1887.* ⊡ *Free.* ☉ *Oct.–Mar., daily 10–5; Apr.–Sept., daily 10–6.*

③⑥ **Fairmont Hotel.** The Fairmont's dazzling opening was delayed a year by the 1906 quake, but since then the marble palace has hosted presidents, royalty, movie stars (Valentino, Dietrich), and local nabobs. Things have changed since its early days, however: On the eve of World War I you could get a room for as low as $2.50 per night, meals included. Nowadays, prices go as high as $8,000, which buys a night in the eight-room, Persian art–filled penthouse suite that was showcased regularly in the TV series *Hotel* (the exterior and some of the interiors of the Fairmont also appeared in the show). On Friday and Saturday from 3 to 6 and on

Sunday from 1 to 6, afternoon tea is served in the plush lobby, all done up Gold Rush style with flamboyant rose-floral carpeting, lush red-velvet chairs, gold faux-marble columns, and gilt ceilings. Don't miss an evening cocktail (the ambience demands you order a mai tai) in the kitschy **Tonga Room,** complete with tiki huts, a sporadic tropical rainstorm, and a floating (literally) bandstand.

Across from the Fairmont, **Brocklebank Apartments,** on the northeast corner of Sacramento and Mason streets and viewable only from a distance, is also a media star. In 1958 it was a major location in Alfred Hitchcock's *Vertigo* and in the 1990s popped up in the miniseries *Tales of the City,* Armistead Maupin's homage to San Francisco. ⊠ *950 Mason St.,* ☎ *415/772–5000.*

❸❹ Grace Cathedral. The seat of the Episcopal Church in San Francisco, this soaring Gothic structure, erected on the site of Charles Crocker's mansion, took 53 years to build. The gilded bronze doors at the east entrance were taken from casts of Ghiberti's Gates of Paradise, which are on the baptistery in Florence, Italy. A black-and-bronze stone sculpture of St. Francis by Beniamino Bufano greets visitors as they enter.

The 35-ft-wide Labyrinth, a large, purplish rug, is a replica of the 13th-century stone labyrinth on the floor of the Chartres Cathedral. All are encouraged to walk the ¼-mi-long labyrinth, a ritual based on the tradition of meditative walking. There's also a terrazzo outdoor labyrinth on the church's north side. The AIDS Interfaith Chapel, to the right as you enter Grace, contains a sculpture by the late artist Keith Haring and panels from the AIDS Memorial Quilt. Especially dramatic times to view the cathedral are during Thursday-night evensong (5:15) and during holiday special programs. ⊠ *1100 California St., at Taylor St.,* ☎ *415/749–6300.* ☉ *Sun.–Fri. 7–6, Sat. 8–6.*

❸❽ Ina Coolbrith Park. This attractive park is unusual because it's vertical—that is, rather than one open space, it's composed of a series of terraces up a very steep hill. A poet and Oakland librarian whose uncle was the Mormon prophet Joseph Smith, Ina Coolbrith (1842–1928) introduced Jack London and Isadora Duncan to the world of books. For years she entertained literary greats in her Macondray Lane home near the park. In 1915 she was named poet laureate of California. ⊠ *Vallejo St. between Mason and Taylor Sts.*

★ ❹⓿ **Lombard Street.** The block-long "Crookedest Street in the World" makes eight switchbacks down the east face of Russian Hill between Hyde and Leavenworth streets. Join the line of cars waiting to drive down the steep hill, or walk down the steps on either side of Lombard. You'll take in super views of North Beach and Coit Tower whether you walk or drive—though if you're the one behind the wheel, you'd better keep your eye on the road lest you become yet another of the many folks who ram the garden barriers. ⊠ *Lombard St. between Hyde and Leavenworth Sts.*

❸⓹ **Mark Hopkins Inter-Continental Hotel.** Built on the ashes of railroad tycoon Mark Hopkins's grand estate (which was built at his wife's urging; Hopkins himself preferred to live frugally), this 19-story hotel went up in 1926. A combination of French château and Spanish Renaissance architecture, with noteworthy terra-cotta detailing, it has hosted statesmen, royalty, and Hollywood celebrities. From the 1920s through the 1940s, Benny Goodman, Tommy Dorsey, and other top-drawer entertainers appeared here regularly. The 11-room penthouse was turned into a glass-walled cocktail lounge in 1939: The **Top of the Mark** (☞ Skyline Bars *in* Chapter 5) is remembered fondly by thousands of World War II veterans who jammed the lounge before leaving for overseas duty. Wives and sweethearts watching the ships depart gave the room's northwest nook its name—Weepers' Corner. With its 360-degree views, the lounge is a wonderful spot for a nighttime drink. ⊠ *1 Nob Hill, at California and Mason Sts.,* ☎ *415/392–3434.*

❸⓽ **San Francisco Art Institute.** A Moorish-tile fountain in a tree-shaded courtyard immediately draws the eye as you enter the institute. The highlight of a visit is Mexican master Diego Rivera's *The Making of a Fresco Showing the Building of a City* (1931), in the student gallery to your immediate left once inside the entrance. Rivera himself is in the fresco—his back is to the viewer—and he's surrounded by his assistants. They in turn are surrounded by a construction scene, laborers, and city notables such as sculptor

Robert Stackpole and architect Timothy Pfleuger. *The Making of a Fresco* is one of only three Bay Area murals painted by Rivera.

The older portions of the Art Institute were erected in 1926. Ansel Adams created the school's fine-arts photography department in 1946, and school directors established the country's first fine-arts film program. Notable faculty and alumni have included painter Richard Diebenkorn and photographers Dorothea Lange, Edward Weston, and Annie Leibovitz. **McBean Gallery** exhibits the often provocative works of established artists. ⊠ *800 Chestnut St.,* ☎ *415/771–7020.* 🎟 *Galleries free.* ☉ *McBean Gallery Tues.–Sat. 10–5 (Thurs. until 8), Sun. noon–5; student gallery daily 9–9.*

Pacific Heights

Some of the city's most expensive and dramatic real estate—including mansions and town houses priced at $2 million and up—is in Pacific Heights. Grand Victorians line the streets, and from almost any point in this neighborhood you get a magnificent view.

Numbers in the margin correspond to numbers on the Downtown San Francisco map.

④① **Broadway and Webster Street estates.** Here you can stroll by some magnificent and prestigious addresses: at **2222 Broadway** is a three-story palace with an intricately filigreed doorway built by Comstock silver mine heir James Flood and later donated to a religious order. The Convent of the Sacred Heart purchased the Grant House at **2220 Broadway.** These two buildings, along with a Flood property at **2120 Broadway,** are all used as school quarters. A gold mine heir, William Bourn II, commissioned Willis Polk to build the nearby mansion at **2550 Webster St.**

④⑤ **Franklin Street buildings.** Don't be fooled by the **Golden Gate Church** (⊠ 1901 Franklin St.)—what at first looks like a stone facade is actually redwood painted white. A Georgian-style residence built in the early 1900s for a coffee merchant sits at **1735 Franklin.** On the northeast corner of Franklin and California streets is a **Christian Science**

church; built in the Tuscan Revival style, it's noteworthy for its terra-cotta detailing. The **Coleman House** (✉ 1701 Franklin St.), is an impressive twin-turreted Queen Anne mansion built for a Gold Rush mining and lumber baron. Don't miss the large stained-glass window on the house's north side. ✉ *Franklin St. between Washington and California Sts.*

➍ Haas-Lilienthal House. A small display of photographs on the bottom floor of this elaborate 1886 Queen Anne house, which cost a mere $18,500 to build, makes clear that it was modest compared with some of the giants that fell victim to the 1906 earthquake and fire. The Foundation for San Francisco's Architectural Heritage operates the home, whose carefully kept rooms provide an intriguing glimpse into late 19th-century life. Volunteers conduct one-hour house tours two days a week and an informative two-hour tour of the eastern portion of Pacific Heights on Sunday afternoon. ✉ *2007 Franklin St., between Washington and Jackson Sts.,* ☎ *415/441–3004.* ▣ *$5.* ☉ *Wed. noon–4 (last tour at 3), Sun. 11–5 (last tour at 4). Pacific Heights tours ($5) leave the house Sun. at 12:30.*

➏ Noteworthy Victorians. Two Italianate Victorians (✉ 1818 and 1834 California St.) stand out on the 1800 block of California. A block farther is the Victorian-era **Atherton House** (✉ 1990 California St.), whose mildly daffy design incorporates Queen Anne, Stick-Eastlake, and other architectural elements. The oft-photographed **Laguna Street Victorians,** on the west side of the 1800 block of Laguna Street, cost between $2,000 and $2,600 when they were built in the 1870s. ✉ *California St. between Franklin and Octavia Sts.*

➌ Spreckels Mansion. This estate was built for sugar heir Adolph Spreckels. His wife, Mrs. Alma Spreckels, was so pleased with her house that she commissioned George Applegarth to design another building in a similar vein: the California Palace of the Legion of Honor (☞ Off the Beaten Path: Lincoln Park and the Western Shoreline, *below*). One of the city's great iconoclasts, Alma Spreckels was the model for the bronze figure atop the Victory Monument in Union Square. ✉ *2080 Washington St., at Octavia St.*

42 **Whittier Mansion.** This was one of the most elegant 19th-century houses in the state, with a Spanish-tile roof and scrolled bay windows on all four sides. An anomaly in a town that lost most of its grand mansions to the 1906 quake, the Whittier Mansion was built so solidly that only a chimney toppled over during the disaster. ✉ *2090 Jackson St.*

OFF THE BEATEN PATH

JAPANTOWN– About 1860 a wave of Japanese immigrants arrived in San Francisco, which they called Soko. After the 1906 earthquake and fire, many of these newcomers settled in the Western Addition. By the 1930s they had opened shops, markets, meeting halls, and restaurants and established Shinto and Buddhist temples. Known as Japantown, this area was virtually deserted during World War II when many of its residents, including second- and third-generation Americans, were forced into so-called relocation camps. Today Japantown, or "Nihonmachi," is centered on the southern slope of Pacific Heights, north of Geary Boulevard between Fillmore and Laguna streets. The Nihonmachi Cherry Blossom Festival is celebrated on two weekends in April.

Though Japantown is a relatively safe area, the Western Addition, which lies to the south of Geary Boulevard, can be dangerous; after dark also avoid straying too far west of Fillmore Street just north of Geary.

Civic Center

The Civic Center—the Beaux-Arts complex between McAllister and Grove streets and Franklin and Hyde streets that includes City Hall, the War Memorial Opera House, the Veterans Building, and the old Public Library (slated to become the Asian Art Museum and Cultural Center by 2002)—is a product of the "City Beautiful" movement of the early 20th century. City Hall, completed in 1915, is the centerpiece. The new main library on Larkin Street between Fulton and Grove streets, completed in 1996, is a modern variation on the Civic Center's architectural theme.

Numbers in the margin correspond to numbers on the Downtown San Francisco map.

Sights to See

48 **City Hall.** This masterpiece of granite and marble was modeled after St. Peter's cathedral in Rome. City Hall's bronze and gold-leaf dome, which is even higher than the U.S. Capitol's version, dominates the area. Arthur Brown Jr., who also designed Coit Tower (☞ North Beach and Telegraph Hill, *above*) and the War Memorial Opera House (☞ *below*), was trained in Paris; his classical influences can be seen throughout the structure. The building was spruced up and seismically retrofitted in the late 1990s, but the sense of history remains palpable. Some noteworthy events that have taken place here include the marriage of Marilyn Monroe and Joe DiMaggio (1954), the hosing—down the central staircase—of civil rights and freedom of speech protesters (1960), the murders of Mayor George Moscone and openly gay Supervisor Harvey Milk (1978), the torching of the lobby by angry members of the gay community in response to the light sentence (eight years for manslaughter, eventually reduced to 5½ years) given to the former supervisor who killed them (1979), and the weddings of scores of gay couples in celebration of the passage of San Francisco's Domestic Partners Act (1991). Because the retrofitting project went $50 million over budget, the reopening festivities in 1999 were subdued. If the building's open, inspect the palatial interior, full of grand arches and with a sweeping central staircase. Across Polk Street is **Civic Center Plaza**, with lawns, walkways, seasonal flower beds, a playground, and an underground parking garage. ⊠ *Between Van Ness Ave., Polk, Grove, and McAllister Sts.*

51 **Louise M. Davies Symphony Hall.** Fascinating and still futuristic looking after two decades, this 2,750-seat hall is the home of the San Francisco Symphony. The glass wraparound lobby and pop-out balcony high on the southeast corner are visible from the outside. Henry Moore created the bronze sculpture that sits on the sidewalk at Van Ness Avenue and Grove Street. The hall's 59 adjustable Plexiglas acoustical disks cascade from the ceiling like hanging windshields. Concerts range from typical symphony fare to more unusual combinations, such as pop-rock singer Elvis Costello performing with a string quartet. San Francisco Symphony leader Michael Tilson-Thomas is the only U.S.-born conductor for a major American orchestra. Scheduled tours (75

minutes), which meet at the Grove Street entrance, take in
Davies and the nearby opera house and Herbst Theatre. ✉
201 Van Ness Ave., ☎ *415/552–8338.* 🎫 *Tours $5.* ☉
Tours Mon. (except holidays) hourly 10–2.

㊼ San Francisco Public Library. The main library, which opened
in 1996, is a modernized version of the old Beaux-Arts library that sits just across Fulton Street. The several specialty
rooms include centers for the hearing and visually im-
paired, a gay and lesbian history center, and African-American and Asian centers. Also here are an auditorium, an art
gallery, a café, and a rooftop garden and terrace. The San
Francisco History Room and Archives contains historic photographs, maps, and other city memorabilia. At the library's core is a five-story atrium with a skylight, a grand
staircase, and murals painted by local artists. Tours of the
library are conducted daily at 2:30 PM. ✉ *100 Larkin St.
between Grove and Fulton Sts.,* ☎ *415/557–4400.* ☉ *Mon.
10–6, Tues.–Thurs. 9–8, Fri. 11–5, Sat. 9–5, Sun. noon–5.*

㊾ Veterans Building. Performing and visual arts organizations occupy much of this 1930s structure. **Herbst Theatre**
(☎ 415/392–4400) hosts lectures and readings, classical ensembles, and dance performances, along with City Arts and
Lectures events. Past City Arts guests have included author
Tom Wolfe and playwright-performer Anna Deavere Smith.
Also in the building are two galleries that charge no admission. The street-level **San Francisco Arts Commission
Gallery** (☎ 415/554–6080), open from Wednesday to Saturday between noon and 5, displays the works of Bay Area
artists. The **San Francisco Performing Arts Library and
Museum** (☎ 415/255–4800) occupies part of the fourth
floor. A small gallery hosts interesting exhibitions, though
the organization functions mainly as a library and research
center, collecting, documenting, and preserving the San
Francisco Bay Area's rich performing arts legacy. The
gallery is open during the afternoon from Wednesday
through Saturday. ✉ *401 Van Ness Ave.*

㊿ War Memorial Opera House. During San Francisco's Barbary Coast days, opera goers smoked cigars, didn't check
their revolvers, and expressed their appreciation with "shrill
whistles and savage yells," as one observer put it. All the

old opera houses were destroyed in the quake, but lusty support for opera continued. The opera didn't have a permanent home until the War Memorial Opera House was inaugurated in 1932 with a performance of *Tosca*. Modeled after its European counterparts, the building has a vaulted and coffered ceiling, marble foyer, two balconies, and a huge silver Art Deco chandelier that resembles a sunburst. The San Francisco Opera performs here from September to December, and the San Francisco Ballet from February to May, with December *Nutcracker* performances. ⊠ *301 Van Ness Ave.,* ☎ *415/621–6600.*

Mission District

The sunny Mission district wins out in San Francisco's system of microclimates—it's always the last to succumb to fog. Home to Italian and Irish communities in the early 20th century, the Mission has been heavily Latino since the late 1960s, when immigrants from Mexico and Central America began arriving. Despite its distinctive Latino flavor, the Mission has in recent years seen an influx of Chinese, Vietnamese, Arabic, and other immigrants, along with a young bohemian crowd enticed by cheap rents and the burgeoning arts and entertainment scene. The district is yet again in transition, as gentrification is leading to higher rents, forcing some longtime residents to move. The Mission, still a bit scruffy in patches, lacks some of the glamour of other neighborhoods, but a walk through it provides the opportunity to mix with a heady cross-section of San Franciscans.

The eight blocks of Valencia Street between 16th and 24th streets—what's come to be known as the Valencia Corridor—typifies the neighborhood's diversity. Businesses on the block between 16th and 17th streets, for instance, include an upscale Vietnamese restaurant, a Lebanese restaurant where in the evening belly dancers writhe gracefully, the Bombay Ice Cream parlor (try a scoop of the zesty cardamom ice cream) and adjacent Indian grocery and sundries store, a tattoo parlor, the yuppie-chic Blondie's bar, pizzerias and taquerias, a Turkish restaurant, a sushi bar, bargain and pricey thrift shops, a cyber café, and the Puerto Allegre restaurant (a hole-in-the-wall whose pack-a-punch margaritas locals revere).

Buena Vista Park, **5**

Castro Theatre, **2**

Grateful Dead House, **6**

Haight/ Ashbury intersection, **7**

Harvey Milk Plaza, **1**

Mission Dolores, **9**

Names Project, **3**

Randall Museum, **4**

Red Victorian Peace Center Bed & Breakfast, **8**

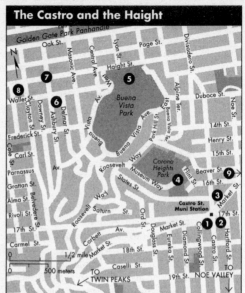

Cinco de Mayo is an important event in the Mission: Music, dance, and parades commemorates the victory, on May 5, 1862, of Mexicans over French troops that had invaded their country. On Memorial Day weekend, the revelers come out in earnest, when **Carnaval** transforms the neighborhood into a northern Rio de Janeiro for three days. Festivities close down several blocks (usually of Harrison Street), where musicians and dancers perform and crafts and food booths are set up. The Grand Carnaval Parade, along 24th and Mission streets, caps the celebration.

Numbers in the margin correspond to numbers on the Castro and the Haight map.

Sights to See

⑨ Mission Dolores. Mission Dolores encompasses two churches standing side by side. Completed in 1791, the small adobe building known as Mission San Francisco de Asís is the oldest standing structure in San Francisco and the sixth of the 21 California missions founded by Father Junípero Serra in the 18th and early 19th centuries. Its ceiling depicts original Ohlone Indian basket designs, executed in vegetable dyes. Frescoes and a hand-painted wooden altar decorate the tiny chapel; some artifacts were brought from Mexico by mule in the late 18th century. There is a small museum, and the pretty little mission cemetery (made famous by a scene in Alfred Hitchcock's *Vertigo*) maintains the graves of mid-19th-century European immigrants. (The remains of an estimated 5,000 Native Americans lie in unmarked graves.) Services are held in both the Mission San Francisco de Asís and next door in the handsome multidome Basilica. ⊠ *Dolores and 16th Sts.,* ☎ *415/621–8203.* ▧ *$2 (audio tour $5).* ☉ *Daily 9–4.*

The Castro

Historians are still trying to discover what drew tens of thousands of gays and lesbians to the San Francisco area during the second half of the 20th century. Some point to the libertarian tradition rooted in Barbary Coast piracy, prostitution, and gambling. Others note that as a huge military embarkation point during World War II, the city was occupied by many single men. Whatever the cause, San Francisco became the city of choice for lesbians and gay men, and in the 1970s Castro Street—nestled at the base of Twin Peaks and just over Buena Vista hill from Haight Street— became its social, cultural, and political center.

The Castro district is one of the liveliest and most welcoming neighborhoods in the city, especially on weekends. Come Saturday and Sunday, the streets teem with folks out shopping, pushing political causes, heading to art films, and lingering in bars and cafés. Cutting-edge clothing stores and gift shops predominate, and pretty young pairs of all genders and sexual persuasions (even heterosexual) hold hands.

Numbers in the margin correspond to numbers on the Castro and the Haight map.

Sights to See

★ ❷ **Castro Theatre.** The neon marquee is the neighborhood's great landmark, and the 1,500-seat theater, which opened in 1922, is the grandest of San Francisco's few remaining movie palaces. Janet Gaynor, who in 1927 won the first Oscar for best actress, worked as an usher here. The

Castro's elaborate Spanish baroque interior is fairly well preserved. Before many shows the theater's pipe organ rises from the orchestra pit and an organist plays pop and movie tunes, usually ending with the Jeanette McDonald standard "San Francisco" (go ahead, sing along). The crowd can be enthusiastic and vocal, talking back to the screen as loudly as it talks to them. Classics like *Who's Afraid of Virginia Woolf?* take on a whole new life, with the assembled beating the actors to the punch and fashioning even snappier comebacks for Elizabeth Taylor. Catch classics, a Fellini film retrospective, or the latest take on same-sex love here. The **Gay and Lesbian Film Festival** (☎ 415/703–8650) takes place in June at the Castro and other venues. ⊠ *429 Castro St.,* ☎ *415/621–6120.*

❶ **Harvey Milk Plaza.** An 18-ft-long rainbow flag, a gay icon, flies above this plaza named for the man who electrified the city in 1977 by being elected to its Board of Supervisors as an openly gay candidate. In the early 1970s, Milk had opened a camera store on the block of Castro Street between 18th and 19th streets. The store became ground zero for his campaign to gain thorough inclusion for gays in the city's social and political life. The liberal Milk hadn't served a full year of his term before he and Mayor George Moscone, also a liberal, were shot in November 1978 at City Hall. The murderer was a conservative ex-supervisor named Dan White, who had recently resigned his post and then become enraged when Moscone wouldn't reinstate him. Milk and White had often been at odds on the board, and White felt that Milk had been part of a cabal to keep him from returning to his post. Milk's assassination shocked the gay community, which became enraged when the famous "Twinkie defense"—that junk food had led to diminished mental capacity—resulted in a manslaughter verdict for White. During the so-called White Night Riot of May 21, 1979, gays and their sympathizers stormed City Hall, torching its lobby and several police cars. Milk, who had feared assassination, had left behind a videotape in which he urged the community to continue the work he began. His legacy is the high visibility of gay people throughout city government. A plaque at the base of the flagpole lists the names of 17 past and present openly gay and lesbian state and local officials. ⊠ *Southwest corner of Castro and Market Sts.*

❸ **Names Project.** Open to anyone who wishes to work on a panel or view the work of those who have, the Names Project has created a gigantic quilt made of more than 42,000 hand-sewn and -decorated panels, pieced together by loved ones to serve as a memorial to those who have died of AIDS. People come from all over the country to this storefront as a labor of love and grief; others have sent panels here by mail. New additions to the quilt are always on display. Next door to the Project is Under One Roof, a gift shop that funnels its profits to area AIDS organizations. ⊠ *2362 Market St.,* ☎ *415/863–1966.* ⊘ *Mon.–Sat. noon–7, Sun. noon–6; quilting bee Wed. 7 pm–10 pm and 2nd Sat. of month 1–5.*

Ⓒ ❹ **Randall Museum.** The highlight of this facility is the educational animal room, popular with children, where you can observe birds, lizards, snakes, spiders, and other creatures that cannot be released to the wild because of injury or other problems. Also here are a greenhouse, woodworking and ceramics studios, and a theater. The Randall sits on 16 acres of public land; the hill that overlooks the museum is variously known as Red Rock, Museum Hill, and, correctly, Corona Heights. ⊠ *199 Museum Way, off Roosevelt Way,* ☎ *415/554–9600.* ⊠ *Free.* ⊘ *Tues.–Sat. 10–5; animal room 10–1 and 2–5.*

The Haight

A continuing fascination with events of the 1960s lead many visitors to the setting of the Summer of Love, a neighborhood known as "the Haight," just east of Golden Gate Park. Despite a fair amount of gentrification, this is still home to a wandering tribe of Deadheads, with anarchist book collectives and shops selling incense and tie-dye T-shirts.

Once an enclave of large middle-class families of European immigrants, the Haight began to change during the late 1950s and early 1960s. Families were fleeing to the suburbs, and the big old Victorians were deteriorating or being chopped up into cheap housing. Young people found the neighborhood an affordable spot in which they could live according to new precepts. By 1966 the Haight had become a hot spot for rock bands like the Grateful Dead—whose members moved into a big Victorian near the corner of Haight and Ashbury streets—and Jefferson Airplane, whose grand mansion was north of the district at 2400 Fulton Street.

The Haight's famous political spirit—it was the first neighborhood in the nation to lead a freeway revolt, and it continues to host regular boycotts against chain stores—exists alongside some of the finest Victorian-lined streets in the city. The area is also known for its vintage merchandise, including clothes, records, and books, and miscellany like crystals, jewelry, and candles.

The avowedly radical Bound Together Anarchist Book Collective at 1369 Haight Street has been "fighting the good fight" against capitalism for decades. Whatever your political persuasion, you may find the collection of political literature intriguing. For a 1960s flashback, head across the street to Pipedreams, at Number 1376. This head shop keeps the hippie era alive with merchandise like hookahs and bongs.

The flashbacks continue as you cross Masonic Avenue. You can't miss the brightly colored building on the southwest corner of Haight and Masonic that houses Positively Haight Street. Here you can purchase tie-dye T-shirts, dresses, and scarves, along with Grateful Dead paraphernalia.

Numbers in the margin correspond to numbers on the Castro and the Haight map.

Sights to See

⑤ Buena Vista Park. Great city views can be had from this eucalyptus-filled park. Although it's not exactly sedate (drug deals are common), it's a very pretty park, especially on a sunny day. Don't wander here after dark. ⊠ *Haight St. between Lyon St. and Buena Vista Ave. W.*

⑥ Grateful Dead house. Nothing unusual marks the house of legend. On the outside, it's just one more well-kept Victorian on a street that's full of them—but true fans of the Dead may find some inspiration here. The three-story house (closed to the public) is tastefully painted in sedate mauves, tans, and teals (no bright tie-dye colors). ⊠ *710 Ashbury St., just past Waller St.*

❼ Haight/Ashbury intersection. On October 6, 1967, hippies took over the intersection of Haight and Ashbury streets to proclaim the "Death of Hip." If they thought hip was dead then, they'd find absolute confirmation of it today, what with the Gap holding court on one quadrant of the famed corner. (There's a Ben and Jerry's, too, an environmentally conscious enterprise whose ethos some might say shows traces of the hippie philosophy.)

Everyone knows the Summer of Love had something to do with free love and LSD, but the drug and other excesses of the Summer of Love have tended to obscure the residents' serious attempts to create an America more spiritually oriented, more environmentally aware, and less caught up in commercialism. The Diggers, a radical group of actors and populist agitators, for example, operated a free shop a few blocks off Haight Street. Everything really was free at the free shop; people brought in things they didn't need and took things they did. The Diggers also distributed free food in Golden Gate Park every day.

Among the folks who hung out in or near the Haight during the late 1960s were writers Richard Brautigan, Allen Ginsberg, Ken Kesey, and Gary Snyder; anarchist Abbie Hoffman; rock performers Marty Balin, Jerry Garcia, Janis Joplin, and Grace Slick; LSD champion Timothy Leary; and filmmaker Kenneth Anger.

❽ Red Victorian Peace Center Bed & Breakfast. By even the most generous accounts the Summer of Love quickly crashed and burned, and the Haight veered sharply away from the higher goals that inspired the fabled summer. In 1977 Sami Sunchild acquired the Red Vic, built as a hotel in 1904, with the aim of preserving the best of 1960s ideals. She decorated her rooms with 1960s themes—one chamber is called the Flower Child Room—and on the ground floor opened the Peace Art Center. Here you can buy her paintings, T-shirts, and "meditative art," along with books about the Haight and prayer flags. There's also a meditation room. ⊠ *1665 Haight St.,* ☎ *415/864–1978.*

NEED A
BREAK?   Boisterous **Cha Cha Cha** (✉ 1801 Haight St., at Shrader St.,
          ☎ 415/386–5758) serves island cuisine, a mix of Cajun,
          southwestern, and Caribbean influences. The decor is Tech-
          nicolor tropical plastic, and the food is hot and spicy. Try
          the fried calamari or chili-spiked shrimp. Reservations are
          not accepted. Expect a wait for dinner.

The Northern Waterfront

For the sights, sounds, and smells of the sea, hop the Powell–Hyde cable car from Union Square and take it to the
end of the line. The views as you descend Hyde Street
down to the bay are breathtaking—tiny sailboats bob in
the whitecaps, Alcatraz hovers ominously in the distance,
and the Marin Headlands form a rugged backdrop to the
Golden Gate Bridge. Once you reach sea level at the cable
car turnaround, Aquatic Park and the National Maritime
Museum are immediately to the west, and the commercial
attractions of the Fisherman's Wharf area are to the east.
Bring good walking shoes and a jacket or sweater for mid-
afternoon breezes or foggy mists.

Each day street artists—jewelers, painters, potters, photographers, and leather workers—and others offer their
wares for sale. Beauty, of course, is always in the eye of the
beholder, but some of the items may be overpriced and of
questionable quality. Bargaining is always possible.

*Numbers in the margin correspond to numbers on the
Northern Waterfront/Marina and the Presidio map.*

Sights to See

★ **Alcatraz Island.** The boat ride to the island is brief (15 minutes) but affords beautiful views of the city, Marin County,
and the East Bay. The audio tour, highly recommended, includes observations of guards and prisoners about life in
one of America's most notorious penal colonies. A separate ranger-led tour surveys the island's ecology. Plan your
schedule to allow at least three hours for the visit and boat
rides combined. Reservations, even in the off-season, are
recommended. ✉ *Pier 41,* ☎ *415/773–1188 (boat schedules and information); 415/705–5555; 800/426–8687
(credit-card ticket orders); 415/705–1042 (park informa-*

tion). 🖃 *$11 or $7.75 without audio ($18.50 for evening tours, which includes audio); add $2 per ticket to charge by phone.* ☉ *Ferry departures Sept.–May 23, daily 9:30– 2:15 (4:20 for evening tour); May 24–Aug., daily 9:30–4:15 (6:30 and 7:30 for evening tour).*

Angel Island. For an outdoorsy adventure, consider a day at Angel Island, northwest of Alcatraz. Discovered by Spaniards in 1775 and declared a U.S. military reserve 75 years later, the island was used from 1910 until 1940 as a screening ground for Asian immigrants, who were often held for months, even years, before being granted entry. In 1963 the government designated Angel Island a state park. Today people come for picnics and hikes—a scenic 5-mi path winds around the perimeter of the island—as well as guided tours that explain the park's history. Twenty-five bicycles are permitted on the regular ferry on a first-come, first-served basis, and you can rent mountain bikes for $10 per hour or $25 per day at the landing. ⊠ *Pier 41,* ☎ *415/435–1915 for park information and ferry schedules; 415/705–5555; 800/426–8687 for tickets.* 🖃 *$10.* ☉ *Ferry sailing days and departure times vary; call for schedule.*

❷ Cannery. This three-story structure was built in 1894 to house what became the Del Monte Fruit and Vegetable Cannery. Today the Cannery is home to shops, art galleries, a comedy club (Cobb's), and some unusual restaurants. The **Museum of the City of San Francisco** (☎ 415/928–0289), on the third floor, displays historical items, maps, and photographs, as well as the 500-pound head of the Goddess of Progress statue, which crowned the City Hall building that crumbled during the 1906 earthquake. Admission to the museum is free. ⊠ *2801 Leavenworth St.,* ☎ *415/771–3112.*

Ferries. Alcatraz Island and Angel Island are just two of the destinations served by the **Blue and Gold Fleet** (⊠ Pier 41, ☎ 415/705–5555). Alcatraz is the best deal—you get all the fun of bay cruise and a great tour of the prison. But the boats are a fine way to day-trip to Sausalito and Tiburon. Blue and Gold also runs ferries to Oakland, Alameda, and Vallejo. The Vallejo boat docks near Six Flags Marine World. The **Red and White Fleet** (⊠ Pier 43½, ☎ 415/447– 0591 or 800/229–2784) operates bay and other cruises.

48

Northern Waterfront/Marina and the Presidio

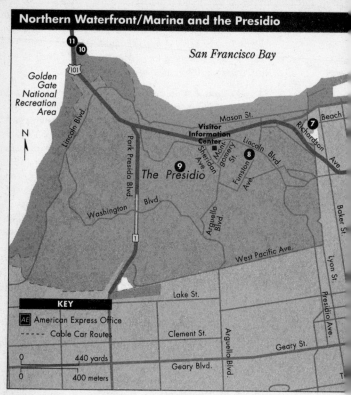

San Francisco Bay

Golden Gate National Recreation Area

N

The Presidio

KEY

AE American Express Office

----- Cable Car Routes

0 — 440 yards
0 — 400 meters

Cannery, **2**
Exploratorium, **7**
Fisherman's Wharf, **4**
Fort Mason Center, **6**
Fort Point, **10**
Ghirardelli Square, **1**

Golden Gate Bridge, **11**
Hyde Street Pier, **3**
Palace of Fine Arts, **7**
Pier 39, **5**
Presidio, **9**

Presidio Museum, **8**

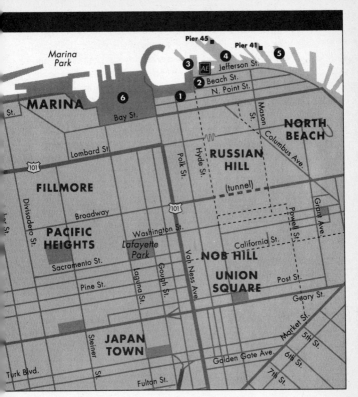

Marina
Park

Pier 45 ■

Pier 41 ■

3 ❸

AE

4 ❹ Jefferson St.

5 ❺

2 ❷ Beach St.

1 ❶ N. Point St.

MARINA

St.

6 ❻

Bay St.

Mason St.

NORTH BEACH

Columbus Ave.

Lombard St.

101

FILLMORE

Hyde St.

Polk St.

RUSSIAN HILL

(tunnel)

Broadway

101

Grant Ave.

Divisadero St.

ey St.

PACIFIC HEIGHTS

Washington St.

Lafayette Park

Powell St.

California St.

NOB HILL

Sacramento St.

Van Ness Ave.

Gough St.

Laguna St.

Pine St.

UNION SQUARE

Post St.

Geary St.

Steiner St.

JAPAN TOWN

Market St.

5th St.

Golden Gate Ave.

6th St.

Turk Blvd.

7th St.

Fulton St.

☝ ❹ **Fisherman's Wharf.** Ships creak at their moorings; seagulls cry out for a handout. By mid-afternoon the fishing fleet is back to port. The chaotic streets of the wharf are home to numerous seafood restaurants, among them sidewalk stands where shrimp and crab cocktails are sold in disposable containers. T-shirts and sweats, gold chains galore, redwood furniture, acres of artwork (precious little of it original), and generally amusing street artists also beckon visitors. Everything's overpriced, especially the so-called novelty museums, which can provide a diversion if you're touring with antsy kids. The best of the lot, though mostly for its kitsch value, is **Ripley's Believe It or Not** (✉ 175 Jefferson St., ☎ 415/771–6188). King Tut and latter-day celebs populate the **Wax Museum** (✉ 145 Jefferson St., ☎ 415/885–4975). For an intriguing if mildly claustrophobic glimpse into life on a submarine during World War II, drop by the **USS *Pampanito*** (✉ Pier 45, ☎ 415/775–1943). The sub, open daily from 9 to 6 (until 8 between Memorial Day and Labor Day), sank six Japanese warships and damaged four others. Admission is $7. ✉ *Jefferson St. between Leavenworth St. and Pier 39.*

❶ **Ghirardelli Square.** Most of the redbrick buildings in this early 20th-century complex were part of the Ghirardelli chocolate factory. Now they house name-brand emporiums, restaurants, and galleries that sell everything from crafts and knickknacks to sports memorabilia. Placards throughout the square describe the factory's history. ✉ *900 North Point,* ☎ *415/775–5500.*

❸ **Hyde Street Pier.** The pier, one of the wharf area's best bargains, always crackles with activity. Depending on the time of day, you might see boatbuilders at work or children manning a ship as though it were still the early 1900s. The highlight of the pier is its collection of historic vessels, all of which can be boarded: the *Balclutha,* an 1886 full-rigged three-masted sailing vessel that sailed around Cape Horn 17 times; the *Eureka,* a side-wheel ferry; the *C. A. Thayer,* a three-masted schooner; and the *Hercules,* a steam-powered tugboat. ✉ *Hyde and Jefferson Sts.,* ☎ *415/556–3002 or 415/556–0859.* 🎫 *$4.* ☉ *Daily 9:30–5; summer, daily 10–6.*

☝ ❺ **Pier 39.** This is the most popular—and commercial—of San Francisco's waterfront attractions, drawing millions of visitors each year to browse through its dozens of shops. Ongoing free entertainment, accessible validated parking, and nearby public transportation ensure crowds most days. Check out the **Marine Mammal Store & Interpretive Center** (☎ 415/289–7373), a quality gift shop and education center whose proceeds benefit Sausalito's Marine Mammal Center, and the **National Park Store** (☎ 415/433–7221), with books, maps, and collectibles sold to support the National Park Service. Brilliant colors enliven the double-decker **Venetian Carousel,** often awhirl with happily howling children. The din on the northwest side of the pier comes courtesy of the hundreds of sea lions that bask and play on the docks. At **Underwater World** (☎ 415/623–5300 or 888/732–3483), moving walkways transport visitors through a space surrounded on three sides by water filled with indigenous San Francisco Bay marine life, from fish and plankton to sharks. The **California Welcome Center,** inside the Citibank Cinemax Theater, is open from 9 to 5:30 daily. Parking is at the Pier 39 Garage, off Powell Street at the Embarcadero. ⊠ *Beach St. at the Embarcadero.*

The Marina and the Presidio

The Marina district was a coveted place to live until the 1989 earthquake, when the area's homes suffered the worst damage in the city—largely because the Marina is built on landfill. Many home owners and renters fled in search of more solid ground, but young professionals quickly replaced them, changing the tenor of this formerly low-key neighborhood. The number of upscale coffee emporiums skyrocketed. A bank became a Williams-Sonoma and the local grocer gave way to a Pottery Barn. On weekends, a fairly homogeneous well-to-do crowd frequents these and other establishments. One unquestionable improvement was the influx of contemporary cuisine in this former bastion of coffee shops and outdated Italian fare. Even before the quake, though, the Marina Safeway, at Laguna Street and Marina Boulevard, was a famed pickup place for young heterosexual singles.

West of the Marina is the sprawling Presidio, a former military base turned park, with superb views and the best hiking and biking areas in San Francisco.

Numbers in the margin correspond to numbers on the Northern Waterfront/Marina and the Presidio map.

Sights to See

★ ☾ **7** **Exploratorium.** The curious of all ages flock to this fascinating "museum of science, art, and human perception" within the Palace of Fine Arts. The more than 650 exhibits focus on sea and insect life, computers, electricity, patterns and light, language, the weather, and much more. "Explainers"—often high school students on their days off from school—provide help and demonstrate scientific principles (lasers, dissection of a cow's eye). Reservations are required to crawl through the pitch-black, touchy-feely **Tactile Dome,** an adventure of 15 minutes. The object is to crawl and climb through the space relying solely on the sense of touch. ⊠ *3601 Lyon St. at Marina Blvd.,* ☏ *415/561–0360 for general information; 415/561–0362 for Tactile Dome reservations.* ☒ *$9; free 1st Wed. of month; Tactile Dome admission $3 extra.* ☉ *Memorial Day–Labor Day, daily 10–6, Wed. 10–9; Labor Day–Memorial Day, Tues., Thurs.–Sun., and most Mon. holidays 10–5, Wed. 10–9.*

6 **Fort Mason Center.** Originally a depot for the shipment of supplies to the Pacific during World War II, Fort Mason was converted into a cultural center in 1977. In business here are the popular vegetarian restaurant Greens and shops, galleries, and performance spaces, most of which are closed on Monday.

The **Mexican Museum** (⊠ Bldg. D, ☏ 415/441–0404) showcases Mexican, Mexican-American, and Chicano art—everything from pre-Columbian Indian terra-cotta figures and Spanish colonial religious images to exhibits about Mexican-American and Chicano culture. This facility is scheduled to close in late 2000 prior to the museum's move in early 2001 to a building adjacent to Yerba Buena Gardens. La Tienda, the museum shop, stocks colorful Mexican folk art, posters, books, and catalogs from museum exhibitions.

Two interesting small museums are in Building C. The **Museo Italo-Americano** (☏ 415/673–2200) mounts impressive exhibits of the works of Italian and Italian-American artists—paintings, sculpture, etchings, and photographs.

The exhibits at the **San Francisco African-American Historical and Cultural Society** (☎ 415/441–0640) document past and contemporary black arts and culture. In Building A is the **San Francisco Craft and Folk Art Museum** (☎ 415/775–0990), an airy space with exhibits of American folk art, tribal art, and contemporary crafts. The museum shop is a sure bet for whimsical gifts from around the world. Next door to the Craft and Folk Art Museum is the **SFMOMA Rental Gallery** (☎ 415/441–4777), where the art is available for sale or rent. Most of the museums and shops at Fort Mason close by 6 or 7. The museum admission fees range from pay-what-you-wish to $3. ✉ *Buchanan St. and Marina Blvd.,* ☎ *415/979–3010 for event information.*

★ ⓫ **Golden Gate Bridge.** The suspension bridge that connects San Francisco with Marin County has long wowed sightseers with its rust-color beauty, 750-ft towers, and simple but powerful Art Deco design. At nearly 2 mi, the Golden Gate, completed in 1937 after four years of construction, was built to withstand winds of more than 100 mph. Though frequently gusty and misty (walkers should wear warm clothing), the bridge offers unparalleled views of the Bay Area. The east walkway yields a glimpse of the San Francisco skyline as well as the islands of the bay. The view west takes in the wild hills of the Marin Headlands, the curving coast south to Land's End, and the majestic Pacific Ocean. A vista point on the Marin side affords a spectacular view of the city. On sunny days sailboats dot the water, and brave windsurfers test the often-treacherous tides beneath the bridge. Muni Buses 28 and 29 make stops at the Golden Gate Bridge toll plaza, on the San Francisco side. ✉ *Lincoln Blvd. near Doyle Dr. and Fort Point,* ☎ *415/921–5858.* ⊙ *Open daily, 24 hrs for cars and bikes, 5 am–9 pm for pedestrians.*

★ ❼ **Palace of Fine Arts.** San Francisco's rosy rococo Palace of Fine Arts is at the western end of the Marina. The palace is the sole survivor of the many tinted plaster buildings (a temporary classical city of sorts) built for the 1915 Panama-Pacific International Exposition, the world's fair that celebrated San Francisco's recovery from the 1906 earthquake and fire. The expo lasted for 288 days and the buildings extended about a mile along the shore. Bernard Maybeck

designed this faux Roman Classic beauty, which was re-
constructed in concrete and reopened in 1967. The massive columns, great rotunda (dedicated to the glory of
Greek culture), and swan-filled lagoon have been used in
countless fashion layouts and films. ⊠ *Baker and Beach
Sts.,* ☎ *415/561–0364 for palace tours.*

❾ Presidio. Part of the Golden Gate National Recreation
Area, the Presidio was a military post for more than 200
years. Don Juan Bautista de Anza and a band of Spanish
settlers first claimed the area in 1776. It became a Mexican garrison in 1822 when Mexico gained its indepen-
dence from Spain; U.S. troops forcibly occupied the Presidio
in 1846. The U.S. Sixth Army was stationed here until October 1994, when the coveted space was transferred into
civilian hands. The more than 1,400 acres of rolling hills,
majestic woods, and redbrick army barracks present an air
of serenity on the edge of the city. There are two beaches,
a golf course, a **visitor center,** and picnic sites, and the
views of the bay, the Golden Gate Bridge, and Marin
County are sublime. ⊠ Presidio: *Between the Marina and
Lincoln Park.* ⊠ Visitor center: Montgomery St., between
Lincoln Blvd. and Sheridan Ave., ☎ 415/561–4323. 🖭 Free.
🕙 Daily 9–5.

❽ Presidio Museum. This is one of the oldest buildings on the
base put up by the U.S. Army. These days, the museum fo-
cuses on the role played by the military in San Francisco's
development. Behind the museum are two cabins that housed
refugees from the 1906 earthquake and fire. Photos on the
wall of one depict rows and rows of temporary shelters at
the Presidio and in Golden Gate Park following the disaster. The Presidio Museum plans to move into the visitor center (☞ *above*) by 2000. ⊠ *Lincoln Blvd. and Funston Ave.,*
☎ *415/561–4331.* 🖭 *Free.* 🕙 *Wed.–Sun. noon–4.*

Golden Gate Park

William Hammond Hall conceived one of the nation's
great city parks and began in 1870 to put into action his
plan for a natural reserve with no reminders of urban life.
Hammond began work in the Panhandle and eastern portions of Golden Gate Park, but it took John McLaren the

length of his tenure as park superintendent, from 1890 to 1943, to complete the transformation of 1,000 desolate brush- and sand-covered acres into a rolling, landscaped oasis. Urban reality now encroaches on all sides, but the park remains a great getaway. On Sunday John F. Kennedy Drive is closed to cars and comes alive with joggers, bicyclists, and in-line skaters. In addition to cultural and other attractions there are public tennis courts, baseball diamonds, soccer fields, and trails for horseback riding. From May to October, **Friends of Recreation and Parks** (☎ 415/263–0991) conducts weekend walking tours. The fog can sweep into the park with amazing speed; always bring a sweatshirt or jacket.

The **Golden Gate Park Explorer Pass** ($14) grants admission to the M. H. de Young and Asian Art museums, plus the California Academy of Sciences and the Japanese Tea Garden. The passes, which are good for up to six months (the length depends on what time of year you buy the pass), can be purchased at the above sights except for the tea garden, or at TIX Bay Area in Union Square (☞ Union Square, *above*).

Because the park is so large, a car will come in handy if you're going to tour it from one end to the other—though you'll still do a fair amount of walking. You can make the jump between the attractions on the eastern edge of the park and the ones near the ocean on public transportation.

On weekends you can park all day for $3 at the University of California at San Francisco garage (enter at Irving Street and 2nd Avenue south of the park); from there a free shuttle leaves every 10 minutes for the park's museums. Muni also serves the park. Bus 5-Fulton stops along its northern edge, and the N-Judah light-rail car stops a block south of the park until 9th Avenue, two blocks the rest of the way west.

Numbers in the margin correspond to numbers on the Golden Gate Park map.

Sights to See

★ ❸ **Asian Art Museum.** The museum's collection includes more than 12,000 sculptures, paintings, and ceramics from 40 countries, illustrating major periods of Asian art. The bulk of the art and artifacts, though, come from China. On the first floor are special exhibitions as well as galleries dedicated to works from Korea and China. On the second floor are treasures from Iran, Turkey, Syria, India, Tibet, Nepal, Pakistan, India, Japan, Afghanistan, and Southeast Asia. This facility will close prior to the museum's move to the Civic Center in 2002. ⊠ *Tea Garden Dr. off John F. Kennedy Dr., near 10th Ave. and Fulton St.,* ☎ *415/668–8921 or 415/379–8801.* ⊠ *$7 ($2 off with Muni transfer), good also· for same-day admission to the M. H. de Young Museum and the Legion of Honor Museum in Lincoln Park; free 1st Wed. of month.* ⊙ *Tues.–Sun. 9:30–5, 1st Wed. of month until 8:45.*

★ ☾ ❺ **California Academy of Sciences.** A three-in-one attraction, the nationally renowned academy houses an aquarium, numerous science and natural-history exhibits, and a planetarium.

Leopard sharks, silver salmon, sea bass, and other fish loop around the mesmerizing Fish Roundabout, the big draw at **Steinhart Aquarium.** Feeding time is 2 PM. At the Touch Tide Pool, you can cozy up to starfish, hermit crabs, and other critters. Elsewhere at Steinhart swim dolphins, sea turtles, piranhas, and manatees. There are also reptile and amphibian displays and an alligator pond. Vibrantly colored fish vie for attention with iridescent coral at the tropical coral reef. Always amusing to watch, the penguins dine at 11:30 AM and 4 PM. The multimedia earthquake exhibit in the Earth and Space Hall at the **Natural History Museum** simulates quakes, complete with special effects. Videos and displays in the Wild California Hall describe the state's wildlife, and there's a re-creation of the environment of the rocky Farallon Islands. Dinosaur bones and a Brontosaurus skull draw dinophiles to the Hall of Fossils. African Hall contains animals (real but stuffed) specific to Africa in their native vegetation; don't miss the sights and sounds of the African watering hole at the end of the room. The natural-history wing's other attractions include the gem and mineral hall, an insect room, Far Side of Science cartoons by Gary Larson, and an open play and learning space for small children.

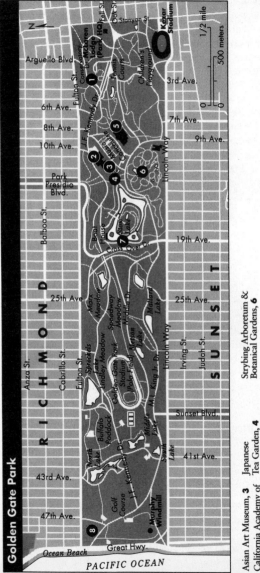

57

Golden Gate Park

Kezar Stadium

1/2 mile

500 meters

Arguello Blvd

Fulton St.
Conservatory
Conservatory
McLaren
Lodge (Park
HQ)

Stanyan St.

Spreckels
Temple
Music
Concourse

Children's
Playground

Tennis
Courts

3rd Ave.

6th Ave.

7th Ave.

8th Ave.

9th Ave.

10th Ave.

Park
Presidio
Blvd.

J.F. Kennedy Dr.

Lincoln Way

Balboa St.

Stow
Lake

Strawberry
Hill

Boat
House

Cross Over Dr.

19th Ave.

25th Ave.

Marx
Meadow

Speedway
Meadow

Middle Dr.

Mallard
Lake

25th Ave.

R I C H M O N D

Anza St.

Cabrillo St.

Fulton St.

Spreckels
Lake

Lindley Meadow

Mur. M.L. King Jr. Dr.

Metson
Lake

Irving St.

Judah St.

S U N S E T

Lincoln Way

Golden Gate Park
(Polo Fields)

Stadium

Sunset Blvd.

43rd Ave.

47th Ave.

North
Lake

Buffalo
Paddock

J.F. Kennedy Dr.

Middle Lake

Swan
Lake

41st Ave.

Golf
Course

Murphy
Windmill

Great Hwy.

Ocean Beach

PACIFIC OCEAN

Asian Art Museum, **3**
California Academy of
  Sciences, **5**
Conservatory of
  Flowers, **1**
Dutch Windmill **8**

Japanese
  Tea Garden, **4**
M.H. de Young
  Memorial Museum, **2**
Stow Lake, **7**

Strybing Arboretum &
  Botanical Gardens, **6**

There is an additional charge (up to $2.50) for **Morrison Planetarium** shows (☎ 415/750–7141 for schedule), which you enter through the Natural History Museum. Daily multimedia shows present the night sky through the ages under a 55-ft dome, complete with special effects and music. The **Laserium** presents evening laser-light shows (☎ 415/750–7138 for schedule and fees) at Morrison Planetarium, accompanied by rock, classical, and other types of music; educational shows outline laser technology. A cafeteria is open daily until one hour before the museum closes. ⊠ *Music Concourse Dr. off South Dr., across from Asian Art and de Young museums,* ☎ *415/750–7145.* ☜ *$8.50; $1 discount with Muni transfer; free 1st Wed. of month.* ☉ *Memorial Day–Labor Day, daily 9–6; Labor Day–Memorial Day, daily 10–5; 1st Wed. of month closes at 8:45 pm.*

❶ **Conservatory of Flowers.** The oldest building in the park and the last remaining wood-frame Victorian conservatory in the country, the Conservatory, which was built in the late 1870s, is a copy of the one in the Royal Botanical Gardens in Kew, England. Heavily damaged during a 1995 storm, the whitewashed facility is closed indefinitely but its architecture and gardens make it a worthy stop nonetheless. The gardens in front of the Conservatory are planted seasonally, with the flowers often fashioned like billboards—trumpeting a Super Bowl victory by the 49ers football team or depicting the Golden Gate Bridge or other city sights. On the east side of the Conservatory (to the right as you face the building), cypress, pine, and redwood trees surround the **Fuchsia Garden,** which blooms in summer and fall. To the west several hundred feet on John F. Kennedy Drive is the **Rhododendron Dell.** The dell contains the most varieties—850 in all—of any garden in the country. It's especially beautiful in March when many of the flowers bloom and is a favorite spot of locals for Mother's Day picnics. ⊠ *John F. Kennedy Dr. at Conservatory Dr.*

❽ **Dutch Windmill.** Two windmills anchor the western end of the park. The restored 1902 Dutch Windmill once pumped 20,000 gallons of well water per hour to the reservoir on Strawberry Hill (☞ Stow Lake, *below*). With its heavy cement bottom and wood-shingled arms and upper section the windmill cuts quite the sturdy figure. The structure overlooks the equally photogenic **Queen Wilhelmina Tulip Garden**, which bursts into full bloom in early spring and late summer. The **Murphy Windmill**, on Martin Luther King Jr. Drive near the Great Highway, was the world's largest windmill when it was built in 1905. Now in disrepair, its wings clipped, the Murphy Windmill also pumped water to the Strawberry Hill reservoir. ⊠ *Between 47th Ave. and the Great Hwy.*

★ ❹ **Japanese Tea Garden.** A serene 4-acre landscape of small ponds, streams, waterfalls, stone bridges, Japanese sculptures, *mumsai* (planted bonsai) trees, perfect miniature pagodas, and some nearly vertical wooden "humpback" bridges, the tea garden was created for the 1894 Mid-Winter Exposition. Go in the spring if you can (March is particularly beautiful), when the cherry blossoms are in bloom. ⊠ *Tea Garden Dr. off John F. Kennedy Dr.,* ☎ *415/752–4227 or 415/752–1171.* 🎫 *$3.50.* ☉ *Mar.–Sept., daily 9–6:30; Oct.–Feb., daily 8:30–6.*

❷ **M. H. de Young Memorial Museum.** Works on display at the de Young include American paintings, sculpture, textiles, and decorative arts from Colonial times through the 20th century. The John D. Rockefeller III Collection of American Paintings is especially noteworthy, with more than 200 paintings of American masters like John Singleton Copley, Thomas Eakins, George Caleb Bingham, and John Singer Sargent. Frederic Church's moody, almost psychedelic *Rainy Season in the Tropics* dominates the room of landscapes. Within the gallery of American still lifes are the trompe l'oeil paintings of William Harnett. The de Young also has collections of African and Native American art, including sculpture, baskets, and ceramics. Ongoing textile installations showcase everything from tribal clothing to couture. The museum hosts traveling exhibitions that sometimes involve extra admission charges and extended hours. The **Café de Young** has outdoor seating in the lovely Oakes Garden. ⊠ *Tea Garden Dr. off John F. Kennedy Dr., near 10th Ave. and Fulton St.,* ☎ *415/863–3330.* 🎫 *$7 ($2 off with Muni transfer), good also for same-day admission to the Asian Art Museum and the Legion of Honor Museum in Lincoln Park; free 1st Wed. of month until 5.* ☉ *Tues.–Sun. 9:30–5, 1st Wed. of month until 8:45.*

➐ Stow Lake. One of the most picturesque spots in Golden Gate Park, this placid body of water surrounds Strawberry Hill. A couple of bridges allow you to cross over and ascend the hill (the old 19th-century stone bridge on the southwest side of the lake is especially quaint). A waterfall cascades down from the top of the hill, and panoramic views make it worth the short hike up here. Down below, rent a boat, surrey, or bicycle or stroll around the perimeter. Just to the left of the waterfall sits the elaborate Chinese Pavilion, a gift from the city of Taipei. It was shipped in 6,000 pieces and assembled on the shore of Strawberry Hill Island in 1981. ⊠ *Off John F. Kennedy Dr. ½ mi west of 10th Ave.,* ☎ *415/752–0347.*

➏ Strybing Arboretum & Botanical Gardens. The 55-acre arboretum specializes in plants from areas with climates similar to that of the Bay Area, such as the west coast of Australia, South Africa, and the Mediterranean; more than 8,000 plant and tree varieties bloom in gardens throughout the grounds. Among the highlights are the Biblical, fragrance, California native plants, succulents, and primitive gardens, the new and old world cloud forests, and the duck pond. The exhaustive reference library holds approximately 18,000 volumes, and the bookstore is a great resource. Maps are available at the main and Eugene L. Friend entrances. ⊠ *9th Ave. at Lincoln Way,* ☎ *415/661–1316.* ▣ *Free.* ☺ *Weekdays 8–4:30, weekends and holidays 10–5. Tours leave the bookstore weekdays at 1:30, weekends at 10:30.*

....

OFF THE
BEATEN
PATH

Lincoln Park and the Western Shoreline – From the historic Cliff House south to the sprawling San Francisco Zoo, the Great Highway and Ocean Beach run along the western edge of the city, revealing incredible ocean and bay views. If you can pull yourself away from its spectacular setting and head indoors, the **California Palace of the Legion of Honor** (⊠ 34th Ave. at Clement St.; Geary St. bus 38 from Union Square; ☎ 415/863–3330) is a wonderful repository of European art from the 14th to the 20th century, including a noteworthy Rodin collection. Admission is $8; $2 off with Muni transfer. More than 1,000 birds and animals reside at the **San Francisco Zoo** (⊠ Sloat Blvd. and the Great Hwy.; Muni L-Taraval streetcar from downtown; ☎ 415/753–7080) including more than 130 endangered species, such as the jaguar and Asian elephant. A popular resident is Prince Charles, a rare white tiger and the first of its kind to be exhibited in the West. Admission is $9; $1 off with Muni transfer. From Land's End in Lincoln Park (⊠ Entrance at 34th Ave. at Clement St.) you'll have some of the best views of the Golden Gate (the name was originally given to the opening of San Francisco Bay long before the bridge was built) and the Marin Headlands. Note that the wind is often strong along the shoreline (carry a jacket) and the water is cold and usually too rough for swimming. ⊠ *Along Great Hwy. and Clement St.*

3 Dining

SAN FRANCISCO HAS MORE RESTAU-
RANTS per capita than any other city in
the United States, and nearly every eth-
nic cuisine is represented. We have chosen several restaurants to represent each popular style of dining in various
price ranges, in most cases because of the superiority of the
food but in some instances because of the view or ambience.

By Sharon
Silva

The areas of town most frequented by visitors have received
the greatest attention. This has meant leaving out some great
places in the more distant districts, such as the Mission,
Haight-Ashbury, the Sunset, and the Richmond. The out-
lying restaurants that are recommended were chosen because they offer an experience not available elsewhere. All
listed restaurants serve lunch and dinner unless otherwise
specified. The restaurants here are organized by neighborhood, which are listed alphabetically.

Smoking is banned in all Bay Area workplaces, including
restaurants, bars, and supper clubs.

The price ranges listed below are for an average three-
course meal.

CATEGORY	COST*
$$$$	over $50
$$$	$30–$50
$$	$20–$30
$	under $20

*per person for a three-course meal, excluding drinks, ser-
vice, and 8.5% sales tax*

The Castro

Contemporary

$$$ ✕ **Mecca.** This sleek bar and restaurant on the edge of the
Castro is a mecca for both local Armani-clad cocktailers
and Bay Area foodies. If clubbing is not your thing, reserve
a seat in the dining area, away from the always crowded,
velvet-curtained circular bar that anchors the cavernous
space. In late 1998, Mike Fennelly took over the kitchen,
delivering an American menu with strong Cajun and Asian

Acquerello, **14**

Aqua, **32**

Beach Chalet, **61**

Bistro Aix, **5**

Bix, **26**

Bizou, **56**

Black Cat, **24**

Boulevard, **34**

Café Marimba, **4**

Campton Place, **43**

Cassis Bistro, **8**

Charanga, **65**

Des Alpes, **21**

Enrico's Sidewalk Cafe, **23**

Eos Restaurant & Wine Bar, **63**

Farallon, **45**

Fattoush, **67**

Fleur de Lys, **47**

Fog City Diner, **17**

42 Degrees, **58**

Fringale, **57**

Gaylord's, **2**

Globe, **27**

Great Eastern, **25**

Greens, **1**

Harris', **12**

Harry Denton's, **35**

Hawthorne Lane, **55**

Hayes Street Grill, **60**

Il Fornaio, **16**

Izzy's Steak & Chop House, **6**

Jardinière, **59**

Kyo-ya, **41**

La Folie, **11**

La Taqueria, **67**

Laghi, **48**

Le Central, **39**

L'Osteria del Forno, **19**

LuLu, **53**

Masa's, **37**

Downtown San Francisco Dining

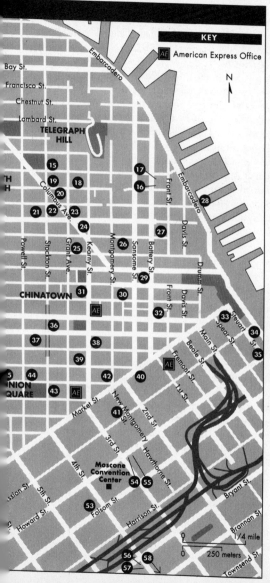

Maykadeh, **18**

Mecca, **68**

McCormick &
Kuleto's, **3**

Mifune, **50**

Moose's, **15**

One Market, **33**

Perry's, **42**

Plouf, **38**

PlumpJack
Café, **7**

Postrio, **46**

R&G Lounge, **31**

Ritz-Carlton
Dining
Room and
Terrace, **36**

Rose Pistola, **20**

Rose's Café, **9**

Rubicon, **30**

Sanppo, **49**

Scala's Bistro, **44**

Slanted Door, **69**

Stars, **52**

Tavolino, **22**

Thep
Phanom, **62**

Thirstybear, **54**

Ti Couz, **70**

2223, **71**

Vineria, **72**

Vivande Porta
Via, **13**

Vivande
Ristorante, **51**

The Waterfront
Restaurant, **28**

Yank Sing, **29, 40**

Zarzuela, **10**

Zuni Café &
Grill, **64**

accents. Choices include an iced shellfish platter, curried potato samosas with pineapple salsa, shrimp dumplings with a spicy tahini sauce, roast chicken, and lemon-mascarpone cheesecake. ⊠ *2029 Market St.,* ☎ *415/621–7000. AE, DC, MC, V. No lunch.*

$$–$$$ ✕ **2223.** Opened in the mid-1990s, when the Castro was a dining-out wasteland, the smart, sophisticated 2223—the address became the name when the principals couldn't come up with a better one—was an instant success and has continued to attract a loyal clientele. That means you'll need a strong pair of lungs, however, as the restaurant's popularity and absence of sound buffers make conversation difficult. Thin-crust pizzas, earthy seasonal soups, chicken with garlic-mashed potatoes, pork loin with wilted escarole, and duck confit salad are among the kitchen's best dishes. For Saturday and Sunday brunch there might be French toast or eggs Benedict on a tasty herb scone. ⊠ *2223 Market St.,* ☎ *415/431–0692. MC, V. No lunch weekdays.*

Chinatown

Chinese

$–$$ ✕ **Great Eastern.** Cantonese chefs are known for their expertise with seafood, and the kitchen at Great Eastern lives up to that venerable tradition. In the busy dining room, large tanks are filled with Dungeness crabs, black bass, abalone, catfish, shrimp, rock cod, and other creatures of the sea, and a wall-hung menu in both Chinese and English specifies the cost of selecting what can be pricey indulgences. Sea conch stir-fried with yellow chives, crab with vermicelli in a clay pot, and steamed fresh scallops with garlic sauce are among the chef's many specialties. In the wee hours Chinese night owls often drop in for a plate of noodles or a bowl of *congee* (rice gruel). ⊠ *649 Jackson St.,* ☎ *415/986–2550. AE, MC, V.*

$–$$ ✕ **R&G Lounge.** The name conjures up an image of a dark bar with a cigarette-smoking piano player, but the restaurant, on two floors, is actually as bright as a new penny. Downstairs (entrance on Kearny Street) is a no-tablecloth dining room that is always packed at lunch and dinner. The classier upstairs space (entrance on Commercial Street), complete with shoji-lined private rooms, is a favorite stop for Chinese businessmen on expense accounts and anyone seeking exceptional Cantonese banquet fare. A menu with photographs helps diners decide among the many exotic dishes, from dried scallops with seasonal vegetables to steamed clams with eggs to deep-fried salt-and-pepper Dungeness crab. ⊠ *631 Kearny St.,* ☎ *415/982–7877 or 415/982–3811. AE, DC, MC, V.*

Civic Center

Contemporary

$$$ ✕ **Jardinière.** One of the city's most talked-about restau-
★ rants since its opening in late 1997, Jardinière continues to be *the* place to dine before a performance at the nearby Opera House and Davies Symphony Hall. The chef-owner is Traci Des Jardins, who made her name at the fashionable Rubicon. The sophisticated interior, with its eye-catching oval atrium and curving staircase, is the work of designer Pat Kuleto. First courses of rabbit rillettes, duck confit, and foie gras are pricey but memorable ways to launch any repast. Alas, not all the main courses reach the same culinary heights, but the finely honed service helps you to forget the few shortcomings. A temperature-controlled cheese room lets you trade in a wedge of chocolate torte for a more European finish. The special three-course "staccato menu" puts music-loving diners in their orchestra seats before the curtain goes up. ⊠ *300 Grove St.,* ☎ *415/861–5555. Reservations essential. AE, DC, MC, V. No lunch.*

$$$ ✕ **Stars.** It has been around for more than a decade, but
★ this culinary hot spot, the domain of superchef Jeremiah Tower, remains a must on every traveling gourmet's itinerary. It's also where many of the local movers and shakers hang out and is a popular place for dining before an evening at the opera or symphony. Although it underwent a pleasing face-lift in 1998—white slipcovered chairs, striking star-shape light fixtures, a new star-patterned carpet—Stars didn't lose its famous clublike ambience. The food ranges from grills to ragouts to sautés—some daringly creative and some classical. Those on a budget can order a stylish hamburger, thin-crusted pizza, or chicken tacos at the counter, or slowly enjoy a flute of champagne at the mile-long bar. ⊠ *150 Redwood Alley, at Van Ness Ave.,* ☎ *415/861–7827. Reservations essential. AE, DC, MC, V. No lunch.*

Italian

$$$　✕ **Vivande Ristorante.** Owner-chef Carlo Middione, a highly regarded authority on the food of southern Italy, has long run a smart take-out shop and casual dining room in Lower Pacific Heights (☞ Vivande Porta Via, *below*). His larger *ristorante,* within walking distance of the Opera House and Symphony Hall, features the same rustic fare found at the original location, like stuffed calamari, risotto laced with seafood, pasta tossed with a tangle of mushrooms, and a hearty osso buco. The spacious room is welcoming, and a late-supper menu lets music lovers grab a bite after performances. ⊠ *670 Golden Gate Ave.,* ☎ *415/673–9245. AE, MC, V.*

Mediterranean

$$$　✕ **Zuni Café & Grill.** Zuni's Italian-Mediterranean menu and
★　its unpretentious atmosphere pack in an eclectic crowd from early morning to late evening. A spacious, window-filled balcony dining area overlooks the large bar, where shellfish, one of the best oyster selections in town, and drinks are dispensed. A whole roast chicken and Tuscan bread salad for two is a popular order here, as are the grilled meats and vegetables. Even the hamburgers have an Italian accent—they're topped with Gorgonzola and served on herbed focaccia. Don't miss the kitchen's addictive shoestring potatoes. ⊠ *1658 Market St.,* ☎ *415/552–2522. Reservations essential. AE, MC, V. Closed Mon.*

Seafood

$$–$$$　✕ **Hayes Street Grill.** Up to 15 different kinds of seafood are chalked on the blackboard each night at this extremely popular restaurant. The fish is simply grilled, with a choice of sauces ranging from tomato salsa to a spicy Sichuan peanut concoction to beurre blanc. Fresh crab slaw and superb crab cakes are regular appetizers, and for dessert, the crème brûlée is legendary. ⊠ *320 Hayes St.,* ☎ *415/863–5545. Reservations essential. AE, D, DC, MC, V. No lunch weekends.*

Cow Hollow/Marina

American

$–$$　✕ **Perry's.** This popular watering hole and meeting place for the button-down singles set and inveterate sports enthusiast serves good, honest saloon food—London broil, corned beef hash, calves' liver, one of the best hamburgers in town, and a great breakfast. Brunch is served on weekends. A second location, **Perry's Downtown**, serves the same signature burgers and other Perry's standards in a clubby, mahogany-lined space although the kitchen is generally less reliable. ⊠ *1944 Union St.,* ☎ *415/922–9022;* ⊠ *185 Sutter St.,* ☎ *415/989–6895. AE, MC, V.*

French

$–$$ ✕ **Bistro Aix.** This lively bistro is a comfortable space composed of light wood banquettes, paper-top tablecloths, and a heated patio. The friendly service and attractive prices draw diners from the surrounding neighborhood and beyond. On weekdays, an early bird two-course prix fixe dinner is available for not much more than the price of a movie ticket. Addictive cracker crust pizzas, superb steamed mussels, crisp-skinned roast chicken, and *steak frites* are additional draws. ⊠ *3340 Steiner St.,* ☎ *415/202–0100. MC, V. No lunch.*

$–$$ ✕ **Cassis Bistro.** Take a seat at the tiny bar and enjoy a glass of wine while you wait for a free table in this sunny yellow, postage stamp–size operation that recalls the small bistros tucked away on side streets in French seaside towns. The servers have solid Gallic accents; the food—onion tart, veal ragout, braised rabbit, tarte Tatin—is comfortingly home style; and the prices are geared toward the penurious. Bare hardwood floors make conversations a challenge on busy nights. ⊠ *2120 Greenwich St.,* ☎ *415/292–0770. No credit cards. Closed Sun.–Mon. No lunch.*

Italian

$–$$ ✕ **Rose's Café.** Chef Reed Hearon opened this more casual kin of Rose Pistola (☞ North Beach *below*) in 1997. Breakfast, lunch, and dinner can be taken in the dining room or outside on a heater-equipped patio. In the morning, folks line up for seductive breads and frittatas. Midday is the time for a hot hero sandwich, a grilled chicken salad, or a pizza topped with arugula and prosciutto. Evening hours find customers working their way through a grilled hangar steak or roast chicken with mashed potatoes and vegetables. For dessert try the memorable *affogato* (vanilla and chocolate ice cream doused with chocolate sauce and served with piping-hot espresso for pouring over the top). ⊠ *2298 Union St.,* ☎ *415/775–2200. AE, MC, V.*

Mediterranean

$$–$$$ ✕ **PlumpJack Café.** This clubby dining room, with its
   ★   smartly attired clientele of bankers and brokers, socialites
and society scions, takes its name from an opera composed
by famed oil tycoon and music lover Gordon Getty, whose
sons are two of the partners here. The regularly changing
menu spans the Mediterranean, with creamy risottos, an
herbed chicken flanked by polenta, and crispy duck confit
among the possibilities. The café is an offshoot of the
nearby highly regarded wine shop of the same name, which
stocks the racks that line the dining room with some of the
most reasonably priced vintages in town. ⌧ *3127 Fillmore
St.,* ☎ *415/463–4755. AE, MC, V. Closed Sun. No lunch
Sat.*

Mexican

$–$$ ✕ **Café Marimba.** Fanciful folk art adorns the walls of this
colorful Mexican café, where an open kitchen turns out contemporary renditions of regional specialties: silken *mole
negro* (sauce of chilies and chocolate) from Oaxaca, served
in tamales and other dishes; shrimp prepared with roasted
onions and tomatoes in the style of Zihuatanejo; and
chicken with a marinade from Yucatán stuffed into an excellent taco. Although the food is treated to many innovative touches, authenticity plays a strong role—even the
guacamole is made to order in a *molcajete,* the three-legged
lava-rock version of a mortar. Fresh fruit drinks and tangy
margaritas are good thirst quenchers. A young, lively crowd
shows up in force, which makes quiet conversation nearly
impossible. ⌧ *2317 Chestnut St.,* ☎ *415/776–1506. AE,
MC, V. No lunch Mon.*

Steak

$$–$$$ ✕ **Izzy's Steak & Chop House.** Izzy Gomez was a legendary
San Francisco saloon keeper, and his namesake eatery carries on the tradition. Here you'll find terrific steaks, chops,
and seafood plus all the trimmings, from cheesy scalloped
potatoes to creamed spinach. A collection of Izzy memorabilia and antique advertising art covers almost every inch
of wall space. There's validated parking at the Lombard
garage. ⌧ *3345 Steiner St.,* ☎ *415/563–0487. AE, DC, MC,
V. No lunch.*

Vegetarian

$$
★
✕ Greens. Long popular with vegetarians and carnivores alike, this beautiful restaurant with expansive bay views is owned and operated by the Green Gulch Zen Buddhist Center of Marin County. The dining room offers a wide, eclectic, and creative spectrum of meatless cooking—corn fritters, black bean soup, thin-crust pizzas, Southwestern-inspired savory tarts. The on-site bakery is an irresistible stop on your way out. Dinners are à la carte on weeknights, but only a five-course prix fixe dinner is served on Saturday. Sunday brunch is a good time to watch local sailboat owners take out their crafts. There's public parking at Fort Mason Center. ✉ *Bldg. A, Fort Mason (enter across Marina Blvd. from Safeway)*, ☎ *415/771–6222. MC, V. No lunch Mon., no dinner Sun.*

Embarcadero North

American

$$ **✕ Fog City Diner.** The diner is an American institution, and Fog City Diner is arguably among the sleekest examples of that beloved national tradition. The long, narrow dining room emulates a luxurious railroad car, with dark wood paneling, huge windows, shiny chrome fixtures, and comfortable booths. The menu is both classic and contemporary, from burgers and fries, chili dogs and hot fudge sundaes to crab cakes and salads of baby lettuce with candied walnuts. The shareable "small plates" are a fun way to go. Grumblers have complained of inconsistent service, but the booths remain full at lunch and dinner. ✉ *1300 Battery St.,* ☎ *415/982–2000. D, DC, MC, V.*

Italian

$$–$$$ **✕ Il Fornaio.** An offshoot of the Il Fornaio bakeries, this handsome tile-floored, wood-paneled complex combines a café, bakery, and upscale trattoria with outdoor seating. The Tuscan cooking, laid out in a sizable menu, features crisp, thin pizzas from a wood-burning oven, house-made pastas and gnocchi, grilled poultry like duck with a balsamic vinegar sauce, and meats like a veal chop with sage and rosemary. Anticipate a wait for a table. Il Fornaio has become as comfortable as an old shoe, which means the kitchen has

a tendency to rest on past laurels. ⊠ *Levi's Plaza, 1265 Battery St.,* ☎ *415/986–0100. AE, DC, MC, V.*

Seafood

$$$ ✕ **The Waterfront Restaurant.** A two-story restaurant has occupied this space for more than three decades, but only in the past few years could it claim a kitchen of such high caliber. On the top floor try the exquisite—and pricey—East-West menu with such exotic pairings as Maine lobster and Japanese shiso leaves, monkfish stew in lotus leaves, and grilled sea bass flavored with Thai kaffir lime. In the more casual downstairs, where both indoor and outdoor seating is available, the menu offers simpler seafood at lower prices. ⊠ *Pier 7,* ☎ *415/391–2696. Reservations essential for upstairs. AE, D, DC, MC, V. No lunch weekends.*

Embarcadero South

American

$$ ✕ **Harry Denton's.** Every night's a party at this madcap waterfront hangout, where singles congregate in a Barbary Coast–style bar, and the rugs are rolled up at 10:30 on Thursday, Friday, and Saturday nights for dancing in the dining room. At lunchtime the place is quieter, attracting diners with its fine bay view and earthy menu that offers everything from pasta to old-fashioned pot roast with mashed potatoes. Wise regulars don't challenge the kitchen, sticking mostly to burgers and pizzas from the wood-fired oven. ⊠ *161 Steuart St.,* ☎ *415/882–1333. AE, DC, MC, V. No lunch weekends.*

Contemporary

$$$ ✕ **Boulevard.** Two of San Francisco's top restaurant talents—chef Nancy Oakes and designer Pat Kuleto—are responsible for this highly successful eatery in one of the city's most magnificent buildings. The setting is the 1889 Audiffred Building, a Parisian look-alike that was one of the few downtown buildings to survive the 1906 earthquake and fire. Oakes's menu is seasonally in flux, but you can always count on her signature juxtaposition of delicacies such as foie gras with homey comfort foods like maple-cured pork loin and roasted chicken. For those who can't find or afford a table during regular hours, Boulevard offers a less formal weekday afternoon bistro service. Portions are generous in either case, so come with an appetite. ⊠ *1 Mission St.,* ☎ *415/543–6084. Reservations essential. AE, D, DC, MC, V. No lunch weekends.*

$$$ ✕ **One Market.** A giant among American chefs, Bradley Ogden gained fame at Campton Place and later at his Lark Creek Inn in Marin County. In 1993 he and partner Michael Dellar opened this huge, bustling brasserie across from the Ferry Building. The handsome two-tier dining room, done in mustard tones, seats 170, and a spacious bar-café serves snacks, including addictive wire-thin onion rings and oysters on the half shell, beginning at noon. The kitchen has had its ups and downs, however, due to a serious spate of executive chef turnover. ⊠ *1 Market St.,* ☎ *415/777–5577. Reservations essential. AE, DC, MC, V. Closed Sun. No lunch Sat.*

Financial District

Chinese

$ ✕ **Yank Sing.** The city's oldest teahouse, Yank Sing began
★ in Chinatown but moved to the Financial District several years ago. The kitchen offers five dozen or so varieties of dim sum on a rotating basis. The Battery Street location seats 300, while the older Stevenson Street site is far smaller, a cozy refuge for Market Street office workers who fuel up on steamed buns and parchment chicken at lunchtime. Take-out counters in both establishments make a meal-on-the-run a delicious compromise. ⊠ *427 Battery St.,* ☎ *415/362–1640;* ⊠ *49 Stevenson St., at Market St.,* ☎ *415/ 541–4949. AE, DC, MC, V. Stevenson branch closed weekends. No dinner.*

Contemporary

$$$ ✕ **Rubicon.** With investors like Robin Williams, Robert De Niro, and Francis Ford Coppola, this sleek, cherry wood–lined restaurant, an offshoot of New York's famed Drew Nierporent restaurant empire, was destined to be famous. Set in a stately stone building dating from 1908, Rubicon has the dignified air of a men's club in the downstairs dining room and a somewhat less appealing atmosphere in the more ascetic upstairs space. The excellent fare,

primarily sophisticated renditions of seafood, meats, and poultry such as sea bass with leeks, lobster-crowned gnocchi, and grilled quail, is served on both floors to Hollywood big shots and San Francisco's glamorous set. ⊠ *558 Sacramento St.,* ☎ *415/434–4100. AE, DC, MC, V. Closed Sun. No lunch Sat.*

$$–$$$ ✕ **Globe.** This smart spot with brick walls, slip-covered chairs, and terra-cotta floors seats less than four dozen diners and never lacks for eager customers, so book ahead. The sophisticated fare, which delivers a Californian punch with a thick Mediterranean accent, includes salad of frisée and lardoons of pancetta topped with a poached egg, sea-fresh grilled sardines, and a lavish T-bone steak with all the trimmings. The building, a former livery stable completed in 1911, is a historic gem that makes eating here all the more enjoyable. The doors stay open until after midnight. ⊠ *290 Pacific Ave.,* ☎ *415/391–4132. Reservations essential. AE, DC, MC, V. Closed Sun. No lunch Sat.*

French

$$–$$$ ✕ **Le Central.** This venerable institution is the quintessential French brasserie: noisy and crowded, with tasty but not-so-subtly cooked classics, such as garlicky pâtés, leeks vinaigrette, steak with Roquefort sauce, cassoulet, and grilled blood sausage with crisp french fries. Local power brokers, even an occasional rock star such as Mick Jagger, snag noontime tables. Staff from the nearby French consulate dine here as well, giving the place an air of authenticity. A traditional zinc bar provides a good perch for people-watching. ⊠ *453 Bush St.,* ☎ *415/391–2233. AE, DC, MC, V. Closed Sun.*

$–$$ ✕ **Plouf.** This sleek spot, handsomely turned out in chrome and the color of the sea, is a gold mine for mussel lovers, with seven generously portioned, reasonably priced preparations from which to choose. Among them are *marinière* (garlic and parsley), apple cider, leeks and cream, and crayfish and tomato. Plouf means "splash," and the appetizers maintain the seaside theme, with plenty of raw oysters on the half shell and a seafood salad of rock shrimp, mussels, and octopus among the offerings. Main courses run the gamut from *steak frites* to steamed sea bass. French vintages are well represented on the carefully selected wine list.

✉ *40 Belden Pl.,* ☎ *415/986–6491. MC, V. Closed Sun.*
No lunch Sat.

Japanese

$$–$$$$ ✕ **Kyo-ya.** Rarely replicated outside Japan, the refined ex-
★ perience of dining in a fine Japanese restaurant has been
introduced with extraordinary authenticity at this show-
place within the Palace Hotel. In Japan a "kyo-ya" is a non-
specialized restaurant that serves a wide range of food. Here,
the range is spectacular, encompassing tempuras, one-pot
dishes, deep-fried and grilled meats, and three dozen sushi
selections. The lunch menu is more limited than dinner but
does include a *shokado,* a sampler of four dishes encased
in a lacquered box. *Kaiseki* meals, multicourse seasonal din-
ners, are also offered, priced for an emperor. ✉ *Palace Hotel,*
2 New Montgomery St., at Market St., ☎ *415/546–5000.*
AE, D, DC, MC, V. Closed Sun. No lunch Mon. and Sat.

Seafood

$$$–$$$$ ✕ **Aqua.** This quietly elegant and ultrafashionable spot,
★ heavily mirrored and populated by a society crowd, is
among the city's most lauded seafood restaurants—and
among the most expensive. Chef-owner Michael Mina cre-
ates contemporary versions of French, Italian, and Amer-
ican classics. Mussel, crab, or lobster soufflé; chunks of
lobster alongside lobster-stuffed ravioli; and the signature
ultrarare ahi tuna paired with foie gras are especially good.
Desserts are miniature museum pieces—try the warm choco-
late tart—and the wine list is superb. ✉ *252 California St.,*
☎ *415/956–9662. Reservations essential. Jacket and tie.*
AE, DC, MC, V. Closed Sun. No lunch Sat.

The Haight

Contemporary

$$$ ✕ **Eos Restaurant & Wine Bar.** The culinary marriage of Cal-
ifornia cuisine and the Asian pantry is the specialty of chef-
owner Arnold Wong, who serves an impressive East-West
menu at this popular spot. Grilled skirt steak is marinated
in a Thai red curry and served with mashed potatoes and
bok choy; rock shrimp cakes arrive with a gingery may-
onnaise; and blackened catfish is paired with lemongrass
risotto. Sometimes diners may find the competing flavors

dizzying, but Wong's faithful following keeps his innovative kitchen in motion. The wine bar next door shelves some 400 vintages, any of which is available at your table. ⊠ *901 Cole St.,* ☎ *415/566–3063. Reservations essential. AE, MC, V. No lunch.*

Thai

$–$$ ✕ **Thep Phanom.** The fine Thai food and the lovely interior at this lower Haight institution keep local food critics and restaurant goers singing its praises. Duck is deliciously prepared in a variety of ways—in a fragrant curry, minced for salad, resting atop a bed of spinach. Other specialties are seafood in various guises, stuffed chicken wings, and fried quail. A number of daily specials supplement the regular menu, and a wonderful mango sorbet is sometimes offered for dessert. ⊠ *400 Waller St.,* ☎ *415/431–2526. AE, D, DC, MC, V. No lunch.*

Japantown

Japanese

$–$$ ✕ **Sanppo.** This modestly priced, casual spot has an enormous selection of almost every type of Japanese food: yakis, nabemono dishes, donburi, udon, and soba, not to mention featherlight tempura and sushi. Grilled eel on rice in a lacquered box and a tempting array of small dishes for snacking make Sanppo a favorite of locals and visitors alike. Seating is Western style. Ask for validated parking at the Japan Center garage. ⊠ *1702 Post St.,* ☎ *415/346–3486. Reservations not accepted. MC, V.*

$ ✕ **Mifune.** Thin, brown soba and thick, white udon are the specialties at this North American outpost of an Osaka-based noodle empire. A line often snakes out the door, but the house-made noodles, served both hot and cold and with more than a score of toppings, are worth the wait. Seating is at rustic wooden tables, where diners can be heard slurping down big bowls of such traditional Japanese combinations as fish cake–crowned udon and *tenzaru* (cold noodles and hot tempura with a gingery dipping sauce) served on lacquered trays. Validated parking is available at the Japan Center garage. ⊠ *Japan Center, Kintetsu Bldg., 1737 Post St.,* ☎ *415/922–0337. Reservations not accepted. AE, D, DC, MC, V.*

Lower Pacific Heights

Italian

$$–$$$ ✕ **Laghi.** For many years, Laghi was a much-loved trattoria in the Richmond District, where it was housed in a small storefront with little available parking. In late 1998, chef-owner Gino Laghi moved his estimable operation to this much larger space, complete with open kitchen, big banquettes, and a sleek wine bar. Old customers and new fans quickly flocked here to enjoy the pastas, including pumpkin-filled ravioli with butter and sage; creamy risottos with everything from fiddlehead ferns to porcini mushrooms to truffles; and roasted rabbit and other game. The wine list of Italian labels is reasonably priced, and the service is friendly and helpful. ✉ *2101 Sutter St.,* ☎ *415/931–3774. AE, DC, MC, V.*

$$–$$$ ✕ **Vivande Porta Via.** Tucked in among the boutiques on upper Fillmore Street, this pricey Italian delicatessen-restaurant, operated by well-known chef and cookbook author Carlo Middione, draws a crowd at lunch and dinner for both its take-out and sit-down fare. Glass cases holding prosciutto di Parma, creamy balls of mozzarella, sweet-and-sour *caponatina* (eggplant antipasto), mile-high *torta rustica* (savory cheese pie), and dozens of other delicacies span one wall. The rest of the room is given over to seating and shelves laden with wines, olives, oils, vinegars, dried pastas, and other Italian gourmet goods. The regularly changing menu includes half a dozen pastas and risottos, including such satisfying southern Italian plates as classic Sicilian pasta *alla Norma* (with eggplant) or spaghetti with fresh tuna and olives, and such northern specialties as risotto with radicchio, pancetta, and pine nuts. Cap off your meal with a lemon tartlet. ✉ *2125 Fillmore St.,* ☎ *415/346–4430. MC, V.*

The Mission District

Contemporary

$$–$$$ ✕ **42 Degrees.** Chef Jim Moffat is the culinary brains behind this sleek, industrial-style space with a curving metal staircase and a seductive view of the bay. The name refers to the latitude on which Provence, Tuscany, and northern Spain lie. The California menu, infused with Mediterranean touches, changes weekly and ranges from creamy bone marrow on toast to duck breast with fiddlehead ferns. Small appetites can graze on a selection of tapas-size plates from the chalkboard menu. Nightly jazz keeps late-night patrons—mostly a younger crowd with bucks to spend—tapping their toes. ⊠ *235 16th St.,* ☎ *415/777–5558. MC, V. Closed Sun. No dinner Mon. and Tues.*

French

$ ✕ **Ti Couz.** Big, thin crêpes just like you find in Brittany are the specialty here, filled with everything from savory ham and Gruyère cheese to bittersweet chocolate. The blue-and-white dining room is always crowded. Rounding out the menu at this Gallic spot are traditional, buttery buckwheat cakes and French hard cider served in classic pottery bowls. ⊠ *3108 16th St.,* ☎ *415/252–7373. MC, V.*

Italian

$–$$ ✕ **Vineria.** The North Mission is home to a continually ex-
★   panding population of eateries, but this is arguably the finest kitchen in the neighborhood. The talented duo behind Vineria are the same women who run the highly successful L'Osteria del Forno in North Beach (☞ *below*), and many of the offerings are identical, including a full list of wonderful panini. There are, however, more pastas at this slightly larger space. The all-Italian wine list is small but superb. ⊠ *3228 16th St.,* ☎ *415/552–3889. MC, V. Closed Mon.–Tues. No lunch.*

Latin

$–$$ ✕ **Charanga.** Cozy and lively, this neighborhood tapas restaurant, named for a Cuban salsa style that relies on flute and violins, serves an eclectic mix of small plates, from mushrooms cooked with garlic and sherry to *patatas a la brava,* twice-fried potatoes with a roasted-tomato sauce. Asian influences show up on this Latin table as well, in such dishes as shrimp and calamari with coconut rice and ginger sauce. The small dining room, with its walls of exposed brick and soothing green, is a friendly, fun place to eat and socialize. Order a pitcher of sangria and enjoy yourself. ⊠ *2351 Mission St.,* ☎ *415/282–1813. Reservations not accepted. MC, V. Closed Sun.–Mon. No lunch.*

Mexican

$ ✕ **La Taqueria.** Although there are a number of taquerias in the Mission, this attractive spot, with its arched exterior and modest interior, is one of the oldest and finest. The tacos are superb: a pair of warm corn tortillas topped with your choice of meat—*carne asada* (grilled steak) and *carnitas* (slowly cooked pork) are favorites—and a spoonful of perfectly fresh salsa. Big appetites may want to try one of the burritos, a large flour tortilla wrapped around hearty spoonfuls of meat, rice, beans, and salsa. Chase your chili-laced meal with a cooling *agua fresca* (fresh fruit cooler) of watermelon or pineapple. ✉ *2889 Mission St.,* ☎ *415/ 285–7117. No credit cards.*

Vietnamese

$$ ✕ **Slanted Door.** Behind the canted facade of this trendy north Mission restaurant, you'll find what owner Charles Phan describes as "real Vietnamese home cooking." There are fresh spring rolls packed with rice noodles, pork, shrimp, and pungent mint leaves, and fried vegetarian imperial rolls concealing bean thread noodles, cabbage, and taro. Five-spice chicken, green papaya salad, and a special of steamed sea bass fillet are among the best dishes. The kitchen, alas, falters more than the crowded tables would have you believe. The menu changes every two weeks or so, but popular dishes are never abandoned. ✉ *584 Valencia St.,* ☎ *415/861–8032. MC, V. Closed Mon.*

Nob Hill

French

$$$–$$$$ ✕ **Ritz-Carlton Dining Room and Terrace.** There are two dis-
★ tinctly different places to eat in this neoclassic Nob Hill show-place. The Dining Room is formal and elegant and has a harpist playing. It serves only three- to five-course dinners, priced by the course, not by the item. The Terrace, a cheerful, informal spot with a large garden patio for outdoor dining, serves breakfast, lunch, dinner, and a Sunday jazz brunch, with piano music at lunchtime and a jazz trio at weekend dinners. In the Dining Room executive chef Sylvain Portay, who was previously chef de cuisine at New York's Le Cirque, turns out an urbane seasonal French

menu—squab with foie gras, lobster salad with caviar cream, a dreamy chocolate soufflé. ⊠ *600 Stockton St.,* ☎ *415/296–7465. AE, D, DC, MC, V. Closed Sun. No lunch.*

Noe Valley

Middle Eastern

$$ ✕ **Fattoush.** Blue tile floors, comfortable banquettes, and bright white walls contribute to the inviting character of this restaurant. Lamb shanks paired with pureed spinach-chickpea sauce and a Palestinian dish of lamb chunks cooked in yogurt with rice and pine nuts are just two of the half dozen fine lamb dishes available. *Sambusak,* phyllo pastry filled with spinach, mushrooms, and nuts served with tahini, is a perfect vegetarian main course. A selection of hot and cold appetizers are offered, including the familiar baba ghanoush and a rich hummus strewn with sumac-dusted onions. Brunch is offered on weekends, and outdoor tables are available on sunny days. ⊠ *1361 Church St.,* ☎ *415/641–0678. MC, V. No lunch Mon.*

North Beach

American

$$$ ✕ **Bix.** In a historic building that was an assay office in Gold Rush days, this old-fashioned supper club was the brain-child of the owners of Fog City Diner. Bix is reminiscent of a theater, with a bustling bar—memorable martinis and generous gin fizzes—and dining tables downstairs and ban-quettes on the balcony. Opt for the lower level; the acoustics upstairs are dreadful. The menu offers contemporary renditions of classic American fare, from Waldorf salad to bananas Foster. There's piano music in the evening. ⊠ *56 Gold St.,* ☎ *415/433–6300. AE, D, DC, MC, V. No lunch weekends.*

Contemporary

$$–$$$ ✕ **Black Cat.** The menu at this combination restaurant and jazz lounge, the latter called the Blue Bar, is made up of dishes that reflect the city's ethnic diversity. You'll find the Wharf's shellfish soups and sand dabs with tartar sauce, North Beach's pastas, Chinatown's roast duck and chow mein, and the Barbary Coast's chops and grills here. The name

is taken from a famous San Francisco café-bar, a bohemian hangout for everyone from artists to trade unionists from the 1930s to the 1960s. The ambience is a spirited one, with live jazz and a tempting bar menu—barbecued salmon spring rolls, terrine of foie gras—served up until the wee hours in the seriously blue lounge. ⊠ *501 Broadway,* ☎ *415/981–2233. Reservations essential. AE, DC, MC, V.*

$$ ✕ **Enrico's Sidewalk Café.** For years this historic North Beach hangout was more a drinking spot than a dining destination, but a reliable kitchen has changed all that. Diners regularly tuck into the Caesar salad, thin-crust pizzas, grilled fish, and nicely done pastas, while gently swaying to first-rate live music. Grazers will be happy to find a slew of eclectic tapas, from smoked salmon bruschetta to fried oysters. The crowd includes local power brokers, struggling writers, twentysomethings, and out-of-towners—all of them hooked on the freewheeling atmosphere. An outdoor patio is outfitted with heat lamps to keep the serious people-watchers warm until closing. ⊠ *504 Broadway,* ☎ *415/982–6223. AE, DC, MC, V.*

French

$ ✕ **Des Alpes.** Opened in 1908, this spot has long been where the savvy diner finds a Basque meal at a rock-bottom price: soup, salad, two entrées—sweetbreads on puff pastry and rare roast beef are a typical pair—and ice cream are included in the budget tariff. It's a haven for ravenous souls, with wood-paneled walls and bright checkered cloths on the tables. Service is family style, and the *intime* bar that fronts the dining room is a delightful step back in time. ⊠ *732 Broadway,* ☎ *415/788–9900. D, DC, MC, V. Closed Mon. No lunch.*

Italian

$$–$$$ ✕ **Rose Pistola.** Chef-owner Reed Hearon's popular 130-
★ seat spot draws huge crowds. The name honors one of North Beach's most revered barkeeps, and the food celebrates the neighborhood's Ligurian roots. A wide assortment of small cold and hot antipasti—roasted peppers, house-cured fish, fava beans and pecorino cheese, crostini topped with cheese, arugula, and figs—and pizzas from the wood-burning oven are favorites, as is the classic San Francisco seafood stew called cioppino. A large and inviting bar area opens

onto the sidewalk, and an immense exhibition kitchen lets customers keep an eye on their orders. ✉ *532 Columbus Ave.,* ☎ *415/399–0499. Reservations essential. AE, MC, V.*

$–$$ ✕ **Tavolino.** A snacker's paradise, this light, airy space celebrates the Venetian tradition of *cicchetti,* small plates usually consumed in a neighborhood bar with a glass of local wine. Some of the offerings fit right in with the classics, such as deep-fried anchovy-stuffed olives, *tramezzini* (triangular sandwiches) filled with mozzarella and sliced tomatoes, fried calamari, and green beans dressed with olive oil. Other dishes are just shrunken versions of Italian *primi* or main dishes, such as squid ink risotto, house-made sausage with polenta, and a hearty lasagna. Tavolino is a nice place to stop for an afternoon sandwich and a glass of wine, or later in the evening for a serious cocktail and an order of sea bass marinated in vinegar with onions. ✉ *401 Columbus Ave.,* ☎ *415/392–1472. AE, DC, MC, V.*

$ ✕ **L'Osteria del Forno.** An Italian-speaking staff, a small, unpretentious dining area, and irresistible aromas drifting from the open kitchen make customers who pass through the door of this modest storefront operation feel as if they've just stumbled into Italy. The kitchen produces small plates of simply cooked vegetables, a few baked pastas, a roast of the day, creamy polenta, and wonderful thin-crust pizzas—including a memorable "white" pie topped with porcini mushrooms and mozzarella. At lunch try one of the delectable focaccia sandwiches. ✉ *519 Columbus Ave.,* ☎ *415/982–1124. Reservations not accepted. No credit cards. Closed Tues.*

Mediterranean

$$–$$$ ✕ **Moose's.** Restaurateur Ed Moose's latest venture was destined to become a celebrity hangout from the moment it opened in 1992, with politicians and media types following him from his former digs at Washington Square Bar & Grill. In 1997, Brian Whitmer, who has done stints at Montrachet in New York and Montrio in Carmel, joined Moose's as executive chef and managing partner, introducing a Mediterranean menu with heavy French, Italian, and Californian accents. Among his popular creations are the warm shiitake and buffalo mozzarella salad, risotto with wild mushrooms, and sturgeon wrapped in pancetta. The surroundings are classic and comfortable, with views of Washington Square and Russian Hill from a front café area. Counter seats have a view of the open kitchen. There's live music at night and a fine Sunday brunch. ⊠ *1652 Stockton St.,* ☎ *415/989–7800. Reservations essential. AE, DC, MC, V. No lunch Mon.–Wed.*

Middle Eastern

$$ ✕ **Maykadeh.** Although it sits in the middle of a decidedly Italian neighborhood, this authentic Persian restaurant serves a large following of faithful customers. Lamb dishes with rice are the specialties, served in a setting so elegant that the modest check comes as a surprise. The chicken, lamb, and beef kabobs and the *chelo* (Persian pilaf) are popular choices. Carnivores will appreciate first courses of lamb tongue in a sour cream-and-lime sauce and grilled lamb brains with saffron. ⊠ *470 Green St.,* ☎ *415/362–8286. MC, V.*

Northern Waterfront

Indian

$$–$$$ ✕ **Gaylord's.** You'll find a vast selection of mildly spiced northern Indian food here, along with meats and breads from the tandoor ovens and a wide range of vegetarian dishes. Although the kitchen sometimes stumbles, the elegantly appointed dining room goes a long way in soothing disappointments. So do the prime bay views. Validated parking is offered at the Ghirardelli Square garage. ⊠ *Ghirardelli Sq.,* ☎ *415/771–8822. AE, D, DC, MC, V.*

Seafood

$$ ✕ **McCormick & Kuleto's.** This seafood emporium in Ghirardelli Square is a visitor's dream come true: a fabulous view of the bay from every seat in the house; an Old San Francisco atmosphere; and dozens of varieties of fish and shellfish prepared in scores of globe-circling ways, from tacos, pot stickers, and fish cakes to grills, pastas, and stew. The food has its ups and downs—stick with the simplest preparations, such as oysters on the half shell and grilled fish—but even on foggy days you can count on the view. Validated parking is available in the Ghirardelli Square garage. ⊠ *Ghirardelli Sq. at Beach and Larkin Sts.,* ☎ *415/929–1730. AE, D, DC, MC, V.*

Russian Hill

French

$$$$ ✕ **La Folie.** Long a favorite of dedicated Francophiles, this
★   small, terribly Parisian establishment underwent a refur-
bishing in 1998, making the storefront café even lovelier.
But the food is the true star here, especially the five-course
discovery menu that allows a sample of such rarified mouth-
fuls as lobster salad with a mango vinaigrette and quail with
white truffles. Much of the food is edible art—whimsical
presentations in the form of savory terrines, *galettes* (flat,
round cakes), and napoleons—or such elegant accompa-
niments as bone-marrow flan. The exquisite food and professional service come at a hefty price, so save this special
place for a very special occasion. ⊠ *2316 Polk St.,* ☎ *415/
776–5577. Reservations essential. AE, D, DC, MC, V.
Closed Sun. No lunch.*

Italian

$$$ ✕ **Acquerello.** This elegant restaurant—white tablecloths,
fresh flowers, exquisite china—is one of the most roman-
tic spots in town. Both the service and the food are exem-
plary, and the menu covers the full range of Italian cuisine.
The gnocchi and tortellini are memorable, as are the fish
dishes. Chef Suzette Gresham's fine creations include a
first course of squab paired with greens and pine nuts, and
a main of beef fillet stuffed with prosciutto and Parmesan
cheese. ⊠ *1722 Sacramento St.,* ☎ *415/567–5432. AE, D,
DC, MC, V. Closed Sun.–Mon. No lunch.*

Spanish

$$ ✕ **Zarzuela.** Until the mid-'90s San Francisco lacked a
great tapas restaurant—but Spanish-born chef Lucas Gasco
changed all that when he and partner Andy Debanne
opened their charming Zarzuela. The small, crowded storefront serves nearly 40 different hot and cold tapas plus some
dozen main courses. There is a tapa to suit every palate,
from poached octopus atop new potatoes and hot garlic-
flecked shrimp to slabs of Manchego cheese with paper-thin
slices of serrano ham. ⊠ *2000 Hyde St.,* ☎ *415/346–0800.
Reservations not accepted. D, MC, V. Closed Sun.*

Steak

$$$ ✕ **Harris'.** Ann Harris knows her beef. She grew up on a
★ Texas cattle ranch and was married to the late Jack Har-
ris of Harris Ranch fame. In her own large, New York–style
restaurant she serves some of the best dry-aged steaks in
town, but don't overlook the starter of spinach salad or the
entrée of calves' liver with onions and bacon. Be sure to
include a side of the fine creamed spinach. If you're a mar-
tini drinker, don't pass up the opportunity to enjoy a su-
perb example of the art form. ✉ *2100 Van Ness Ave.,* ☎
415/673–1888. AE, D, DC, MC, V. No lunch.

South of Market

Contemporary

$$$ ✕ **Hawthorne Lane.** In 1995 Anne and David Gingrass, of
★ Postrio fame (☞ *Union Square, below*), joined the boom-
ing bevy of SoMa eateries with this instantly popular establishment on a quiet alley a block or so from the Moscone
Center and the Museum of Modern Art. In the large, high-
ceiling bar there's a selection of irresistible small plates—
Thai-style squid, skewers of grilled chicken, and
tempura-battered green beans with mustard sauce. Patrons
in the light-flooded dining room engage in more serious eating, from perfectly seared foie gras to grilled quail on scalloped potatoes, all turned out with Mediterranean and
Asian touches. The breadbasket is full of house-made de-
lights, including biscuits, bread sticks, rye, and rolls. The
desserts are suitably decàdent. ✉ *22 Hawthorne St.,* ☎ *415/
777–9779. Reservations essential. D, DC, MC, V. No lunch
weekends.*

French

$$–$$$ ✕ **Bizou.** Chef Loretta Keller, who once cooked alongside
Jeremiah Tower at Stars, has developed her own distinctive French country menu here. Partisans of her rustic cooking cite the thin, crisp pizza topped with caramelized onions,
fried snap beans with aioli or fig sauce, and panfried skate
in brown butter as evidence of her talents. The space itself
is small and unpretentious. Outsized windows means it's
also sunny and bright. Although service can sometimes be

uneven, Keller's faithful following doesn't seem to mind.
☒ 598 4th St., ☎ 415/543–2222. AE, MC, V. Closed Sun.
No lunch Sat.

\$\$–\$\$\$ ✕ **Fringale.** The bright yellow paint on this dazzling bistro
★   stands out like a beacon on an otherwise bleak industrial
street, attracting a well-dressed clientele. They come for the
reasonably priced French Basque–inspired creations of
Biarritz-born chef Gerald Hirigoyen, whose classic *frisée
aux lardoons* (curly salad greens with crisp bacon cubes and
a poached egg), *steak frites,* steamed mussels, and flaky apple
tart are hallmarks. Small tables covered with cloths and white
paper, a sensible wine list, and a crew of waiters sporting
Gallic accents will have you practicing your French. ☒ 570
4th St., ☎ 415/543–0573. Reservations essential. AE, MC,
V. Closed Sun. No lunch Sat.

Latin

\$\$ ✕ **Thirstybear.** Just around the corner from the cathedral-
like San Francisco Museum of Modern Art, Thirstybear is
a combination brew pub and tapas outpost. The cavernous
interior of concrete floors, rustic brick walls, and shiny tanks
holding homemade brews is cool and utilitarian, but the
small plates of garlic-and-sherry-infused fish cheeks, steamed
mussels, grilled garlic-studded shrimp, and white beans
with sausage and aioli will warm you right up. Bigger ap-
petites can dig into paella Valenciana. ☒ 661 Howard St.,
☎ 415/974–0905. MC, V. No lunch Sun.

Mediterranean

\$\$–\$\$\$ ✕ **LuLu.** Since its opening day in 1993, a seat at this bois-
★   terous restaurant has been one of the hottest tickets in town,
although the throngs have faded somewhat since founding
chef Reed Hearon divorced himself from the operation in
1996. The food, under the watchful eye of executive chef
Jody Denton, has remained satisfyingly uncomplicated and
delectable. Under the high barrel-vaulted ceiling, beside a
large open kitchen, diners feast on sizzling mussels roasted
in an iron skillet, plus pizzas, pastas, and wood-roasted
poultry, meats, and shellfish. Sharing dishes is the custom
here. A smaller, quieter room off to one side makes conversation easier. The café on the opposite side serves food
from morning until late at night. ☒ 816 Folsom St., ☎ 415/
495–5775. Reservations essential. AE, DC, MC, V.

Sunset District

Contemporary

$$ ✕ **Beach Chalet.** In a historic colonnaded building with hand-some Works Project Administration–produced murals de-picting San Francisco in the mid-'30s, the Beach Chalet is the place to watch the sun set over the Pacific. The micro-brewery beers run the gamut from a light pilsner to Play-land pale ale, named for a now-gone nearby amusement park that entertained generations of San Franciscans. The food is an eclectic mix of steamed mussels and pizzette, but-termilk-dipped onion rings and house-made chorizo, thick burgers, and seafood gumbo. It's a 40-minute ride on the N Judah streetcar from downtown—and well worth the trip. ✉ *1000 Great Hwy.,* ☎ *415/386–8439. MC, V.*

Union Square

Contemporary

$$$$ ✕ **Campton Place.** This elegant, ultrasophisticated small hotel
★ put new American cooking on the local culinary map with famed opening chef Bradley Ogden, who was followed by the nearly equally celebrated Jan Birnbaum, and later by yet another favorite, Todd Humphries, who left in early 1999. The kitchen continues to offer a refined American table that relies on the freshest local ingredients and hand-some presentation. A small side bar is a comfortable spot for sipping a martini while waiting for a table in the sub-tly appointed dining room. Brunch and breakfast are major events. ✉ *340 Stockton St.,* ☎ *415/955–5555. Reservations essential. AE, D, DC, MC, V.*

$$$–$$$$ ✕ **Postrio.** There's always a chance to catch a glimpse of some celebrity here, including Postrio's owner, superchef Wolfgang Puck, who periodically commutes from Los An-geles to make an appearance in the restaurant's open kitchen. A stunning three-level bar and dining area is high-lighted by palm trees and museum-quality contemporary paintings. Attire is formal. The food is Puckish Californian with Mediterranean and Asian overtones: Chinese roast duck with mango sauce, house-cured salmon on a giant blini, and irresistible pastries. Substantial breakfast and bar menus (with great pizza) can be found here as well. Although rip-ples of dissatisfaction with the fare have been heard from some quarters, reservations are still tough to come by. ✉ *545 Post St.,* ☎ *415/776–7825. Reservations essential. AE, D, DC, MC, V.*

French

$$$$ ✕ **Fleur de Lys.** The creative cooking of French chef-partner Hubert Keller has brought every conceivable culinary award to this romantic spot, which some consider the best French restaurant in town. The menu changes constantly, but such dishes as seared foie gras, truffled vichyssoise, and venison medallions with tender braised greens are Keller hallmarks. Perfectly smooth service adds to the overall enjoyment of eating here. There are tasting menus for both omnivores and vegetarians, and the elaborately canopied dining room is reminiscent of a sheikh's tent. ✉ *777 Sutter St.,* ☎ *415/673–7779. Reservations essential. Jacket required. AE, DC, MC, V. Closed Sun. No lunch.*

$$$$ ✕ **Masa's.** Julian Serrano headed up the kitchen at this pretty,
★   flower-filled dining spot in the Vintage Court hotel for more than a dozen years, carrying on the tradition of the restaurant's late founder, Masa Kobayashi. In 1998, the torch was passed to Chad Callahan, who had served as the number two chef for several years. Time will tell if Callahan can develop his own style in this celebrated food temple, but regulars have generally been pleased with the silky smooth transition. Dinners are prix fixe, with two menus offered, a four-course menu du jour and a five-course menu, both laced with truffles and foie gras and both priced at a king's ransom. ✉ *648 Bush St.,* ☎ *415/989–7154. Reservations essential. Jacket and tie. AE, D, DC, MC, V. Closed Sun.–Mon. and 1st 2 wks of Jan. No lunch.*

Italian

$$–$$$ ✕ **Scala's Bistro.** Smart leather-and-wood booths, an extravagant mural along one wall, and an appealing menu of Italian plates make this one of downtown's most attractive destinations. A large open kitchen stands at the rear of the fashionable dining room, where regulars and out-of-town visitors alike sit down to breakfast, lunch, and dinner. Grilled Portobello mushrooms and a tower of fried calamari or zucchini are among the favorite antipasti, and the pastas and grilled meats are satisfying. ✉ *432 Powell St.,* ☎ *415/395–8555. AE, D, DC, MC, V.*

Seafood

$$$ ✗ **Farallon.** Outfitted with sculpted purple-and-pink jelly-
★ fish lamps, kelp-covered columns, sea urchin chandeliers,
and seashell covered walls, this swanky Pat Kuleto–de-
signed restaurant is loaded with style *and* customers. Chef
Mark Franz, who gained his fame at Stars, cooks up
exquisite seafood that draws serious diners from coast to
coast. Such showy concoctions as spot prawns, scallops,
and lobster suspended in a pyramid of aspic, and truffled
mashed potatoes doused with a sauce of crab and sea
urchin are regular fare here. The desserts, including a very
adult peppermint patty, are by former Stars whiz Emily
Luchetti. ⊠ *450 Post St.,* ☎ *415/956–6969. AE, DC, MC,
V. No lunch Sun.*

4 Lodging

FEW CITIES IN THE UNITED STATES can rival
San Francisco's variety in lodging. There
are plush hotels ranked among the finest
in the world, renovated older buildings with a European
flair, and the popular chain hotels found in most American cities. One of the brightest spots in the lodging picture
is the proliferation of small bed-and-breakfasts housed in
elegant Victorian edifices, where evening hors d'oeuvres and
wine service are common practice.

Updated
by Andy
Moore

The **San Francisco Convention and Visitors Bureau** (☎ 415/
391–2000) publishes a free lodging guide with a map and
listings of San Francisco and Bay Area hotels; or call 888/
782–9673 to reserve a room at over 60 visitors bureau–recommended hotels in the city or near the airport. **San Francisco Reservations** (☎ 800/677–1500) handles advance
reservations at over 250 Bay Area hotels, often at special
discount rates. Reservations are always advised, especially
during the peak seasons (May–October and December).

No matter what their location, the hotels listed below are
on or close to public transportation lines. A few properties on Lombard Street and in the Civic Center area have
free parking, while hotels in the Union Square and Nob Hill
areas almost invariably charge $17–$26 a day for a spot
in their garage.

San Francisco hotel prices may come as a not-so-pleasant surprise. Weekend rates for double rooms downtown and at the
wharf start at about $130 and average over $100 per night
city-wide (slightly less on weekdays and off-season). Adding
to the expense is the city's 14% transient occupancy tax, which
can significantly boost the cost of a lengthy stay. The good
news is that because of the hotel building boom of the late
1980s, there is now an oversupply of rooms, which has led
to frequent discounts. Check for special rates and packages
when making reservations. For those in search of true budget accommodations (under $60), try the **Adelaide Inn** (☞
Union Square/Downtown, *below*) or the **YMCA Central
Branch** (✉ 220 Golden Gate Ave., ☎ 415/885–0460).

An alternative to hotels and motels is staying in private homes
and apartments, available through **American Family Inn/Bed**

& Breakfast San Francisco (✉ Box 420009, San Francisco 94142, ☎ 415/931–3083, ℻ 415/921–2273), **Bed & Breakfast California** (✉ 205 Park Rd., Suite 209, Burlingame 94010, ☎ 650/696–1690 or 800/872–4500, ℻ 650/696–1699), and **American Property Exchange** (✉ 2800 Van Ness Ave., San Francisco 94109, ☎ 415/447–2040, ℻ 415/447–2058).

CATEGORY	COST*
$$$$	over $200
$$$	$120–$200
$$	$80–$120
$	under $80

All prices are for a standard double room, excluding 14% tax.

Union Square/Downtown

The largest variety and greatest concentration of hotels is in the city's downtown hub, Union Square, where you can find the best shopping, the theater district, and convenient transportation to every spot in San Francisco. If the grand hotels right on Union Square are beyond your budget, consider the more modest establishments a few blocks to the west, between Mason and Jones streets—but be careful when walking there late at night.

$$$$ 🏨 **Campton Place.** Behind a simple brownstone facade
★ with a white awning, quiet reigns. Highly attentive personal service—from unpacking assistance to nightly turndown—begins the moment uniformed doormen greet guests outside the marble-floor lobby. Rooms, though a little smaller than those at other luxury hotels, are supremely elegant, decorated with Asian touches in light, subtle tones. They overlook an atrium, which lends a cozy, residential feel. The Campton Place Restaurant, listed as one of San Francisco's best by *Gourmet* magazine in 1998, is famed for its breakfasts. ✉ *340 Stockton St., 94108, ☎ 415/781–5555 or 800/ 235–4300, ℻ 415/955–5536. 107 rooms, 10 suites. Restaurant, bar, in-room safes, minibars, no-smoking rooms, room service, dry cleaning, concierge, meeting rooms, parking (fee). AE, DC, MC, V.*

$$$$ ⊞ **The Clift.** Towering over San Francisco's theater district is the venerable Clift. Its crisp, forest-green awnings and formal door service provide subtle hints of the elegance within. In the lobby, dark paneling and enormous chandeliers lend a note of grandeur. Rooms—some rich with dark woods and burgundies, others refreshingly pastel—all have large writing desks. Be sure to sample a cocktail in the dramatic Art–Deco Redwood Room lounge, complete with chandeliers and a sweeping redwood bar. ⊠ *495 Geary St., 94102,* ☎ *415/775–4700 or 800/652–5438,* 🖷 *415/441–4621. 218 rooms, 108 suites. Restaurant, bar, in-room data ports, minibars, no-smoking floor, room service, exercise room, laundry service and dry cleaning, concierge, meeting rooms, parking (fee). AE, DC, MC, V.*

$$$$ ⊞ **Hotel Monaco.** The hottest hotel in town, with its yellow beaux-arts facade, stands in stark contrast to its more ★ stately neighbor, the Clift. The contrast continues inside, where a French inglenook fireplace climbs almost two stories above the lobby toward the three huge domes of a vaulted ceiling, which is hand-painted with hot-air balloons, World War I–era planes, and miles of blue sky. Though small, the rooms are comfortable and inviting, with Chinese-inspired armoires and high-back upholstered chairs; in the outer rooms, bay window seats overlook the theater district. Though the riot of stripes and colors may strike some guests as a bit outré, it's all been done so tastefully you can't help but appreciate the flair. The Grand Café and Bar, in which hotel guests get preferred seating, features a French-California menu. ⊠ *501 Geary St., 94102,* ☎ *415/292–0100 or 800/214–4220,* 🖷 *415/292–0111. 177 rooms, 24 suites. Restaurant, bar, in-room data ports, in-room safes, minibars, no-smoking rooms, room service, spa, laundry service and dry cleaning, business services, parking (fee). AE, D, DC, MC, V.*

$$$$ ⊞ **Pan Pacific Hotel.** Exotic flower arrangements and elegant Asian touches set this business hotel apart from others. A graceful sculpture, *Joie de Dance,* encircles the fountain in the lobby, where two fireplaces add to the refined atmosphere. Guest rooms feature such business amenities as in-room fax machines and modem lines, not to mention elegant bathrooms lined with terra-cotta Portuguese marble. Complimentary personal valet service and the hotel's

Downtown San Francisco Lodging

Chestnut St.

Lombard St.

Greenwich St.

Filbert St.

Union St.

Green St.

Vallejo St.

Broadway

Pacific Ave.

Jackson St.

Alta Plaza

PACIFIC HEIGHTS

Lafayette Park

RUSSIAN HILL

Green St.

Vallejo St.

Broadway

Broadway Tunnel

Pacific Ave.

Jackson St.

Washington St.

Clay St.

Sacramento St.

California St.

Pine St.

Bush St.

JAPANTOWN

Post St.

Geary St.

O'Farrell St.

Ellis St.

Eddy St.

Sutter St.

Post St.

Geary St.

O'Farrell St.

Ellis St.

Eddy St.

Turk St.

Golden Gate Ave.

Greenwich St. • Filbert St. • Union St. • Green St. • Vallejo St. • Broadway • Pacific Ave. • Jackson St.

Scott St. • Pierce St. • Steiner St. • Fillmore St. • Webster St. • Buchanan St. • Laguna St. • Octavia St. • Gough St. • Franklin St. • Van Ness Ave. • Polk St. • Larkin St. • Hyde St. • Leavenworth St. • Jones St.

1 · 2 · 3 · 4 · 5 · 6 · 7 · 8 · 9 · 43 · 44 · 45 · 46

Adelaide Inn, **45**

The Archbishop's Mansion, **8**

Bed and Breakfast Inn, **3**

Bijou, **38**

Campton Place, **29**

The Clarion, **37**

The Clift, **42**

Commodore International, **22**

Embassy Suites San Francisco Airport—Burlingame, **33**

Galleria Park, **30**

Grant Plaza Hotel, **24**

Harbor Court, **26**

Hotel Bohème, **13**

Hotel Del Sol, **1**

Hotel Diva, **41**

Hotel Majestic, **6**

Hotel Monaco, **43**

Hotel Rex, **19**

Hotel Sofitel–San Francisco Bay, **34**

Hotel Triton, **27**

The Huntington, **18**

Hyatt Regency San Francisco Airport, **35**

Inn at the Opera, **9**

Inn at Union Square, **40**

Mandarin Oriental, **25**

Mark Hopkins Inter–Continental, **17**

Nob Hill Lambourne, **23**

Palace Hotel, **31**

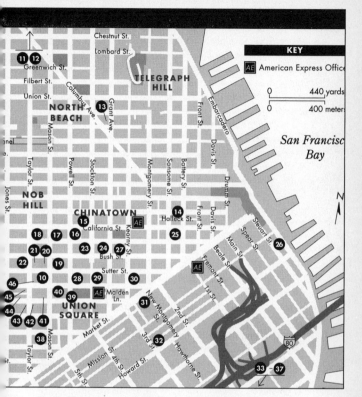

Chestnut St.

Lombard St.

TELEGRAPH HILL

Greenwich St.

Filbert St.

Union St.

NORTH BEACH

Chestnut St.

Columbus Ave.

Grant Ave.

Front St.

Embarcadero

San Francisco Bay

KEY

AE American Express Office

0   440 yards
0   400 meters

Mason St.

Taylor St.

Jones St.

Powell St.

Stockton St.

Montgomery St.

Sansome St.

Battery St.

Davis St.

Front St.

Davis St.

Drumm St.

NOB HILL

CHINATOWN

California St.

Kearny St.

Halleck St.

Sutter St.

Bush St.

Maiden Ln.

UNION SQUARE

Market St.

Mission St.

Howard St.

5th St.

4th St.

3rd St.

2nd St.

New Montgomery St.

1st St.

Fremont St.

Beale St.

Main St.

Spear St.

Steuart St.

Mason St.

Taylor St.

Hawthorne St.

80

N

Pan Pacific Hotel, **10**	San Francisco Residence Club, **16**	Tuscan Inn, **11**
Park Hyatt, **14**	San Remo, **12**	Union Street Inn, **4**
Petite Auberge, **21**	Shannon Court Hotel, **44**	W San Francisco, **32**
Prescott Hotel, **46**	Sherman House, **5**	Westin St. Francis, **39**
Radisson Miyako Hotel, **7**	Sir Francis Drake Hotel, **28**	White Swan Inn, **20**
Red Roof Inn, **36**	Town House Motel, **2**	
The Ritz–Carlton, San Francisco, **15**		

fleet of luxury cars serving as shuttles for guests add to a pampering experience. The hotel's restaurant, Pacific, is well regarded for its California cuisine. ⊠ *500 Post St., 94102,* ☎ *415/771–8600 or 800/327–8585,* FAX *415/398–0267. 311 rooms, 19 suites. Restaurant, bar, lobby lounge, in-room data ports, in-room safes, minibars, no-smoking floors, refrigerators, room service, exercise room, piano, laundry service and dry cleaning, concierge, business services, meeting rooms, parking (fee). AE, D, DC, MC, V.*

$$$$ **Prescott Hotel.** A gourmet's delight might be the best way
★   to describe this plush hotel, thanks to its partnership with Wolfgang Puck's Postrio, one of San Francisco's best restaurants. Cuisine-conscious guests can order room service from the restaurant or dine at tables reserved for hotel guests—no small perk considering it can otherwise take months to get a reservation at Postrio. The Prescott's rooms, which vary only in size and shape, are traditional in style and decorated in a rich hunter green; bathrooms have marble-top sinks and gold fixtures. There's a brick-and-wood fireplace in the hunting-lodge-style living room—a perfect setting for the complimentary coffee and tea services and evening wine and cheese receptions. ⊠ *545 Post St., 94102,* ☎ *415/563–0303 or 800/283–7322,* FAX *415/563–6831. 134 rooms, 30 suites. Restaurant, bar, lobby lounge, in-room data ports, minibars, no-smoking floors, room service, concierge, business services, meeting rooms, parking (fee). AE, D, DC, MC, V.*

$$$$ **Westin St. Francis.** Guests as illustrious as Emperor Hirohito, Queen Elizabeth II, and many presidents have stayed here since it opened in 1904. No wonder; with an imposing facade, black marble lobby, and gold-top columns, the St. Francis looks more like a great public building than a hotel. The effect is softened by the columns and exquisite woodwork of the Compass Rose bar and restaurant, a romantic retreat from the bustle of Union Square. Many rooms in the original building are small by modern standards, but all retain their original Victorian-style moldings and are decorated with Empire-style furnishings. Rooms in the modern tower are larger, with Oriental-style lacquered furniture. Ask for a room above the 15th floor for a spectacular view of the city. ⊠ *335 Powell St., 94102,* ☎ *415/ 397–7000,* FAX *415/774–0124. 1,108 rooms, 84 suites. 3* restaurants, 2 bars, in-room data ports, in-room safes, no-smoking floors, room service, exercise room, nightclub, laundry service and dry cleaning, concierge, business services, meeting rooms, travel services, parking (fee). AE, D, DC, MC, V.

$$$–$$$$ 🖬 **Galleria Park.** A few blocks east of Union Square, this
★ hotel with a black marble facade is close to the Chinatown Gate and Crocker Galleria, one of San Francisco's most elegant shopping areas. The staff is remarkably pleasant and helpful. The comfortable rooms all have floral bedspreads, stylish striped wallpaper, and white furniture that includes a writing desk. In the lobby, dominated by a massive fireplace, complimentary coffee and tea are served in the mornings, wine in the evenings. The third-floor rooftop Cityscape Park features an outdoor jogging track. Adjoining the hotel is Perry's Downtown, a casual steak-and-burger eatery where singles like to congregate. ⊠ 191 Sutter St., 94104, ☎ 415/781–3060; 800/792–9639; 800/792–9855 in CA; FAX 415/433–4409. 162 rooms, 15 suites. 2 restaurants, in-room data ports, minibars, no-smoking floors, room service, exercise room, jogging, dry cleaning, laundry service, concierge, business services, meeting rooms, parking (fee). AE, D, DC, MC, V.

$$$–$$$$ 🖬 **Hotel Rex.** Literary and artistic creativity are celebrated
★ at the stylish Hotel Rex, where thousands of books, largely antiquarian, line the 1920s-style lobby. Original artwork adorns the walls, and the proprietors even host book readings and roundtable discussions in the common areas, which are decorated in warm, rich tones. Upstairs, quotations from works by California writers are painted on the terra-cotta-color walls near the elevator landings. Rooms have writing desks and lamps with whimsically hand-painted shades. Striped bedspreads and carpets and restored period furnishings evoke the spirit of 1920s salon society, but rooms also have modern amenities like voice mail and CD players. ⊠ 562 Sutter St., 94102, ☎ 415/433–4434 or 800/433–4434, FAX 415/433–3695. 92 rooms, 2 suites. Bar, lobby lounge, in-room data ports, minibars, no-smoking rooms, laundry service and dry cleaning, concierge, parking (fee). AE, D, DC, MC, V.

$$$–$$$$ 🖬 **Hotel Triton.** This just may be the zaniest place to stay in town. Guests enter via a whimsical lobby of three-leg fur-

niture, star-pattern carpeting, and inverted gilt pillars—stylized spoofs of upside-down Roman columns. The hotel caters to fashion, entertainment, music, and film-industry types, who seem to appreciate the iridescent multicolor rooms with S-curve chairs, curly-neck lamps, and oddball light fixtures. On the downside, rooms are uncommonly small. If you care about space, try a king room or junior suite. Twenty-four rooms have been designated environmentally sensitive. They feature extra air and water filtration, biodegradable toiletries, and all-natural linens. The trendy newsstand–coffeehouse–dining room Café de la Presse, which serves as a gathering place for foreign visitors to the city, is attached to the hotel. ⊠ *342 Grant Ave., 94108,* ☎ *415/394–0500 or 888/364–2622,* 𝔽𝔸𝕏 *415/394–0555. 133 rooms, 7 suites. In-room data ports, minibars, no-smoking floors, exercise room, laundry service and dry cleaning, business services, meeting rooms, parking (fee). AE, D, MC, V.*

$$$–$$$$ 🏨 **Sir Francis Drake Hotel.** Beefeater-costumed doormen (including the internationally renowned Tom Sweeney) welcome you into the regal lobby, which has wrought-iron balustrades, chandeliers, and Italian marble. The guest rooms have a simpler decor with California-style furnishings and floral-print fabrics. On the top floor, Harry Denton's Starlight Room has been all the rage since its opening in 1995. The hotel's surprisingly affordable restaurant, Scala's Bistro, serves excellent food in its dramatic though somewhat noisy dining room. ⊠ *450 Powell St., 94102,* ☎ *415/392–7755 or 800/227–5480,* 𝔽𝔸𝕏 *415/395–8559. 394 rooms, 23 suites. 2 restaurants, in-room data ports, minibars, no-smoking rooms, exercise room, nightclub, concierge, meeting rooms, parking (fee). AE, D, DC, MC, V.*

$$$–$$$$ 🏨 **Inn at Union Square.** With its tiny but captivating lobby with trompe l'oeil bookshelves painted on the walls, this inn feels like someone's home. Comfortable rooms with sumptuous goose-down pillows promote indolence. Brass lion's-head door knockers are a unique touch. Guests like to lounge in front of the wood-burning fireplaces found in each floor's tiny sitting area, and with good reason: By the time the staff clears away the afternoon tea and pastries, they're already setting out the complimentary evening wine and hors d'oeuvres. Tips are not accepted, and the hotel is

In case you want to see the world.

At American Express, we're here to make your journey
a smooth one. So we have over 1,700 travel service locations in over 130 countries ready to help. What else
would you expect from the world's largest travel agency?

do more AMERICAN EXPRESS

Travel

Call 1 800 AXP-3429 or visit
www.americanexpress.com/travel

In case you want to be welcomed there.

We're here to see that you're always welcomed at establishments everywhere. That's why millions of people carry the American Express® Card – for peace of mind, confidence, and security, around the world or just around the corner.

do more

Cards

In case you're running low.

We're here to help with more than 190,000 Express Cash locations around the world. In order to enroll, just call American Express at 1 800 CASH-NOW before you start your vacation.

do more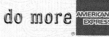

Express Cash

And in case you'd rather be safe than sorry.

We're here with American Express® Travelers Cheques. They're the safe way to carry money on your vacation, because if they're ever lost or stolen you can get a refund, practically anywhere or anytime. To find the nearest place to buy Travelers Cheques, call 1 800 495-1153. Another way we help you do more.

do more AMERICAN EXPRESS

Travelers Cheques

completely no-smoking. ✉ *440 Post St., 94102,* ☎ *415/ 397–3510 or 800/288–4346,* 🖷 *415/989–0529. 30 rooms. In-room data ports, parking (fee). AE, DC, MC, V.*

$$$ 🖬 **Hotel Diva.** A gray awning and burnished silver facade give this reasonably priced hotel a slick, high-tech look that sets it apart from others in San Francisco. Fresh from a 1998 renovation, the futuristic decor extends to the somewhat small rooms, which have angular sofas, wire-frame chairs, and black-lacquer furniture. Although the Diva's proximity to the Curran Theater attracts actors, musicians, and others of an artistic bent, the hotel is also popular with business travelers, who have free access to the tiny business center, and families, who entertain themselves with the in-room Nintendo and VCRs. A complimentary Continental breakfast is delivered to guests' rooms. ✉ *440 Geary St., 94102,* ☎ *415/885–0200 or 800/553–1900,* 🖷 *415/346–6613. 79 rooms, 32 suites. Restaurant, in-room data ports, in-room safes, minibars, no-smoking floors, room service, in-room VCRs, exercise room, laundry service and dry cleaning, concierge, business services, meeting room, parking (fee). AE, D, DC, MC, V.*

$$$ 🖬 **Shannon Court Hotel.** Passing through the elaborate wrought-iron and glass entrance into the marble-tiled lobby of the Shannon Court evokes the old world charm of turn-of-the-century San Francisco. This hotel has some of the most spacious standard rooms in the Union Square area; many have sofa beds for families. Two of the luxury suites on the 16th floor have rooftop terraces with lofty city views. Complimentary morning coffee and afternoon tea and cookies are served in the lobby area. The hotel's restaurant, City of Paris, is open all day until midnight and serves California French cuisine in a casual atmosphere, with good live jazz on weekends. ✉ *550 Geary St., 94102,* ☎ *415/775–5000 or 800/228–8830,* 🖷 *415/928–6813. 172 rooms, 4 suites. Restaurant, bar, lobby lounge, no-smoking floor, refrigerators, laundry service and dry cleaning, concierge, parking (fee). AE, D, DC, MC, V.*

$$$ 🖬 **White Swan Inn.** The White Swan has all the comforts of home—personal front-door keys, complimentary soft drinks, and free copies of the *San Francisco Chronicle*. Rooms are large, with dark wood furniture and an English country theme. Each room has a fireplace (there are 26 guest rooms and 30 fireplaces on the property). Afternoon tea, appetizers, and wine are served in the lounge, where comfortable chairs and sofas invite lingering. The breakfasts (included in the room rate) here are famous, and guests can purchase the inn's cookbook to try to duplicate their crab and cheese souffle toasts, chocolate scones, or artichoke pesto puffs at home. The entire inn is no-smoking. ⊠ *845 Bush St., 94108,* ☎ *415/775–1755 or 800/999–9570,* ℻ *415/775–5717. 23 rooms, 3 suites. Breakfast room, in-room data ports, no-smoking floors, concierge, meeting rooms, parking (fee). AE, MC, V.*

$$–$$$ 🎞 **Bijou.** With plush velvet upholstery and rich detailing, this hotel is decorated as a nostalgic tribute to 1930s cinema. The mini lobby theater, Le Petit Theatre Bijou, shows movies from the hotel's collection of 65 San Francisco–themed films to guests. The smallish rooms are named after these films and decorated with black-and-white prints from them. The staff is friendly, but the service is definitely no-frills. The handcrafted chrome ticket booth in the lobby offers a hot line to current San Francisco film shoots and casting calls for extras. ⊠ *111 Mason St., at Eddy St., 94102,* ☎ *415/771–1200 or 800/771–1022,* ℻ *415/346–3196. 65 rooms. No-smoking rooms, laundry service, concierge, parking (fee). AE, D, DC, MC, V.*

$$–$$$ 🎞 **Commodore International.** Entering the lobby is like stepping onto the main deck of an ocean liner of yore: Neodeco chairs look like the backdrop for a film about transatlantic crossings; and steps away is the Titanic Café, where goldfish bowls and bathysphere-inspired lights add to the sea-cruise mood. The fairly large rooms with monster closets are painted in soft yellows and golds and decorated with photographs of San Francisco landmarks. If red is your color, you may find yourself glued to a seat in the hotel's Red Room, a startlingly scarlet cocktail lounge. ⊠ *825 Sutter St., 94109,* ☎ *415/923–6800 or 800/338–6848,* ℻ *415/923–6804. 113 rooms. Restaurant, in-room data ports, no-smoking rooms, nightclub, laundry service and dry cleaning, concierge, parking (fee). AE, D, MC, V.*

$$–$$$ 🎞 **Petite Auberge.** The dozens of teddy bears in the reception area may seem a bit precious, but the rooms in this re-creation of a French country inn never stray past the mark. Rooms are small, but each has a teddy bear, bright flowered

wallpaper, an old-fashioned writing desk, and a much-needed armoire—there's little or no closet space. Most rooms have working fireplaces; the suite has a whirlpool tub. Afternoon tea, wine, and hors d'oeuvres are served in the lobby by the fire, and a full breakfast is included. The entire inn is no-smoking. ⊠ *863 Bush St., 94108, ☎ 415/928–6000 or 800/365–3004, FAX 415/775–5717. 25 rooms, 1 suite. Breakfast room, parking (fee). AE, DC, MC, V.*

$–$$ 🏨 **Grant Plaza Hotel.** One block in from the Chinatown Gate guarded by its famous stone lions, this hotel may seem worlds away from Union Square, yet it and the Financial District are only a stone's throw away. Amazingly low room rates for this part of town make the Grant Plaza a find for budget travelers wanting to look out their window at the exotic architecture and fascinating street life of Chinatown. The smallish rooms, all with private baths, are very clean and modern. All rooms have electronic locks, voice mail, and satellite TV. The two large, beautiful stained-glass windows near the top floor elevator area are worth a look. ⊠ *465 Grant Ave., 94108, ☎ 415/434–3883 or 800/472–6899, FAX 415/434–3886. 72 rooms, 1 suite. Concierge, parking (fee). AE, DC, MC, V.*

$ 🏨 **Adelaide Inn.** The bedspreads at this quiet retreat may not match the drapes or carpets, and the floors may creak, but the rooms are sunny, clean, and remarkably cheap. Tucked away in an alley, the funky European-style pension hosts many guests from Germany, France, and Italy, making it fun to chat over complimentary coffee and rolls downstairs in the mornings. Baths are shared. ⊠ *5 Isadora Duncan Ct., at Taylor St. between Geary and Post Sts., 94102, ☎ 415/441–2474 or 415/441–2261, FAX 415/441–0161. 18 rooms. Breakfast room, refrigerators. AE, MC, V.*

Financial District

High-rise growth in San Francisco's Financial District has turned it into a mini-Manhattan and a spectacular sight by night. Shoppers and sightseers enjoy easy access to nearby Union Square, the Embarcadero, Pier 39 at Fisherman's Wharf, Market Street's shops, and the burgeoning South of Market (SoMa) area with its many restaurants and nightclubs. Don't expect much nightlife in the Financial District itself, though. Many restaurants and bars in the neighborhood close soon after the last commuters catch their BART train home.

$$$$ 🏨 **Mandarin Oriental.** Since the Mandarin comprises the
★   top 11 floors (38 to 48) of San Francisco's third-tallest building—the First California Center—all rooms provide panoramic vistas of the city and beyond. The glass-enclosed sky bridges that connect the front and back towers of the hotel are almost as striking as the views. Rooms are decorated in light creamy yellow with black accents; those in the front tower fill up quickly because of their dramatic ocean views. The Mandarin Rooms in each tower have bathtubs flanked by windows; enjoy a decadent bathing experience with loofah sponges, plush robes, and silk slippers. The second-floor restaurant, Silks, earns rave reviews for its innovative California cuisine with Asian touches. ⊠ *222 Sansome St., 94104,* ☎ *415/276–9888 or 800/622– 0404,* 𝔽𝔸𝕏 *415/433–0289. 154 rooms, 4 suites. Lobby lounge, in-room data ports, minibars, no-smoking floors, room service, health club, laundry service and dry cleaning, concierge, business services, meeting rooms, parking (fee). AE, D, DC, MC, V.*

$$$$ 🏨 **Palace Hotel.** This landmark hotel—with a guest list that has included Enrico Caruso, Woodrow Wilson, and Amelia Earhart—was the epitome of luxury when it opened in 1875. Today its historic splendor is best seen in the stunning entryway and the belle epoque Garden Court restaurant, with its graceful chandeliers and lead-glass ceiling. After the lavish public spaces, the rooms seem uninspired, although modern conveniences, like TVs inside mahogany armoires, are well integrated into the decor. Though service is sometimes disappointing, the hotel is a logical choice for business travelers, with a prime location near the Financial District, a business center, a health club, and an indoor lap pool. One of the restaurants, Maxfield's, is named for the Maxfield Parrish Pied Piper mural hanging over the bar. The modern Kyo-ya restaurant is to the immediate right of the hotel entrance. ⊠ *2 New Montgomery St., 94105,* ☎ *415/ 512–1111,* 𝔽𝔸𝕏 *415/543–0671. 517 rooms, 33 suites. 3 restaurants, bar, room service, health club, laundry service, parking (fee). AE, D, DC, MC, V.*

$$$$ 🏨 **Park Hyatt.** Contemporary in design but with a touch of old world style, the Park Hyatt is a well-managed property across Battery Street from the Embarcadero Center. Convenient to the waterfront, downtown, and the South of Market area, the hotel's public areas feature large floral displays and fine artworks on the walls. The good-size rooms are decorated with Australian lacewood, polished granite, stylish furniture, and fresh flowers. Amenities include voice mail and Neutrogena toiletries. The Park Grill restaurant serves upscale California cuisine, and an elegant afternoon tea is served in the Lounge. Complimentary car service is offered within downtown San Francisco. ⊠ *333 Battery St., 94111,* ☎ *415/392–1234 or 800/492–8822,* ℻ *415/421–2433. 322 rooms, 38 suites. Restaurant, 2 bars, in-room data ports, minibars, room service, laundry service and dry cleaning, business services, parking (fee). AE, D, DC, MC, V.*

$$$–$$$$ 🏨 **Harbor Court.** Within shouting distance of the Bay Bridge
★ and the hot South of Market area with its plentiful night-clubs and restaurants, this cozy hotel, formerly an Army/Navy YMCA, is noted for the exemplary service of its warm, friendly staff. Some guest rooms, with double sets of sound-proof windows, overlook the bay; others face a dressed-up rooftop. In the evening complimentary wine is served in the cozy lounge, sometimes accompanied by live guitar. Guests have free access to YMCA facilities (including a 150-ft heated indoor pool), on one side of the hotel, and a convenient entrance to Harry Denton's Bar and Grill, with its turn-of-the-century mahogany bar and plush saloon atmosphere, on the other. There's also a complimentary limousine service to the Financial District. ⊠ *165 Steuart St., 94105,* ☎ *415/882–1300 or 800/346–0555,* ℻ *415/882–1313. 136 rooms. In-room data ports, minibars, no-smoking floors, room service, laundry service and dry cleaning, business services, parking (fee). AE, D, DC, MC, V.*

South of Market (SoMa)

This up-and-coming area is a convenient spot for leisure and business travelers to bed down. The San Francisco Museum of Modern Art and the Yerba Buena Gardens are nearby, among other attractions.

$$$$ ▣ **W San Francisco.** The city's first newly built hotel in 10 years, the W San Francisco's 31-story tower opened in May 1999, nodding architecturally to two of its neighbors, the landmark Pacific Telephone Building and SFMOMA. Across the street from the Yerba Buena Center for the Arts and Moscone Convention Center, the W's gray facade is trimmed with black granite piping, and its octagonal 3-story glass entrance leads into a lobby decorated—like the entire hotel—in modern high-style. Stone, corrugated metal, frosted glass, and other urban-industrial elements are offset by accents of polished mahogany, floor-to-ceiling yellow-green mohair drapes, and broad-striped carpeting. Each guest room has either a cozy corner sitting area or a padded window seat perch overlooking the city. The snugly beds have pillow-top mattresses, goose-down comforters and pillows, and 250-thread count linens. Cordless phones and Aveda bath products are added bonuses. ⊠ *181 Third St., 94103,* ☎ *415/626–0777,* ☏ *415/817–7848. 418 rooms, 5 suites. Restaurant, bar, café, in-room data ports, in-room safes, minibars, no-smoking floor, refrigerators, room service, in-room VCRs, indoor pool, hot tub, massage, exercise room, laundry service and dry cleaning, concierge, business services, meeting rooms, parking (fee). AE, D, DC, MC, V.*

Nob Hill

Synonymous with San Francisco's high society, Nob Hill contains some of the city's best-known luxury hotels. All have spectacular views and noted restaurants. Cable car lines that cross Nob Hill should help you avoid the short but very steep trek from Union Square.

$$$$ ▣ **The Huntington.** The family-owned Huntington provides an oasis of gracious personal service in an atmosphere of understated luxury. The privacy of the hotel's many celebrated guests, from Bogart and Bacall to Picasso and Pavarotti, has always been impeccably preserved. Rooms and suites, many of which have great views of Grace Cathedral, the bay, or the city skyline, are large because they used to be residential apartments. Most rooms have wet bars, all have large antique desks, and some suites have kitchens. The hotel's famous Big Four Restaurant, named after railroad magnates Charles Crocker, Leland Stanford, Mark Hopkins, and C. P. Huntington, serves contemporary American cuisine in an elegant clublike setting filled with San Francisco and Western memorabilia. ⊠ *1075 California St., 94108,* ☎ *415/474–5400; 800/227–4683; 800/652–1539 in CA;* FAX *415/474–6227. 101 rooms, 36 suites. Restaurant, bar, in-room data ports, in-room safes, no-smoking rooms, room service, laundry service and dry cleaning, concierge, meeting rooms, parking (fee). AE, D, DC, MC, V.*

$$$$ ⌕ **Mark Hopkins Inter-Continental.** The circular drive to this regal Nob Hill landmark leads to a lobby with floor-to-ceiling mirrors and marble floors. The rooms, with dramatic neoclassic furnishings of gray, silver, and khaki and bold leaf-print bedspreads, lead into bathrooms lined with Italian marble (at press time, a renovation of rooms is scheduled which will include changes in decor). Rooms on high floors have views of either the Golden Gate Bridge or the downtown cityscape. No visit would be complete without a visit to the vibrant Top of the Mark, *the* rooftop cocktail lounge in San Francisco since 1939, featuring panoramic views with live bands and dancing in the evenings. ⊠ *999 California St., 94108,* ☎ *415/392–3434 or 800/662–4455,* FAX *415/421–3302. 361 rooms, 30 suites. Restaurant, 2 bars, room service, exercise room, laundry service and dry cleaning, concierge, business services, meeting rooms, car rental, parking (fee). AE, D, DC, MC, V.*

$$$$ ⌕ **The Ritz-Carlton, San Francisco.** Consistently rated one
★ of the top hotels in the world by *Condé Nast Traveler,* the Ritz-Carlton is a stunning tribute to beauty, splendor, and warm, sincere service. Beyond the neoclassic facade, crystal chandeliers illuminate an opulent lobby adorned with Georgian antiques and a collection of museum-quality 18th- and 19th-century paintings. The hotel's fitness center is a destination in its own right, with an indoor swimming pool, saunas, and a whirlpool; you can even get an in-room massage. The renowned Dining Room features a three-, four-, or five-course seasonal menu with modern French accents by celebrated chef Sylvain Portay, originally from New York's beloved Le Cirque. Afternoon tea in the Lobby Lounge—which overlooks the hotel's beautifully landscaped garden courtyard—is a San Francisco institution. ⊠ *600 Stockton St., at California St., 94108,* ☎ *415/296–7465 or*

800/241–3333, ⓕ*AX 415/296–8261. 276 rooms, 60 suites. 2 restaurants, bar, lobby lounge, health club, laundry service and dry cleaning, concierge, business services, meeting rooms, parking (fee). AE, D, DC, MC, V.*

$$$ 🏨 **Nob Hill Lambourne.** This urban retreat, designed with
★ the traveling executive in mind, takes pride in pampering business travelers with personal computers, fax machines, and personalized voice mail; an on-site spa with massages, body scrubs, manicures, and pedicures helps them relax. If that's not enough, videos on such topics as stress reduction and yoga are available on request. Rooms have queen-size beds with hand-sewn mattresses, silk-damask bedding, and contemporary furnishings in muted colors. All rooms have modern kitchenettes and stereos. A deluxe Continental breakfast and evening wine service are complimentary. ✉ *725 Pine St., at Stockton St., 94108,* ☎ *415/433–2287 or 800/274–8466,* ⓕ*AX 415/433–0975. 14 rooms, 6 suites. Lobby lounge, in-room data ports, no-smoking floors, in-room VCRs, spa, business services, parking (fee). AE, D, DC, MC, V.*

$–$$$ 🏨 **San Francisco Residence Club.** In contrast to the neighboring showplace hotels, the Residence Club, once an apartment building, is a humble guest house with million-dollar views and a money-saving meal plan. Though it has a fancy Nob Hill address, the building has seen better days and most of the very modest rooms share baths. Many of the rooms, however, have sweeping views of the city and the bay; some have TVs and refrigerators. The club's dedicated international clientele ranges from leisure travelers and business professionals to longer-term residents who enjoy the full American breakfast *and* dinner included in the daily, weekly, or monthly room rate. The dining room is a great place to meet interesting people, and the garden patio is a pleasant place to relax. ✉ *851 Powell St., 94108,* ☎ *415/421–2220,* ⓕ*AX 415/421–2335. 84 rooms. Dining room, lobby lounge, coin laundry. No credit cards; $100 advance deposit via check required.*

Fisherman's Wharf/North Beach

All accommodations in Fisherman's Wharf are within a few blocks of restaurants, shops, and cable car lines. Because of city ordinances, no hotel exceeds four stories, so this is not the area for fantastic views of the city or the bay. Reservations are always necessary, sometimes weeks in advance during peak summer months when rates rise by as much as 30%. Some street-side rooms can be noisy. Nearby North Beach has surprisingly few lodgings. A few small B&Bs, however, hide in unassuming Victorians on the neighborhood's side streets.

$$$–$$$$ 🏨 **Tuscan Inn.** The major attraction here is the friendly, attentive staff, which provides such services as a complimentary limousine to the Financial District. The condolike exterior of the inn—reddish brick with white concrete—gives little indication of the charm of the relatively small, Italian-influenced guest rooms, with their white-pine furniture and floral bedspreads and curtains. Room service is provided by Cafe Pescatore, the Italian seafood restaurant off the lobby. Morning coffee, tea, and biscotti are complimentary, and wine is served in the early evening. ✉ *425 N. Point St., at Mason St., 94133,* ☎ *415/561–1100 or 800/648–4626,* ℻ *415/561–1199. 208 rooms, 12 suites. Restaurant, minibars, no-smoking rooms, room service, laundry service and dry cleaning, meeting rooms, parking (fee). AE, D, DC, MC, V.*

$$–$$$ 🏨 **Hotel Bohème.** In the middle of historic North Beach, this little bargain gives guests a taste of the area's historical bohemian flair. The small rooms, decorated with European armoires, bistro tables, and memorabilia from the 1950s and '60s, recall the beat generation; rumor has it that the late poet Allen Ginsberg used to stay here. Coral-color walls and handmade lampshades complete the nostalgic mood. Enjoy complimentary sherry in the lobby while you decide which of the many nearby Italian restaurants and cafés to visit. ✉ *444 Columbus Ave., 94133,* ☎ *415/433–9111,* ℻ *415/362–6292. 15 rooms. In-room data ports. AE, D, MC, V.*

$ 🏨 **San Remo.** This three-story, blue-and-white Italianate Victorian just a few blocks from Fisherman's Wharf has reasonably priced rooms and a down-home, slightly faded elegance. The smallish rooms are crowded with furniture: vanities; rag rugs; pedestal sinks; ceiling fans; antique armoires; and brass, iron, or wooden beds. Guests share six black-and-white-tile shower rooms, one bathtub chamber, and six scrupulously clean toilets with brass pull chains and oak tanks. The penthouse has a wonderful 360-degree view of the city and a private bath and is often requested by honeymooners and other romantics. ⊠ *2237 Mason St., 94133,* ☎ *415/776–8688 or 800/352–7366,* FAX *415/776–2811. 61 rooms, 1 suite. No-smoking rooms, coin laundry, parking (fee). AE, DC, MC, V.*

Pacific Heights, Cow Hollow, and the Marina

Lombard Street, a major traffic corridor leading to the Golden Gate Bridge, stretches past San Francisco's poshest neighborhoods: Pacific Heights, Cow Hollow, and the Marina. The cheapest accommodations are along Lombard Street. If you prefer to be out of the hustle and bustle, opt for lodgings on smaller side streets. Wherever you stay in this area, it's a short walk to the Marina, where sailboats bob on the bay and park goers fly kites.

$$$$ **⊞ Sherman House.** This magnificent Italianate mansion at
★   the foot of residential Pacific Heights is San Francisco's most luxurious small hotel. Rooms are individually decorated with Biedermeier, English Jacobean, or French Second Empire antiques. The decadent mood is enhanced by tapestry-like canopies over four-poster featherbeds, wood-burning fireplaces with marble mantels, and sumptuous bathrooms, some with whirlpool baths. The six romantic suites attract honeymooners from around the world, and the elegant in-house dining room serves superb French-inspired cuisine. Room rates include a full breakfast, as well as evening wine and hors d'oeuvres in the Gallery, an upstairs sitting room. ⊠ *2160 Green St., 94123,* ☎ *415/563–3600 or 800/424–5777,* FAX *415/563–1882. 8 rooms, 6 suites. Dining room, room service, in-room VCRs, piano, concierge, airport shuttle. AE, DC, MC, V.*

$$$–$$$$ **⊞ Union Street Inn.** Innkeeper David Coyle was a chef for
★   the Duke and Duchess of Bedford, England, and his partner Jane Bertorelli has been innkeeping for 15 years. With the help of her many family heirlooms, they've made this ivy-draped 1902 Edwardian a delightful B&B inn filled with antiques and unique artwork. Equipped with candles, fresh flowers, and wine glasses, rooms are very popular

with honeymooners. The private Carriage House, which has its own whirlpool tub, is separated from the main house by an old-fashioned English garden complete with lemon trees. An elaborate complimentary breakfast is served to guests in the parlor, in the garden, or in their rooms. Afternoon tea and evening hors d'oeuvres are also complimentary. Late sleepers should avoid the English Garden room, which can be noisy mornings. ✉ *2229 Union St., 94123,* ☎ *415/346–0424,* FAX *415/922–8046. 6 rooms. Breakfast room, no-smoking rooms, parking (fee). AE, MC, V.*

$$–$$$ 🏨 **Bed and Breakfast Inn.** Hidden in an alleyway off Union Street, between Buchanan and Laguna, this ivy-covered Victorian contains English country–style rooms full of antiques, plants, and floral paintings. Though the rooms with shared baths are quite small, they are inexpensive at $80 a night. The Mayfair, a private apartment above the main house, comes complete with a living room, kitchenette, and spiral staircase leading to a sleeping loft. The Garden Suite, a larger, more deluxe apartment, has a cozy country kitchen, whirlpool bath, and plenty of room for four guests. ✉ *4 Charlton Ct., at Union St., 94123,* ☎ *415/921–9784. 9 rooms, 5 with bath, 2 apartments. Breakfast room, parking (fee). No credit cards.*

$$–$$$ 🏨 **Hotel Del Sol.** Once a typical '50s-style motor court, the Hotel Del Sol has been converted into an anything-but-typical artistic statement playfully celebrating California's vibrant (some might say wacky) culture. The sunny courtyard and yellow and blue three-story building are candy for the eyes. Rooms face boldly striped patios, citrus trees, and a heated swimming pool and hammock under towering palm trees. Even the carports have striped dividing drapes. Rooms evoke a beach house feeling with plantation shutters, tropical-stripe bedspreads, and rattan chairs. Some rooms have brick fireplaces, and one named "The Sandbox" features bunk beds, child-friendly furnishings, toys, and games. There are even free kites for kids. ✉ *3100 Webster St., 94123,* ☎ *415/921–5520 or 877/433–5765,* FAX *415/931–4137. 47 rooms, 10 suites. In-room data ports, in-room safes, no-smoking rooms, pool, sauna, laundry service, concierge, free parking. AE, D, DC, MC, V.*

$–$$ 🏨 **Town House Motel.** What this family-oriented motel lacks in luxury and ambience, it makes up for in value: The sim-

ple rooms, most with refrigerators, are nicely furnished with
a southwestern pastel color scheme and lacquered-wood
furnishings. Continental breakfast in the lobby is complimentary. ⊠ *1650 Lombard St., 94123,* ☎ *415/885–5163
or 800/255–1516,* 🅵🅰🅇 *415/771–9889. 24 rooms. No-smoking rooms, airport shuttle, free parking. AE, D, DC, MC, V.*

Civic Center/Van Ness

Though the city's government buildings here have been hidden under scaffolding for the last few years, major projects
like the construction of the San Francisco Public Library
and the renovation of the War Memorial Opera House have
been completed, and the neighborhood is experiencing a
renaissance of sorts. Fine restaurants, including Jeremiah
Tower's famous Stars, flank Van Ness Avenue, and smaller,
hipper places have opened west of Van Ness Avenue on
Hayes Street.

$$$–$$$$ 🏨 **The Archbishop's Mansion.** Everything at the Arch-
  ★   bishop's Mansion is extravagantly romantic, starting with
the cavernous common areas, where a chandelier used in
the movie *Gone With the Wind* hangs above a 1904 Bech-
stein grand piano once owned by Noël Coward. The 15 guest
rooms, each named for a famous opera, are individually
decorated with intricately carved antiques; many have
Jacuzzi tubs or fireplaces. Though not within easy walk-
ing distance of many restaurants or attractions, its perch
on the corner of Alamo Square near the Painted Ladies—
San Francisco's famous Victorian homes—makes for a
scenic, relaxed stay. Enjoy the complimentary Continental
breakfast in the ornate dining room or in the privacy of your
own suite. There's also an afternoon wine service. ⊠ *1000
Fulton St., 94117,* ☎ *415/563–7872 or 800/543–5820,* 🅵🅰🅇
*415/885–3193. 10 rooms, 5 suites. Breakfast room, lobby
lounge, no-smoking rooms, in-room VCRs, piano, meet-
ing room, limited free parking. AE, MC, V.*

$$$–$$$$ 🏨 **Radisson Miyako Hotel.** Near the Japantown complex
and not far from Fillmore Street and Pacific Heights, this
pagoda-style hotel is popular with business travelers. Some
guest rooms are in the tower building; others are in the gar-
den wing, which has a traditional Japanese garden with a
waterfall. Japanese-style rooms have futon beds with tatami

mats, while Western rooms have traditional beds with mattresses—but all feature gorgeous Asian furniture and original artwork. Most have their own soaking rooms with a bucket and stool and a Japanese tub (1 ft deeper than Western tubs), and in-room shiatsu massages are available. The hotel's award-winning Yoyo Tsunami Bistro specializes in Asian fusion cuisine. ⊠ *1625 Post St., at Laguna St., 94115,* ☎ *415/922–3200 or 800/533–4567,* FAX *415/921–0417. 209 rooms, 9 suites. Restaurant, bar, in-room data ports, minibars, exercise room, laundry service and dry cleaning, business services. AE, D, DC, MC, V.*

$$$ ☲ **Hotel Majestic.** One of San Francisco's original grand hotels, and once the decade-long residence of screen stars Joan Fontaine and Olivia de Havilland, this five-story white 1902 Edwardian surrounds you with elegance. Most of the romantic guest rooms have gas fireplaces, a mix of French and English antiques, and either a large, hand-painted, four-poster canopied bed or two-poster bonnet twin beds; some have original claw-foot bathtubs. Afternoons bring complimentary sherry and homemade biscotti to the exquisite lobby, replete with black-marble stairs, antique chandeliers, plush Victorian chairs, and a white-marble fireplace. The hotel's Café Majestic has a turn-of-the-century San Francisco mood and an innovative menu of California cuisine with an Asian touch. Glass cases in the bar house a large collection of rare butterflies from Africa and New Guinea. ⊠ *1500 Sutter St., 94109,* ☎ *415/441–1100 or 800/869–8966,* FAX *415/673–7331. 51 rooms, 9 suites. Restaurant, bar, laundry service and dry cleaning, parking (fee). AE, DC, MC, V.*

$$$ ☲ **Inn at the Opera.** This seven-story hotel a block or so ★   from City Hall, Davies Hall, and the War Memorial Opera House has hosted the likes of Pavarotti and Baryshnikov, as well as lesser lights of the music, dance, and opera worlds. Behind the marble-floor lobby are rooms of various sizes, decorated with creamy pastels and dark wood furnishings. The bureau drawers are lined with sheet music, and every room is outfitted with terry robes, a microwave oven, a minibar, and a basket of apples. All rooms have queen-size beds, though the standard rooms are a bit cramped; larger rooms are more expensive. Continental breakfast is included in the room rate. A major attraction is the sumptuous, dimly

lighted Ovation restaurant. Stars congregate in its mahogany and green-velvet interior before and after performances. ⊠ *333 Fulton St., 94102,* ☎ *415/863–8400; 800/325–2708; 800/423–9610 in CA;* 🖅 *415/861–0821. 30 rooms, 17 suites. Restaurant, lobby lounge, room service, concierge, parking (fee). AE, DC, MC, V.*

The Airport

A construction boom near San Francisco International Airport during the mid-'80s brought several new luxury-class hotels to this rather bleak-looking area, where rates are about 20% less than those at in-town counterparts. Airport shuttle buses are provided by all of the following hotels. Because they cater primarily to midweek business travelers, airport hotels often cut weekend prices; be sure to inquire.

$$$$ 🏨 **Hotel Sofitel–San Francisco Bay.** Parisian boulevard lampposts, a Métro sign, and a kiosk covered with posters bring an unexpected bit of Paris to this bay-side hotel. The French-theme public spaces—the Gigi Brasserie, Baccarat Restaurant, and La Terrasse Bar—have a light, open, airy feeling that extends to the rooms, each of which has a minibar and writing desk. ⊠ *223 Twin Dolphin Dr., Redwood City 94065,* ☎ *650/598–9000 or 800/763–4835,* 🖅 *650/598–0459. 377 rooms, 42 suites. 2 restaurants, bar, lobby lounge, health club, laundry service, concierge, meeting rooms, free parking. AE, DC, MC, V.*

$$$–$$$$ 🏨 **Embassy Suites San Francisco Airport–Burlingame.** With
★   excellent service and facilities, this California mission–style hostelry is arguably the most lavish in the airport area. Set on the bay with up-close views of planes taking off and landing, it consists entirely of suites that open onto a nine-story atrium and tropical garden replete with ducks, parrots, fish, and a waterfall. Living rooms all have a work area, sleeper sofa, wet bar, television, microwave, and refrigerator. Rates include a full breakfast and evening cocktail. ⊠ *150 Anza Blvd., Burlingame 94010,* ☎ *650/342–4600 or 800/362–2779,* 🖅 *650/343–8137. 340 suites. Restaurant, bar, no-smoking rooms, room service, indoor pool, sauna, exercise room, concierge, business services, free parking. AE, DC, MC, V.*

$$\text{-}$$$$ ⊞ **Hyatt Regency San Francisco Airport.** The spectacular 29,000-square-ft, eight-story lobby atrium of this dramatic Hyatt Regency 2 mi south of the airport encloses a world of water, light, and air. You'll feel like you're outdoors and the weather is always perfect. This is the largest airport convention hotel in Northern California, boasting a high level of personal service for business and leisure travelers alike. Almost every service and amenity one could think of is here, including several dining options, athletic facilities, and entertainment options. Rooms are modern and well-equipped. Scalini serves upscale northern Italian fare. ⊠ *1333 Bayshore Hwy., Burlingame 94010,* ☎ *650/347–1234,* FAX *650/696–2669. 793 rooms, 42 suites. Restaurant, café, deli, lobby lounge, piano bar, sports bar, in-room data ports, no-smoking floor, room service, pool, outdoor hot tub, exercise room, jogging, laundry service and dry cleaning, concierge, business services, convention center, meeting rooms, airport shuttle, car rental, free parking. AE, D, DC, MC, V.*

$$\text{-}$$$ ⊞ **The Clarion.** This busy hotel 1 mi south of the airport is frequented by airline personnel. Respite from the bustle in the gigantic, glass-front lobby can be found in an adjoining garden area, where wrought-iron benches, a heated pool, and a whirlpool tub are set among pine trees. ⊠ *401 E. Millbrae Ave., Millbrae 94030,* ☎ *650/692–6363 or 800/223–7111,* FAX *650/697–8556. 440 rooms, 6 suites. Restaurant, bar, in-room data ports, no-smoking floors, room service, outdoor pool, outdoor hot tub, exercise room, jogging, meeting rooms, airport shuttle, parking (fee). AE, DC, MC, V.*

$ -$$ ⊞ **Red Roof Inn.** This five-story hotel, which attracts families and business travelers, underwent an extensive renovation in 1998. The reasonably priced rooms are plain but very clean, with light wood furnishings. Upper floors facing the airport and San Francisco have better views but are noisier when planes start flying early in the morning. ⊠ *777 Airport Blvd., Burlingame 94010,* ☎ *650/342–7772 or 800/843–7663,* FAX *650/342–2635. 212 rooms. Restaurant, no-smoking rooms, outdoor pool, free parking. AE, DC, MC, V.*

5 Nightlife and the Arts

THE ARTS

Updated
by Denise
M. Leto

The best guide to arts and entertainment events in San Francisco is the "Datebook" section, printed on pink paper, in the *San Francisco Sunday Examiner and Chronicle*. Also consult any of the free alternative weeklies (☞ Nightlife, *below*). For up-to-date information about cultural and musical events, call the **Convention and Visitors Bureau's Events Hotline** (☎ 415/391–2001).

Half-price, same-day tickets to many local and touring stage shows go on sale (cash only) at 11 AM from Tuesday to Saturday at the **TIX Bay Area** (☎ 415/433–7827) booth, on the Stockton Street side of Union Square, between Geary and Post streets. TIX is also a full-service ticket agency for theater and music events around the Bay Area (open Tuesday, Wednesday, and Thursday from 11 AM until 6 PM and Friday and Saturday until 7 PM).

The city's charge-by-phone ticket service is **BASS** (☎ 415/776–1999 or 510/762–2277), with one of its centers in the TIX booth (☞ *above*) and another at Tower Records (⊠ Bay St. at Columbus Ave., ☎ 415/885–0500), near Fisherman's Wharf. **City Box Office** (⊠ 153 Kearny St., Suite 401, ☎ 415/392–4400) has a downtown charge-by-phone service for many concerts and lectures. The opera, symphony, the San Francisco Ballet's *Nutcracker,* and touring hit musicals are often sold out in advance. Tickets are usually available within a day of the performance for other shows.

Dance

The **San Francisco Ballet** (⊠ 301 Van Ness Ave., ☎ 415/865–2000) has regained much of its luster under artistic director Helgi Tomasson, and both classical and contemporary works have won admiring reviews. The company's primary season runs from February to May. Its repertoire includes such full-length ballets as *Swan Lake* and *Sleeping Beauty*; its annual December presentation of the *Nutcracker* is one of the most spectacular in the nation. The company also performs bold new dances from such star choreographers as William Forsythe and Mark Morris, alongside modern classics by George Balanchine and Jerome

Robbins. Tickets and information are available at the **Opera House** (⊠ 301 Van Ness Ave., ☎ 415/865–2000).

Cal Performances and San Francisco Performances (☞ Music, *below*) are the area's leading importers of world-class dance troupes.

Approximately 30 of the Bay Area's estimated 200 ethnic dance companies and soloists perform at the **Ethnic Dance Festival** (⊠ Palace of Fine Arts Theatre, Bay and Lyon Sts., ☎ 415/474–3914), which takes place in June. Prices are modest.

The **Margaret Jenkins Dance Company** (☎ 415/826–8399) is a nationally acclaimed modern troupe. **Lines Contemporary Ballet** (☎ 415/863–3040) is a good bet for modern ballet. **Smuin Ballets/SF** (☎ 415/665–2222), led by former San Francisco Ballet Director Michael Smuin, is renowned for its fluidity and excitement. The company regularly integrates pop music into its performances. **Lawrence Pech Dance Company** (☎ 415/641–1423), formed in 1996, is considered a new gem in Bay Area dance. **ODC/San Francisco** (☎ 415/863–6606) mounts an annual Yuletide version of *The Velveteen Rabbit* at the Center for the Arts. The **Robert Henry Johnson Dance Company** (☎ 415/824–4782) mounts contemporary productions, usually at Yerba Buena Center for the Arts and Theatre Artaud. The **Dancers Group/Footwork** (☎ 415/824–5044) is a small but significant local company.

Film

The San Francisco Bay Area, including Berkeley and San Jose, is considered one of the nation's most important movie markets. Films of all sorts find an audience here. The area is also a filmmaking center: Documentaries and experimental works are produced on modest budgets, feature films and television programs are shot on location, and some of Hollywood's biggest directors (including George Lucas and Francis Ford Coppola) live in the city or, more often, in Marin County. In San Francisco about a third of the theaters regularly show foreign and independent films.

The **Castro Theatre** (✉ 429 Castro St., near Market St., ☎ 415/621–6120), designed by Art Deco master Timothy Pfleuger, is worth visiting for its decor alone; it also offers revivals as well as foreign and independent engagements. Across the bay, the spectacular Art Deco **Paramount Theatre** (✉ 2025 Broadway, Oakland, near 19th St. BART station, ☎ 510/465–6400) alternates between vintage flicks and live performances.

Foreign and Independent Films

Opera Plaza Cinemas (✉ 601 Van Ness Ave., at Golden Gate Ave., ☎ 415/352–0810). **Lumière** (✉ 1572 California St., near Polk St., ☎ 415/352–0810). **Clay** (✉ 2261 Fillmore St., at Clay St., ☎ 415/352–0810). **Bridge** (✉ 3010 Geary Blvd., near Masonic Ave., ☎ 415/352–0810). **Embarcadero Center Cinemas** (✉ 1 Embarcadero Center, Promenade level, ☎ 415/352–0810).

The **Roxie Cinema** (✉ 3117 16th St., ☎ 415/863–1087) specializes in film noir and new foreign and indie features. The avant-garde **Red Vic Movie House** (✉ 1727 Haight St., ☎ 415/668–3994) screens an adventurous lineup of contemporary and classic American and foreign titles in a funky setting. The **Cinematheque** (☎ 415/558–8129) splits its experimental film and video schedule between the **San Francisco Art Institute** (✉ 800 Chestnut St., ☎ 415/558–8129) and the **Yerba Buena Center for the Arts** (✉ 701 Mission St., between 3rd and Howard Sts., ☎ 415/978–2787).

The **Pacific Film Archive** (✉ University Art Museum, 2625 Durant Ave., Berkeley, ☎ 510/642–1124) screens a comprehensive mix of old and new American and foreign films.

Festivals

The **San Francisco International Film Festival** (☎ 415/931–3456) takes over several theaters for two weeks in late April and early May, primarily the Castro Theatre (☞ *above*) and the AMC Kabuki complex at Post and Fillmore streets. The festival schedules about 150 films from around the globe, many of them American premieres. Marin County's **Mill Valley Film Festival** (☎ 415/383–5256), in early October, is also renowned.

The **Film Arts Festival of Independent Cinema** (☎ 415/552–8760), in November, showcases Bay Area documentary and independent film talent. The **San Francisco International Lesbian and Gay Film Festival** (☎ 415/703–8650), the world's oldest and largest of its kind, takes place in late June at various venues. The **San Francisco Jewish Film Festival** (☎ 415/621–0556) takes place in July. Look for the **Asian American Film Festival** (☎ 415/863–0814) in March, and the **Latino Film Festival** (☎ 415/553–8135) in September. The **American Indian Film Festival** (☎ 415/554–0525) takes place in November at the Palace of Fine Arts Theater.

Music

San Francisco's symphony, opera, and ballet are all based in the Civic Center. The symphony and other musical groups also perform in the smaller, 928-seat Herbst Theatre in the War Memorial Building, the Opera's "twin" at Van Ness Avenue and McAllister Street. Musical ensembles can be found all over the city: in churches and museums, in restaurants and parks, not to mention in Berkeley and on the peninsula. Each October, concert halls, clubs, and churches throughout the city host the acclaimed **San Francisco International Jazz Festival** (☎ 415/398–5655), featuring jazz legends alongside world-class up-and-comers.

San Francisco Symphony. The symphony performs from September to May. Michael Tilson Thomas, who is known for his innovative programming of 20th-century American works, is the musical director. Occasional guest conductors include Hugh Wolff and Roger Norrington, with featured soloists of the caliber of Andre Watts, Midori, and Frederica von Stade. Special events include a summer festival built around a particular composer, nation, or musical period, and summer Pops Concerts at various venues. Tickets run $12–$100. ✉ *Davies Symphony Hall, 201 Van Ness Ave., at Grove St.,* ☎ *415/864–6000.*

Berkeley Symphony Orchestra. This East Bay ensemble has risen to considerable prominence under artistic director Kent Nagano's baton. The emphasis is on 20th-century composers from Messiaen to Zappa (including many world premieres), alongside more traditional pieces. The orchestra performs four concerts from August to June. ✉ *Zellerbach Hall, Telegraph Ave. and Bancroft Way, UC Berkeley campus,* ☎ *510/841–2800.*

Cal Performances. This series, running from August to June at various UC Berkeley campus venues, offers the Bay Area's most varied bill of internationally acclaimed artists in all disciplines, from classical soloists to the latest jazz, world music, theater, and dance ensembles. ✉ *Zellerbach Hall, Bancroft Way and Telegraph Ave., Berkeley,* ☎ *510/642–9988.*

San Francisco Performances. San Francisco's equivalent to Cal Performances brings an eclectic array of topflight global music and dance talents to various venues—mostly Civic Center's Herbst Theatre—from October to May. Recent guests have included Andre Watts, Wynton Marsalis, and John Williams. ☎ *415/398–6449.*

Philharmonia Baroque. This ensemble has been called a local baroque orchestra with a national reputation and the nation's preeminent group for performances of early music. Its season of concerts, from fall to spring, celebrates composers of the 17th and 18th centuries, including Handel, Vivaldi, and Mozart. ☎ *415/495–7445.*

Kronos Quartet. Twentieth-century works and a number of premieres make up the programs for this surprisingly avant-garde group, whose following includes both the young and mainstream, debunking all conceptions of string quartets as somber affairs. ☎ *415/731–3533.*

Old First Concerts. This well-respected Friday evening and Sunday afternoon series offers chamber music, vocal soloists, new music, and jazz. Phone for tickets or visit the TIX booth in Union Square (☞ *above*). ✉ *Old First Presbyterian Church, 1751 Sacramento St., at Van Ness Ave.,* ☎ *415/474–1608.*

Pops Concerts. Many members of the symphony perform in the summer Pops series in the 2,400-seat Davies Hall. The schedule includes light classics and Broadway, country, and movie music. Tickets cost as little as a few dollars. ✉ *Davies Symphony Hall, 201 Van Ness Ave., at Grove St.,* ☎ *415/864–6000.*

Stern Grove. The nation's oldest continual free summer music festival hosts Sunday afternoon performances of symphony, opera, jazz, pop music, and dance. The amphitheater is in a eucalyptus grove below street level; dress for cool weather. ⊠ *Sloat Blvd. at 19th Ave.,* ☎ *415/252–6252.*

42nd Street Moon Productions. This group produces delightful "semi-staged" revivals of rare chestnuts from Broadway's musical comedy golden age at the New Conservatory Theatre Center in irregularly scheduled miniseasons throughout the year. ⊠ *25 Van Ness Ave.,* ☎ *415/861–8972.*

Opera

San Francisco Opera. Founded in 1923, this world-renowned company has resided in the Civic Center's War Memorial Opera House since it was built in 1932. Over its season, the opera presents approximately 70 performances of 10 operas from September to December and June to July. The opera uses supertitles: Translations are projected above the stage during almost all non-English operas. Long considered a major international company and the most important operatic organization in the United States outside New York, the opera frequently embarks on coproductions with European opera companies. ⊠ *301 Van Ness Ave., at Grove St.,* ☎ *415/864–3330.*

Ticket prices range from about $22 to $145. Standing-room tickets ($10) are always sold at 10 AM for same-day performances, and patrons often sell extra tickets on the Opera House steps just before curtain time at face value or less. The full-time box office is at 199 Grove Street, at Van Ness Avenue.

Pocket Opera. This lively, modestly priced alternative to grand opera aims to bring opera to a broad audience. The concert performances of popular and seldom-heard works are mostly in English. Offenbach's operettas are frequently on the bill during the February–June season. Concerts are held at various locations. ☎ *415/575–1102.*

Lamplighters. This operatic alternative specializes in Gilbert and Sullivan but presents other light operas as well. The troupe performs at various venues including the Center for the Arts. ☎ *415/227–4797.*

Theater

San Francisco's theaters are concentrated on Geary Street west of Union Square, but a number of additional commercial theaters, as well as resident companies that enrich the city's theatrical scene, are within walking distance of this theater row. The three major commercial theaters are operated by the Shorenstein-Nederlander organization, which books touring plays and musicals, some before they open on Broadway.

The most venerable commercial theater is the **Curran** (✉ 445 Geary St., ☎ 415/551–2000). The **Golden Gate** is a stylishly refurbished movie theater (✉ Golden Gate Ave. at Taylor St., ☎ 415/551–2000), now primarily a musical house. The gorgeously restored 2,500-seat **Orpheum** (✉ 1192 Market St., near the Civic Center, ☎ 415/551–2000) is used for the biggest touring shows.

The city's major nonprofit theater company is the **American Conservatory Theater (ACT)**, which was founded in the mid-1960s and quickly became one of the nation's leading regional theaters. During its season from the early fall to the late spring, ACT presents approximately eight plays, from classics to contemporary works, often in rotating repertory. In December ACT stages a much-loved version of Charles Dickens's *A Christmas Carol*. The ACT ticket office is at 405 Geary Street (☎ 415/749–2228). Next door to ACT is its home, the **Geary Theater.**

The leading producer of new plays is the **Magic Theatre** (✉ Bldg. D, Fort Mason Center, Laguna St. at Marina Blvd., ☎ 415/441–8822). Once Sam Shepard's favorite showcase, the Magic presents works by the latest rising American playwrights, such as Neena Beber, Karen Hartman, and Claire Chafee.

Marines Memorial Theatre (✉ 609 Sutter St., at Mason St., ☎ 415/771–6900) offers touring shows plus some local performances. The **Stage Door Theater** (✉ 420 Mason St., ☎

no phone) is small but dependable. **Theatre on the Square** (⊠ 450 Post St., ☎ 415/433–9500) is a popular smaller venue. For commercial and popular success, nothing beats *Beach Blanket Babylon,* the zany revue that has been running since 1974 at North Beach's **Club Fugazi** (☞ Cabarets *in* Nightlife, *below*). Conceived by the late San Francisco director Steve Silver, it is a hilarious mix of cabaret, show-biz parodies, and tributes to local landmarks.

The **Lorraine Hansberry Theatre** (⊠ 620 Sutter St., ☎ 415/474–8800) specializes in plays by black writers. The **Asian American Theatre Company** (⊠ 1840 Sutter St., ☎ 415/440–5545) is dedicated to working with local actors. **A Traveling Jewish Theatre** (⊠ 470 Florida St., ☎ 415/399–1809) stages various productions, often with Jewish themes. **Theatre Rhinoceros** (⊠ 2926 16th St., ☎ 415/861–5079) showcases gay and lesbian performers. The two-stage **New Conservatory Theatre** (⊠ 25 Van Ness Ave., ☎ 415/861–8972) hosts the annual Pride Season focusing on contemporary gay- and lesbian-themed works. The **San Francisco Shakespeare Festival** (☎ 415/422–2222) offers free weekend performances from Labor Day to October in Golden Gate Park. A uniquely Bay Area summertime freebie is the Tony Award–winning **San Francisco Mime Troupe** (☎ 415/285–1717), whose politically leftist, barbed satires are hardly mime in the Marcel Marceau sense; they perform afternoon shows at area parks from July 4 weekend through September.

Avant-garde theater, dance, opera, and performance art turn up in a variety of locations, not all of them theaters. Major presenting organizations include **Theatre Artaud** (⊠ 450 Florida St., in the Mission District, ☎ 415/621–7797), in a huge, converted machine shop, and the **Yerba Buena Center for the Arts** (⊠ 3rd and Howard Sts., ☎ 415/978–2787), which schedules contemporary theater events, in addition to dance and music.

Notable venues for small-scale plays and experimental works include **George Coates Performance Works** (⊠ 110 McAllister St., ☎ 415/863–4130), **Intersection for the Arts** (⊠ 446 Valencia St., ☎ 415/626–2787), **The Marsh** (⊠ 1062 Valencia St., ☎ 415/826–5750), and **Climate Theatre** (⊠

285 9th St., ☎ 415/978–2345). Solo performers are a local staple and are annually spotlighted at the early fall **Solo Mio Festival,** which takes place at various venues (for information call Climate Theatre). Ground zero for absurdist theater is the **Exit Theatre** (✉ 156 Eddy St., ☎ 415/673–3847), which also presents the annual **Fringe Festival** (☎ 415/931–1094) in September.

Berkeley Repertory Theatre (☎ 510/845–4700), across the bay, is the American Conservatory Theatre's major rival for leadership among the region's resident professional companies. It performs an adventurous mix of classics and new plays from fall to spring in a modern, intimate theater at 2025 Addison Street, near BART's downtown Berkeley station. Tickets are available at the TIX booth in San Francisco's Union Square. **California Shakespeare Festival** (☎ 510/548–9666), the Bay Area's largest outdoor summer theater event, performs in an amphitheater east of Oakland on Gateway Boulevard, just off state Highway 24.

Though San Francisco lacks an outstanding year-round source for live family entertainment, two animal-free, acrobatically inclined new-vaudeville-style groups offer excellent annual shows. **Make-A-Circus** (☎ 415/242–1414), which tours to parks and rec centers statewide in the summer, invites kids to learn circus skills at intermission, then join in during the second act. **The New Pickle Circus** (☎ 415/487–7940) generally performs at indoor locales around Christmastime.

NIGHTLIFE

SAN FRANCISCO HAS A TREMENDOUS potpourri of evening entertainment, from ultrasophisticated cabarets to bawdy bistros that reflect the city's Gold Rush past. Although it's a compact city with the prevailing influences of some neighborhoods spilling into others, the following generalizations should help you find the kind of entertainment you're looking for. **Nob Hill** is noted for its plush piano bars and panoramic skyline lounges. **North Beach,** infamous for its topless and bottomless "dance clubs," has cleaned up its image considerably and yet still maintains a sense of its beatnik past in atmospheric bars and coffeehouses. **Fisherman's Wharf,** although touristy, is great for people-watching and attracts plenty of street performers. Tony **Union Street** is home away from home for singles in search of company. South of Market—**SoMa,** for short—has become a hub of nightlife, with a bevy of popular nightclubs, bars, and lounges in renovated warehouses and auto shops. The gay and lesbian scenes center around the **Castro District** and the clubs and bars along **Polk Street.** Twentysomethings and alternative types should check out the ever-funky **Mission District** and **Haight Street** scenes.

For information on who is performing where, check out the *San Francisco Chronicle*'s pink "Datebook" insert—or consult the *San Francisco Bay Guardian,* free and available in racks around the city, listing neighborhood, avant-garde, and budget-priced events. The *S.F. Weekly* is also free and packed with information on arts events around town. Another handy reference is the weekly magazine *Key,* offered free in most major hotel lobbies and at Hallidie Plaza (Market and Powell streets). For a phone update on musical and cultural events, call the **Convention and Visitors Bureau's Events Hotline** (☎ 415/391–2001).

With the exception of the hotel lounges and discos noted below, casual dress is the norm. A 1998 state law banned smoking in any indoor place of work—including all bars and clubs. In San Francisco, fines have been given out to people caught lighting up. Bars generally close between midnight and 2 AM. Bands and other performers usually begin between 8 PM and 11 PM. The cover charge at smaller clubs ranges from $3 to $10, and credit cards are rarely accepted. At the larger venues the cover may go up to $30, and tickets can often be purchased through **BASS** (☎ 415/776–1999 or 510/762–2277).

Bars

Ever notice how everyone looks so much better when you are visiting another town? Here's where the magic may happen for you.

Balboa Cafe (✉ 3199 Fillmore St., at Greenwich St., ☎ 415/ 921–3944), a jam-packed hangout for the young and up-wardly mobile crowd, is famous for its burgers and its sin-gle clientele.

Gordon Biersch Brewery and Restaurant (✉ 2 Harrison St., at the Embarcadero, ☎ 415/243–8246) is a favorite of the swinging twentysomething set on Friday. The upstairs din-ing room and microbrewery beer is a nightly draw for adults of all ages.

Hard Rock Cafe (✉ 1699 Van Ness Ave., at Sacramento St., ☎ 415/885–1699), part of the famous chain, is filled with a collection of rock-and-roll memorabilia that won't dis-appoint fans.

Harry Denton's (✉ 161 Steuart St., near the Embarcadero, ☎ 415/882–1333), one of San Francisco's liveliest, most upscale saloons, is packed with well-dressed young pro-fessionals. When dinner service is through, there are live bands and dancing after 8 PM Sunday through Thursday, after 10 PM Friday and Saturday.

Perry's (✉ 1944 Union St., at Laguna St., ☎ 415/922–9022), the most famous of San Francisco's singles bars, is usually jam-packed. You can dine here on great hamburgers as well as more substantial fare.

Cabarets

Traditional cabaret is no longer enjoying the strong come-back of recent years, but a few longtime favorites and al-ternative venues continue the tradition, and a new hot spot arrives occasionally to rejuvenate the San Francisco scene.

Club Fugazi (✉ 678 Green St., at Powell St., ☎ 415/421–4222) is most famous for *Beach Blanket Babylon,* a wacky musical revue that has become the longest-running show of its genre. A send-up of San Francisco moods and mores, *Beach Blanket* has run since 1974. Although the choreog-raphy is colorful, the singers brassy, and the songs witty, the real stars are the comically exotic costumes and famous ceiling-high "hats"—worth the price of admission in them-selves. Order tickets as far in advance as possible. The revue has been sold out up to a month in advance. Those under 21 are admitted only to the Sunday matinee.

Finocchio's (✉ 506 Broadway, near Columbus Ave., ☎ 415/982–9388), an amiable, world-famous club, has been generating confusion with its female impersonators since 1936. The scene at Finocchio's (open from Thursday to Saturday) is decidedly retro, which for the most part only adds to its charm.

The Marsh (✉ 1062 Valencia St., near 22nd St., ☎ 415/826–5750), in the Mission District, books an eclectic mix of alternative and avant-garde theater, performance art, comedy, and the occasional musical act, with an emphasis on solo performances and seldom-staged plays. The room is homey and dimly lighted, and you can purchase freshly baked treats and excellent coffee at intermission.

New Orleans Room (✉ 950 Mason St., at California St., ☎ 415/772–5259), in the Fairmont Hotel, has a somewhat tacky 1960s hotel-bar ambience. Still, it's a low-key place to enjoy a cocktail along with show tunes by the pianist.

Comedy Clubs

In the '80s it seemed as if every class clown or life-of-the-party type was cutting it up at a comedy club. The stand-up boom, like others from the decade, has gone bust, except for the two fine clubs listed below.

Cobb's Comedy Club (✉ 2801 Leavenworth St., at Beach St., ☎ 415/928–4320), in the Cannery, books such super stand-up comics as Jake Johannsen, Rick Overton, and Janeane Garofalo.

Punch Line (✉ 444 Battery St., between Clay and Washington Sts., ☎ 415/397–7573), a launching pad for the likes of Jay Leno and Whoopi Goldberg, features some of the area's top talents. Recent headliners have included Will Durst, Johnny Steele, and Dana Gould. Weekend shows often sell out. Buy tickets in advance at BASS outlets or from the club's charge line (☎ 415/397–4337). Eighteen and over only.

Dance Clubs

Some of the rock, blues, and jazz clubs listed below have active dance floors. Some also offer DJ dancing when live acts aren't on the stage. Below are several spots devoted solely to dancing.

DNA Lounge (⊠ 375 11th St., near Harrison St., ☎ 415/626–1409), a longtime, two-floor SoMa haunt, headlines alternative rock, funk, and hip-hop, as well as weekly theme nights. On Wednesday the DJs spin industrial and alternative rock; on Friday look for '70s tunes; Saturdays bring '80s favorites and swing music in the VIP lounge.

El Rio (⊠ 3158 Mission St., at Precita St., ☎ 415/282–3325) is a casual Mission District spot with salsa dancing on Sunday (from 4 PM), lounge music from around the world on Tuesday, Arab dance on Thursday, a global dance party on Friday, and live rock starting at 9 PM on weekends.

Metronome Ballroom (⊠ 1830 17th St., at De Haro St., ☎ 415/252–9000) is at its most lively on weekend nights, when ballroom, Latin, and swing dancers come for lessons and revelry. The ambience is lively but mellow at this alcohol-free spot.

Gay and Lesbian Nightlife

Lesbian Bars

For a place known as a gay mecca, San Francisco has always suffered a surprising drought of seven-days-a-week women's bars. The meager selection is augmented by a few reliable one-nighters; call ahead to verify scheduling. Younger lesbians and gays don't segregate themselves quite as much as the older set. You'll find mixed crowds at a number of the bars listed under Gay Male Bars, *below.*

Blondies' Bar and No Grill (⊠ 540 Valencia St., near 16th St., ☎ 415/864–2052), a mixed bar most of the week, plays host to "Red," a diverse all-women's night every Sunday.

The Box (⊠ 628 Divisadero St., ☎ 415/647–8258), a long-running one-nighter, features "Mixtress" Paige Hodel, who keeps the dressed-to-sweat crowd in constant motion with house, hip-hop, and funk sounds. For your $7 expect to find a mixed, increasingly male crowd shaking their collective bootie every Thursday night to 4 AM.

Club Q (⊠ 177 Townsend St., at 3rd St., ☎ 415/647–8258), a monthly (first Friday of every month) dance party from Paige Hodel's One Groove Productions, is geared to "women and their friends" and is always packed. The cover charge is $7, and doors open at 9 PM.

CoCo Club (⊠ 139 8th St., entrance on Minna St., ☎ 415/626–2337) offers a variety of theme nights, including a drag cabaret, a coed erotic cabaret, and a woman's speakeasy. Every other Friday is "In Bed with Fairy Butch," an all-women's dance night.

G Spot (⊠ 401 6th St., at Harrison St., ☎ 415/337–4962), at SoMa's End Up club, features Top 40, house, and R&B every Saturday from 9 PM; several top San Francisco DJs keep the mix lively.

Hollywood Billiards (⊠ 61 Golden Gate Ave., near Taylor St., ☎ 415/252–2419), a macho pool hall six nights a week, has become the unlikely host of a smoldering lesbian scene every Wednesday during its ladies' night. For women, a table costs just $5 for three hours.

The Lexington Club (⊠ 3464 19th St., at Lexington St., ☎ 415/863–2052) is where, according to the slogan, "Every night is ladies' night." This all-girl club is geared toward the younger lesbian set.

Gay Male Bars

"A bar for every taste, that's the ticket," was how the curious "documentary" *Gay San Francisco* described late-'60s nightlife here. Leather bars, drag-queen hangouts, piano bars, and bohemian cafés were among the many options for gay men back then. The scene remains just as versatile today. Unless otherwise noted, there is no cover charge at the following establishments.

THE SOMA SCENE

SF-Eagle (⊠ 398 12th St., at Harrison St., ☎ 415/626–0880) is one of the few SoMa bars that remains from the days before AIDS and gentrification. International leather legend Mister Marcus often drops by to judge the Mr. SF Leather, Mr. Leather Calendar, and innumerable other contests, most of which are AIDS benefits. The Sunday afternoon "Beer Busts" (3 PM–6 PM) are a social high point.

The Stud (✉ 399 9th St., at Harrison St., ☎ 415/252–7883) is still going strong after more than 30 years. Its DJs mix up-to-the-minute music with carefully chosen highlights from the glory days of gay disco. The ever-changing weekly schedule includes new wave, classic disco, funk, and rock. Tuesday is Trannyshack, a drag cabaret show.

IN THE CASTRO

The Café (✉ 2367 Market St., at 17th St., ☎ 415/861–3846) is in the heart of gay Castro. Always comfortable and often crowded with locals and visitors alike, it's a place where you can chat quietly or dance, as you please. The rare smoking deck means it's a favorite destination for friends of tobacco.

Café Flore (✉ 2298 Market St., at Noe St., ☎ 415/621–8579), more of a daytime destination, attracts a mixed crowd including poets, punks, and poseurs. You can mingle day and night at open-air tables or inside the glass walls over beer, wine, excellent coffee, or tea. A separate concessionaire serves surprisingly tasty food until 10 PM; breakfast is popular.

The Metro (✉ 3600 16th St., at Market St., ☎ 415/703–9750) is a semi-upscale bar with a balcony overlooking the intersection of Noe, 16th, and Market streets. Guppies (gay yuppies) love this place, especially since it has a fairly good restaurant adjoining the bar. Tuesday is Karaoke Night.

Midnight Sun (✉ 4067 18th St., at Castro St., ☎ 415/861–4186), one of the Castro's longest-standing and most popular bars, has riotously programmed giant video screens. Don't expect to be able to hear yourself think.

ON/NEAR POLK STREET

The Cinch (✉ 1723 Polk St., at Clay St., ☎ 415/776–4162), a neighborhood bar with pinball machines and pool tables, is one of several hosts of the gay San Francisco Pool Association's weekly matches.

Kimo's (⌧ 1351 Polk St., at Pine St., ☎ 415/885–4535), a laid-back club, has floor-to-ceiling windows that provide a great view of hectic Polk Street. On Friday and Saturday nights drag, cabaret, and comedy shows take place upstairs.

Motherlode (⌧ 1002 Post St., at Larkin St., ☎ 415/928–6006), around the corner from the Polk Street bars in the rough-and-tumble Tenderloin, is *the* place for transvestites, transsexuals, and their admirers, with frequent stage performances. If you're in town in December, be sure to check out the city's gaudiest Christmas display, right here.

N Touch (⌧ 1548 Polk St., at Sacramento St., ☎ 415/441–8413), a tiny dance bar, has long been popular with Asian–Pacific Islander gay men. In addition to videos, there's dancing to '70s and '80s tunes Monday nights and karaoke Tuesday and Sunday nights; male strippers perform Thursday night. A monthly drag show and go-go dancers on weekends round out the entertainment.

The Swallow (⌧ 1750 Polk St., at Clay St., ☎ 415/775–4152), for those tired of the young and the buff, is a quiet, posh bar that caters to an older gay male clientele. A pianist plays standards nightly beginning at 9 PM, and patrons are often welcome to croon along open-mike style.

AROUND TOWN

Alta Plaza Restaurant & Bar (⌧ 2301 Fillmore St., at Clay St., ☎ 415/922–1444) is an upper Fillmore restaurant-bar that caters to nattily dressed guppies and their admirers. Jazz musicians perform from Sunday to Thursday; a DJ takes over on weekends.

Esta Noche (⌧ 3079 16th St., near Valencia St., ☎ 415/861–5757), a longtime Mission District establishment, draws a steady crowd of Latino gays, including some of the city's wildest drag queens. The latter perform shows every Wednesday, Thursday, and Sunday night.

Lion Pub (⌧ 2062 Divisadero St., at Sacramento St., ☎ 415/241–0205), one of the community's more established enterprises, is a cozy neighborhood bar with an ever-changing array of antiques.

Finally, a travel companion that doesn't snore on the plane or eat all your peanuts.

When traveling, your MCI WorldCom Card is the best way to keep in touch. Our operators speak your language, so they'll be able to connect you back home—no matter where your travels take you. Plus, your MCI WorldCom Card is easy to use, and even earns you frequent flyer miles every time you use it. When you add in our great rates, you get something even more valuable: peace-of-mind. So go ahead. Travel the world. MCI WorldCom just brought it a whole lot closer.

You can even sign up today at www.mci.com/worldphone or ask your operator to make a collect call to 1-410-314-2938.

EASY TO CALL WORLDWIDE

1 Just dial the WorldPhone access number of the country you're calling from.
2 Dial or give the operator your MCI WorldCom Card number.
3 Dial or give the number you're calling.

Argentina	
To call using Telefonica	0-800-222-6249
To call using Telecom	0-800-555-1002
Brazil	**000-8012**
France ◆	**0-800-99-0019**
Ireland	**1-800-55-1001**
United Kingdom	
To call using BT	0800-89-0222
To call using CWC	0500-89-0222
United States	**1-800-888-8000**

For your complete WorldPhone calling guide, dial the WorldPhone access number for the country you're in and ask the operator for Customer Service. In the U.S. call 1-800-431-5402.

◆ Public phones may require deposit of coin or phone card for dial tone.

EARN FREQUENT FLYER MILES

American Airlines
AAdvantage®

Continental Airlines
OnePass

Delta Air Lines
SkyMiles

MILEAGE PLUS.
United Airlines

U·S AIRWAYS
DIVIDEND MILES

MCI WorldCom, its logo and the names of the products referred to herein are proprietary marks of MCI WorldCom, Inc. All airline names and logos are proprietary marks of the respective airlines. All airline program rules and conditions apply.

Fodor's

Distinctive guides packed with up-to-date expert
advice and smart choices for every type of traveler.

Fodor's. For the world of ways you travel.

Jazz

There's been a major revival in San Francisco's jazz scene, thanks largely to a new generation of local performers like the Broun Fellinis and Charlie Hunter, many of whom push the borders between jazz, hip-hop, funk, and reggae. Check the Rock, Pop, Folk, and Blues venues below for special jazz events. More regular options run the gamut from mellow restaurant cocktail lounges to hip SoMa venues.

Bruno's (✉ 2389 Mission St., at 19th St., ☎ 415/550–7455) is a slice of retro heaven in the Mission District. Huge red booths provide a comfy place to ogle the beautiful people ordering swanky cocktails. An excellent menu draws crowds, while two lounges attract rotating local jazz, swing, and retro bands. The surrounding neighborhood isn't the greatest. Take a taxi late at night.

Cafe du Nord (✉ 2170 Market St., at Sanchez St., ☎ 415/861–5016) hosts some of the coolest jazz, blues, and alternative sounds in town. The atmosphere in this basement poolroom bar could be called "speakeasy hip." The music, provided mostly by local talent, is strictly top-notch. Adrian Bermudez offers free salsa lessons Tuesday at 9 PM, and the fabulous Juanda introduces beginners to swing at 8 PM on Sunday—followed by a chance to strut your steps to live music.

Elbo Room (✉ 647 Valencia St., between 17th and 18th Sts., ☎ 415/552–7788) is a convivial spot to hear up-and-coming jazz acts upstairs, or to relax in the dark, moody bar downstairs. Thursday is dance night. Brazilian jazz, world music, and the occasional funk band round out the musical offerings.

Enrico's (✉ 504 Broadway, at Kearny St., ☎ 415/982–6223) was the city's hippest North Beach hangout after its 1958 opening. Following the retirement of famed owner Enrico Banducci—who also brought Woody Allen, Barbra Streisand, and Lenny Bruce to his late, lamented "hungry i" in the early '60s—the luster faded. Today it's hip once again, with an indoor/outdoor café, a fine menu (tapas and Italian), and mellow nightly jazz combos.

Jazz at Pearl's (✉ 256 Columbus Ave., near Broadway, ☎ 415/291–8255) is one of the few reminders of North Beach's

heady beatnik days. With mostly straight-ahead jazz acts
and dim lighting, this club has a mellow feel. The talent level
is remarkably high, especially considering that there is
rarely a cover.

Kimball's East (⊠ 5800 Shellmound St., Emeryville, ☎
510/658–2555), in an East Bay shopping complex just off
Highway 80, hosts such talents as Jeffrey Osborne, Tito
Puente, and Mose Allison. This supper club features an elegant interior and fine food.

Moose's (⊠ 1652 Stockton St., near Union St., ☎ 415/989–
7800), one of North Beach's most popular restaurants,
also features great sounds in its small but stylish bar area.
Combos play classic jazz nightly from 8.

330 Ritch Street (⊠ 330 Ritch St., at Townsend St., ☎ 415/
541–9574), a popular SoMa nightclub, blends stylish modern decor with an extensive tapas menu, a dance floor, and
live jazz acts. The club is closed on Monday and Tuesday.

Up and Down Club (⊠ 1151 Folsom St., between 7th and
8th Sts., ☎ 415/626–2388), a hip restaurant–cum–club
whose owners include supermodel Christy Turlington,
books emerging jazz artists downstairs and offers dancing
to a DJ upstairs every day except Sunday.

Yoshi's (⊠ 510 Embarcadero St., Oakland, ☎ 510/238–
9200) is one of the area's best jazz venues. J. J. Johnson,
Betty Carter, local favorite Kenny Burrell, Joshua Redman,
and Cecil Taylor have played here, along with blues and
Latin performers.

Piano Bars

You only have eyes for her . . . or him. Six quiet spots provide the perfect atmosphere for holding hands and making plans.

Masons (⊠ 650 Mason St., at California St., ☎ 415/772–
5233), an elegant restaurant in the Fairmont Hotel, has fine
jazz, show tunes, and standards by local and national talents.

Ovation (⊠ 333 Fulton St., near Franklin St., ☎ 415/553–
8100), in the Inn at the Opera Hotel, is a popular spot for

a romantic rendezvous. The focal point of this tastefully appointed, intimate restaurant-lounge is a crackling fireplace. A new menu features American grill specialties with an emphasis on seafood.

Redwood Room (⊠ 495 Geary St., near Taylor St., ☎ 415/775–4700), in the Clift Hotel, is an Art Deco lounge with a low-key but sensuous ambience. Klimt reproductions cover the walls, and mellow sounds fill the air.

Ritz-Carlton Hotel (⊠ 600 Stockton St., at Pine St., ☎ 415/296–7465) has a tastefully appointed lobby lounge where a harpist plays during high tea (weekdays 2:30–4:30, weekends 1–4:30). At 5:30, the lounge shifts to piano or a jazz trio for cocktails until 11 PM weeknights and 1 AM on weekends.

Washington Square Bar and Grill (⊠ 1707 Powell St., near Union St., ☎ 415/982–8123), affectionately known as the "Washbag" among San Francisco politicians and newspaper folk, hosts pianists performing jazz and popular standards nightly.

Rock, Pop, Folk, and Blues

In the hip SoMa neighborhood and elsewhere, musical offerings range from straight-up rock to retro jazz to utter cacophony.

Bottom of the Hill (⊠ 1233 17th St., at Texas St., ☎ 415/621–4455), in Potrero Hill, showcases some of the city's best local alternative rock. The atmosphere is ultra low-key, although the occasional blockbuster act—Alanis Morissette, Pearl Jam—has been known to hop on stage.

The Fillmore (⊠ 1805 Geary Blvd., at Fillmore St., ☎ 415/346–6000), San Francisco's most famous rock music hall, serves up a varied menu of national and local acts: rock, reggae, grunge, jazz, folk, acid house, and more. Ticket prices range from $10 to $27.50 and shows are all-ages. Avoid steep service charges by buying tickets at the Fillmore box office on Sunday between 10 and 4.

Freight and Salvage Coffee House (⊠ 1111 Addison St., Berkeley, ☎ 510/548–1761), one of the finest folk houses in the country, is worth a trip across the bay. Some of the most talented practitioners of folk, blues, Cajun, and blue-grass perform in this alcohol-free space, where tickets range from $10 to $15.

Great American Music Hall (✉ 859 O'Farrell St., between Polk and Larkin Sts., ☎ 415/885–0750) is a great eclectic nightclub. Here you can find top-drawer entertainment, with acts running the gamut from the best in blues, folk, and jazz to alternative rock. The colorful marble-pillared emporium (built in 1907 as a bordello) also accommodates dancing at some shows. Pub grub is available most nights.

John Lee Hooker's Boom Boom Room (✉ 1601 Fillmore St., at Geary Blvd., ☎ 415/673–8000) attracts old-timers and hipsters alike with top-notch blues acts and, occasionally, a show by the man himself. It's hard to go wrong no matter which night you go. Live bands play nightly.

Last Day Saloon (✉ 406 Clement St., between 5th and 6th Aves., ☎ 415/387–6343) hosts major entertainers and rising local bands with a varied schedule of blues, Cajun, rock, and jazz.

Lou's Pier 47 (✉ 300 Jefferson St., Fisherman's Wharf, ☎ 415/771–0377) is the place for cool music and hot Cajun seafood on the waterfront nightly.

Paradise Lounge (✉ 1501 Folsom St., at 11th St., ☎ 415/861–6906), a quirky lounge with three stages for eclectic live music and dancing, also has spoken-word shows on Sunday and beyond-the-fringe performances at the adjoining Transmission Theatre. It's a long-favored hangout for San Francisco's alternative scenesters, 21 and over only.

Red Devil Lounge (✉ 1695 Polk St., at Clay St., ☎ 415/921–1695) is a lush, trendy supper club featuring local and up-and-coming live funk, rock, and jazz acts, along with the occasional DJ dance night. Intimate tables line the narrow balcony overlooking the dance floor.

The Saloon (✉ 1232 Grant Ave., near Columbus Ave., ☎ 415/989–7666) is a favorite blues and rock spot among North Beach locals in the know.

Slim's (✉ 333 11th St., near Folsom St., ☎ 415/522–0333), one of SoMa's most popular nightclubs, specializes in national touring acts—mostly classic rock, blues, and jazz. Co-owner Boz Scaggs helps bring in the crowds and famous headliners.

The Warfield (⊠ 982 Market St., at 6th St., ☎ 415/775–7722), once a movie palace, is one of the city's largest rock-and-roll venues. There are tables and chairs downstairs, and theater seating upstairs. Performers range from Porno for Pyros to Suzanne Vega to Harry Connick Jr.

San Francisco's Favorite Bars

Locals patronize all the places listed, but there are several joints they hold near and dear.

Bix (⊠ 56 Gold St., off Montgomery St., ☎ 415/433–6300), a North Beach institution, is occasionally credited with the invention of the martini. It's just an urban legend, but you might believe it anyway at this lively, elegant bar and supper club.

Buena Vista Café (⊠ 2765 Hyde St., at Beach St., ☎ 415/474–5044), the wharf area's most popular bar, introduced Irish coffee to the New World—or so they say. Because it has a fine view of the waterfront, it's usually packed with tourists.

Cypress Club (⊠ 500 Jackson St., at Columbus Ave., ☎ 415/296–8555) is an eccentric restaurant-bar where sensual, '20s-style opulence clashes with Fellini/Dalì frivolity. The decor alone makes it worth a visit, but it's also a fine spot for a before-dinner or after-theater chat. Private dining rooms are available, and live jazz is played nightly.

Edinburgh Castle (⊠ 950 Geary St., near Polk St., ☎ 415/885–4074), cherished by Scots all over town, pours out happy and sometimes baleful Scottish folk tunes. You can work off your fish-and-chips and Scottish brews with a turn at the dart board or pool table. There's live music nightly from Wednesday to Saturday.

Harrington's (⊠ 245 Front St., near Sacramento St., ☎ 415/392–7595), a family-owned Irish saloon, is *the* place to be on St. Patrick's Day. The occasional Celtic rock group provides live music. The restaurant serves American fare except Sunday.

House of Shields (⊠ 39 New Montgomery St., at Market St., ☎ 415/392–7732), a saloon-style bar with a large wine cellar, attracts an older, Financial District crowd after work. Food is served until 8; the bar is closed on weekends.

Specs' (⊠ 12 Saroyan Pl., off Columbus Ave., ☎ 415/421–4112), a hidden hangout for artists and poets, is worth looking for. It's an old-fashioned watering hole, reflecting a sense of the North Beach of days gone by.

The Tonga Room (⊠ 950 Mason St., at California St., ☎ 415/772–5278), on the Fairmont Hotel's terrace level, has given San Francisco a beloved taste of high Polynesian kitsch for over 50 years. Fake palm trees, grass huts, a lake (three-piece combos play pop standards on a floating barge), and faux monsoons—courtesy of sprinkler-system rain and simulated thunder and lightning—create the ambience, which only grows more surreal as you quaff the selection of very potent cocktails. The weekday happy hour (5 PM–7 PM) features $6 Asian finger foods.

Tosca Café (⊠ 242 Columbus Ave., ☎ 415/391–1244), like Specs' and Vesuvio nearby, holds a special place in San Francisco lore. It has an Italian flavor, with opera, big band, and Italian standards on the jukebox, plus an antique espresso machine that's nothing less than a work of art. Known as a hangout for filmmaker Francis Ford Coppola and playwright and actor Sam Shepard (when they're in town), this place positively breathes a film noir atmosphere.

Vesuvio Café (⊠ 255 Columbus Ave., at Broadway, ☎ 415/362–3370), near the legendary City Lights Bookstore, is little altered since its 1960s heyday. The second-floor balcony is a fine vantage point for watching the colorful, slightly seedy Broadway–Columbus intersection.

Skyline Bars

San Francisco is a city of spectacular vistas. Enjoy drinks, music, and sometimes dinner with 360-degree views at any of the bars below.

Carnelian Room (⊠ 555 California St., at Kearny St., ☎ 415/433–7500), on the 52nd floor of the Bank of America Building, has what is perhaps the loftiest view of San Francisco's magnificent skyline. Enjoy dinner or cocktails at 779 ft above the ground; reservations are a must for dinner. The dress code requires jackets, but ties are optional.

Cityscape (⊠ 333 O'Farrell St., at Mason St., ☎ 415/771–1400), in the tower of the Hilton Hotel, offers dancing to Top 40, rock, and pop nightly until 1 AM.

Crown Room (⊠ 650 Mason St., at California St., ☎ 415/772–5131), the aptly named lounge on the 23rd floor of the Fairmont Hotel, is one of the most luxurious of the city's skyline bars. Riding the glass-enclosed Skylift elevator is an experience in itself.

Harry Denton's Starlight Room (⊠ 450 Powell St., ☎ 415/395–8595), on the 21st floor of the Sir Francis Drake Hotel, re-creates the 1950s high life with rose-velvet booths, romantic lighting, and staff clad in tuxes or full-length gowns. Whenever live combos playing jazz and swing aren't holding court over the small dance floor, taped Sinatra rules.

Top of the Mark (⊠ 999 California St., at Mason St., ☎ 415/392–3434), in the Mark Hopkins Hotel, was immortalized by a famous magazine photograph as a hot spot for World War II servicemen on leave or about to ship out. Now folks can dance to the sounds of that era on weekends—in a room with a view.

View Lounge (⊠ 55 4th St., at Market St., ☎ 415/896–1600), on the 39th floor of the San Francisco Marriott, is one of the loveliest of the city's skyline lounges. There's live piano music Monday–Wednesday beginning at 8:30 PM, and live R&B and blues Thursday–Saturday, from 9:30 PM to 1 AM.

Wine Bars

Why not forgo that frothy pint of beer for the more sedate pleasures of the vine? These spots offer tasting "flights," wines grouped together by type for contrast and comparison.

Hayes and Vine (⊠ 377 Hayes St., at Gough St., ☎ 415/626–5301) provides a warm lounge, dominated by a stunning white-onyx bar, where patrons relax and taste a few of the 550 wines available by the bottle, or the 40 selections served by the glass. Cheeses, pâtés, and caviar are served.

London Wine Bar (⊠ 415 Sansome St., at Sacramento St., ☎ 415/788–4811), a warm Financial District spot open on weekdays only, pours 40 wines by the glass from a cellar of 8,000 bottles.

6 Outdoor Activities and Sports

In San Francisco stockbrokers go surfing at noon, weathered old men brave chilling bay waters that not even Alcatraz prisoners could swim, and children flock to the Marina Green to fly kites against a backdrop of sailboats. The temperature rarely drops below 50°F, and parks, beaches, and open space are as plentiful as bay views and fresh air.

Updated
by Denise
M. Leto

BEACHES

Nestled in a quiet cove between the lush hills adjoining Fort Mason, the Municipal Pier, and the crowds at Fisherman's Wharf, **Aquatic Park** has a tiny but sandy beach with gentle water. The distant sound of bongo drums at Fisherman's Wharf adds to the peaceful mood. Keep an eye out for the swim-capped heads of members of the **Dolphin Club** (☎ 415/441–9329), who come every morning for a dip in these ice-cold waters. An especially large and raucous crowd jumps in on New Year's Day.

Baker Beach is a local favorite, with gorgeous views of the Golden Gate Bridge, the Marin Headlands, and the bay. Its strong waves make swimming a dangerous prospect, but the mile-long shoreline is ideal for fishing, building sand castles, or watching sea lions play in the surf. On warm days the entire beach is packed with bodies (some nude) taking in the sun. Look for Baker Beach in the southwest corner of the Presidio, beginning at the end of Gibson Road, which turns off Bowley Street. The beach has picnic tables, grills, and trails that lead all the way to the Golden Gate Bridge.

China Beach was named for the poor Chinese fishermen who once camped here (though it's sometimes marked on maps as James D. Phelan Beach). From April to October the tiny strip of sand offers swimmers gentle waters as well as changing rooms and showers. It's south of Baker Beach and bordered by the gleaming million-dollar homes of the Seacliff neighborhood.

South of the Cliff House, **Ocean Beach** stretches along the western (ocean) side of San Francisco. Though certainly not the city's cleanest beach, it's wide and sandy, stretching for miles and perfect for a long walk or jog. It's popular with surfers, but swimming is not recommended. On summer evenings after sundown, numerous bonfires form a string of lights along the beach; permits are not necessary.

PARTICIPANT SPORTS

Physical fitness and outdoor activities are a way of life in the Bay Area. Joggers, bicyclists, and aficionados of virtually all sports can often find their favorite pastimes within walking distance of downtown hotels. Golden Gate Park has numerous paths for runners, strollers, in-line skaters, and cyclists. Hiking paths with incredible ocean and bay views are abundant throughout the **Golden Gate National Recreation Area** (☎ 415/556–0560), which encompasses the San Francisco coastline, the Marin Headlands, and Point Reyes National Seashore. Lake Merced in San Francisco and Lake Merritt in Oakland are among the most popular areas for joggers; and Berkeley's sprawling Tilden Park is great for hiking and mountain biking.

For a listing of running races, tennis tournaments, bicycle races, and other participant sports, check the monthly issues of *City Sports* magazine, available free at sporting goods stores, tennis centers, and other recreational sites.

The most important running event of the year is the *San Francisco Examiner*'s **Bay-to-Breakers race** on the third Sunday in May. Up to 100,000 serious and not-so-serious runners dress up in crazy costumes—an adult version of Halloween, but twice the fun—and make their way from the Embarcadero to the Pacific Ocean. For race information and entry forms, call ☎ 415/512–5000 ext. 2222.

The **San Francisco Marathon & 5K** is held annually on the second Sunday in July. Beginning at the Golden Gate Bridge, the 26.2-mi marathon passes through downtown and up and over many of the city's steepest hills, drawing up to 7,000 runners. For entry forms and race information call ☎ 415/296–7111.

Bicycling

With its legendary hills, the city offers countless cycling challenges—but also plenty of level ground. A completely flat route, the **Embarcadero** gives you a clear view of open waters and the Bay Bridge on the pier side and sleek high-rises on the other. **Golden Gate Park** is a beautiful maze of roads and hidden bike paths, with rose gardens, lakes, waterfalls, museums, horse stables, bison, and ultimately, a spectacular view of the Pacific Ocean.

Boating and Sailing

A Day on the Bay (☎ 415/922–0227) is ideally located in San Francisco's small craft marina, just minutes from the Golden Gate Bridge and open waters. **Cass' Marina** (✉ 1702 Bridgeway, at Napa St., ☎ 415/332–6789), in Sausalito, has a variety of sailboats that can be rented as long as you have a qualified sailor in the group. **Stow Lake** (☎ 415/752–0347), in Golden Gate Park, has rowboat, pedal boat, and electric boat rentals. The lake is open daily for boating, but call for seasonal hours.

Fishing

Numerous fishing boats leave from San Francisco, Sausalito, Berkeley, Emeryville, and Point San Pablo. They go for salmon and halibut outside the bay or striped bass and giant sturgeon within the bay. In San Francisco lines can be cast from San Francisco Municipal Pier, Fisherman's Wharf, Baker Beach, or Aquatic Park. Trout fishing is possible at Lake Merced. You can rent rods and boats and buy bait at the **Lake Merced Boating and Fishing Company** (✉ 1 Harding Rd., ☎ 415/753–1101). One-day **licenses,** good for ocean fishing only, are available for around $10 on the charters. Some selected sportfishing charters are listed below. Most depart daily from Fisherman's Wharf during the salmon-fishing season, which is from March to October.

Lovely Martha's Sportfishing (✉ Fisherman's Wharf, Berth 3, ☎ 650/871–1691) offers salmon-fishing excursions as well as bay tours. **Wacky Jacky** (✉ Fisherman's Wharf, Pier 45, ☎ 415/586–9800) will take you salmon fishing in a sleek, fast, and comfortable 50-ft boat.

Fitness

The various branches of **24-Hour Fitness** (✉ 1200 Van Ness Ave., ☎ 415/776–2200; ✉ 350 Bay St., ☎ 415/395–9595; ✉ 3741 Buchanan St., ☎ 415/563–3535; ✉ 100 California St., ☎ 415/434–5080; ✉ 303 2nd St., at Folsom

St., ☎ 415/543–7808) are open to the public for a $15 drop-in fee. Facilities and services vary, but most of the clubs have saunas, Jacuzzis, and steam rooms as well as aerobics classes and a complete line of fitness equipment. The **Embarcadero YMCA** (⊠ 169 Steuart St., ☎ 415/957–9622), one of the finest facilities in San Francisco, has racquetball, a 25-m swimming pool, and aerobics classes. The $12 drop-in fee includes use of the sauna, steam room, and whirlpool plus a magnificent view of the bay. **Pinnacle Fitness** has two locations in the heart of the Financial District (⊠ 61 New Montgomery St., ☎ 415/543–1110; ⊠ 1 Post Plaza, at Market St., ☎ 415/781–6400). Both offer day passes for $15, which include use of the lap pool at the Post Plaza location and access to aerobics classes at both. The Post Plaza location offers boxing classes. The **World Gym** (⊠ 260 De Haro St., at 16th St., ☎ 415/703–9650), though a bit off the beaten track, is a must-see for bodybuilding enthusiasts; a lack of extensive spa facilities is a fair trade-off for the extensive weight-training and aerobics equipment. The day rate of $10 includes aerobics classes.

Golf

Call the **golf information line** (☎ 415/750–4653) to get detailed directions to the city's public golf courses or to reserve a tee time ($1 per player) up to seven days in advance. **Harding and Fleming parks** (⊠ Harding Rd. and Skyline Blvd., ☎ 415/664–4690) have an 18-hole, par-72 course and a 9-hole executive course, respectively. **Lincoln Park** (⊠ 34th Ave. and Clement St., ☎ 415/221–9911) has an 18-hole, par-68 course. **Golden Gate** (⊠ 47th Ave. between Fulton St. and John F. Kennedy Dr., ☎ 415/751–8987) is a 9-hole, par-27 course in Golden Gate Park just above Ocean Beach. **Sharp Park,** in Pacifica (⊠ Off Hwy. 1 at the Sharp Park Rd. exit, ☎ 650/359–3380), has 18 holes, par 72. **Glen Eagles Golf Course** (⊠ 2100 Sunnydale Ave., ☎ 415/587–2425) is a challenging 9-hole, par 36 course in McLaren Park. The **Presidio Golf Course** (⊠ 300 Finley Rd., near W. Pacific Ave. and Arguello Blvd., ☎ 415/561–4653) is an 18-hole, par-72 course managed by Arnold Palmer's company.

In-Line Skating

Golden Gate Park is one of the country's best places for in-line skating, with smooth surfaces, manageable hills, and lush scenery. John F. Kennedy Drive, which extends almost to the ocean, is closed to cars on Sunday, when it seems that the city's entire population heads to the park with in-line skates. **Skates on Haight** (✉ 1818 Haight St., ☎ 415/752–8376), near the Stanyan Street entrance to the park, offers free lessons (with a purchase) on Sunday morning and rents recreational and speed skates for $28 per day.

For beginners, the path along **the Marina** offers a 1½-mi (round-trip) easy route on a flat, well-paved surface, with glorious views of San Francisco Bay. **FTC Sports** (✉ 1586 Bush St., ☎ 415/673–8363) rents and sells in-line skates and protective gear. Advanced skaters may want to experience the challenge and take in the brilliant views of **Tilden Park** (☎ 510/843–2137 or 510/525–2233), in the Berkeley Hills. Follow signs to the parking lot at Inspiration Point. There you'll find the trailhead for Nimitz Way, a nicely paved 8-mi (round-trip) recreational path that stretches along a ridge overlooking San Francisco Bay and Mt. Diablo.

Skaters with a competitive edge can take part in the nightly pickup roller hockey games at **Bladium** (✉ 1050 3rd St., ☎ 415/442–5060), where a one-game pass costs $10 and gear can be rented for another $10. Reservations are required three days in advance.

Tennis

The San Francisco Recreation and Park Department maintains 132 public tennis courts throughout the city. All courts are free except those in Golden Gate Park. The largest set of free courts is at **Mission Dolores Park** (✉ 18th and Dolores Sts.), where six courts are available on a first-come, first-served basis. The 16 courts in **Golden Gate Park** (☎ 415/753–7001) are the only public ones for which you can make advance reservations. The fee for visitors is $6 for 90 minutes weekdays and $8 weekends; the resident fees are $4 and $6 respectively. For gorgeous views while you play, head up to the two **Buena Vista Park Courts** (✉ Buena Vista and Duboce Aves., ☎ 415/753–7001). Popular with Marina locals, the four courts at the **George Moscone Recreation Center** (✉ between Chestnut, Bay, Laguna, and Fillmore Sts., ☎ 415/753–7001) sometimes require a wait. Hidden among eucalyptus trees, the **Stern Grove**

Annex (✉ Sloat Blvd. at 19th Ave., ☎ 415/753–7001) only has two courts, but the park's beauty is a great distraction in case you have to wait.

SPECTATOR SPORTS

Baseball

The **San Francisco Giants** play at 3Com Park at Candlestick Point (✉ U.S. 101 at 3Com Park exit, 3 mi south of downtown, ☎ 415/467–8000 or 800/734–4268). Pacific Bell Park, a new downtown bayfront stadium, is scheduled to open in 2000. Game-day tickets are usually available at 3Com. City shuttle buses marked BALLPARK EXPRESS run from numerous bus stops throughout San Francisco; call **Muni** (☎ 415/673–6864) for the stop nearest you. 3Com Park is often windy and cold, so take along extra layers of clothing. The **Oakland A's** play at the Oakland Coliseum (✉ Coliseum Way off I–880, ☎ 510/638–0500 or 510/762–2255). Same-day tickets can usually be purchased at the stadium; on Wednesdays, tickets are often $1. To reach the Oakland Coliseum, take a BART train to the Coliseum stop.

Basketball

The **Golden State Warriors** play NBA basketball at the Oakland Coliseum Arena (✉ Coliseum Way off I–880) from November to April. Tickets are available through **BASS** (☎ 510/762–2277).

Football

The NFC West's **San Francisco 49ers** play at 3Com Park (✉ U.S. 101 at 3Com Park exit, 3 mi south of downtown), but the games are almost always sold out far in advance (☎ 415/468–2249). The AFC West's **Oakland Raiders** play at the Oakland Coliseum (✉ Coliseum Way off I–880). Except for high-profile games, tickets (☎ 510/762–2277) are usually available.

Hockey

Tickets for the NHL's **San Jose Sharks** are available from **BASS** (☎ 510/762–2277). Games are held at the San Jose Arena.

7 Shopping

SHOPPING IN SAN FRANCISCO means much more than driving to the local mall. Major department stores, swank fashion boutiques, discount outlets, art galleries, and specialty stores for crafts, vintage items, and more are scattered among the city's diverse neighborhoods. Most accept at least Visa and MasterCard, and many also accept American Express and Diners Club. Very few accept cash only, and policies vary on traveler's checks. The *San Francisco Chronicle* and *San Francisco Examiner* advertise sales. For smaller shops check the two free weeklies, the *San Francisco Bay Guardian* and *S.F. Weekly*, which can be found on street corners every Wednesday. Store hours vary slightly, but standard shopping times are between 10 and 5 or 6 on Monday, Tuesday, Wednesday, Friday, and Saturday; between 10 and 8 or 9 Thursday; and from noon to 5 on Sunday. Stores on and around Fisherman's Wharf often have longer hours in summer.

Updated by Denise M. Leto

Department Stores

Since most of San Francisco's department stores cluster around Union Square and the San Francisco Shopping Centre, shoppers can hit all the major players without driving or walking from one end of town to the other.

Macy's (⊠ Stockton and O'Farrell Sts., ☎ 415/397–3333; ⊠ 835 Market St., ☎ 415/296–4061) two downtown locations are behemoths. One branch—with entrances on Geary, Stockton, and O'Farrell streets—houses the women's, children's, and housewares departments. The men's department occupies its own building across Stockton Street. A branch carrying mostly furniture is just a block away on Market Street, inside the San Francisco Shopping Centre.

Neiman Marcus (⊠ 150 Stockton St., ☎ 415/362–3900), with its Philip Johnson–designed checkerboard facade, gilded atrium, and stained-glass skylight, is one of the city's most luxurious shopping experiences. Although its high-end prices raise an eyebrow or two, its biannual "Last Call" sales—in January and July—draw a crowd.

Nordstrom (✉ 865 Market St., ☎ 415/243–8500), the store that's known for service, is housed in a stunning building with spiral escalators circling a four-story atrium. Designer fashions, shoes, accessories, and cosmetics are specialties.

Saks Fifth Avenue (✉ 384 Post St., ☎ 415/986–4300) feels like an exclusive, multilevel mall, with a central escalator ascending past a series of designer boutiques. With its extensive lines of cosmetics and jewelry, this branch of the New York–based store caters mostly to women, though there is a small men's department on the fifth floor. The restaurant, also on the fifth floor, overlooks Union Square.

Major Shopping Districts

The Castro/Noe Valley

The Castro, often called the gay capital of the world, is also a major destination for nongay travelers. The Castro is filled with clothing boutiques, home accessory stores, and various specialty stores.

Especially notable is **A Different Light** (☞ Booksellers, *below*), one of the country's premier gay and lesbian bookstores. **Under One Roof** (✉ 2362-B Market St., ☎ 415/252–9430), housed in the same building as the Names Project, donates the profits from its home and garden items, gourmet foods, bath products, books, frames, and cards to northern California AIDS organizations.

Just south of the Castro on 24th Street, largely residential Noe Valley is an enclave of gourmet food stores, used-record and -CD shops, clothing boutiques, and specialty gift stores. At **Panetti's** (✉ 3927 24th St., ☎ 415/648–2414) you'll find offbeat novelty items, whimsical picture frames, journals, and more.

Chinatown

The intersection of Grant Avenue and Bush Street marks the gateway to Chinatown. Here, hordes of shoppers and tourists are introduced to 24 blocks of shops, restaurants, and markets—a nonstop tide of activity. Dominating the exotic cityscape are the sights and smells of food: crates of bok choy, tanks of live crabs, and hanging whole chickens.

Racks of Chinese silks, toy trinkets, colorful pottery, baskets, and carved figurines are displayed chockablock on the sidewalks, alongside fragrant herb shops. The **Great China Herb Co.** (⊠ 857 Washington St., ☎ 415/982–2195), where they add up the bill on an abacus, is one of the biggest herb stores around.

Embarcadero Center

Five modern towers of shops, restaurants, offices, and a popular movie theater—plus the Hyatt Regency Hotel—make up the Embarcadero Center, downtown at the end of Market Street. It's one of the few major shopping centers with an underground parking garage.

Fisherman's Wharf

A constant throng of sightseers crowds Fisherman's Wharf, and with good reason: Pier 39, the Anchorage, Ghirardelli Square, and the Cannery are all here, each with shops and restaurants, as well as outdoor entertainment—musicians, mimes, and magicians. Best of all are the wharf's view of the bay and its proximity to cable car lines, which can shuttle shoppers directly to Union Square.

The Haight

Haight Street is a perennial attraction for visitors, if only to see the sign at Haight and Ashbury streets—the geographic center of the Flower Power movement during the 1960s. These days, in addition to ubiquitous tie-dyed shirts, you'll find high-quality vintage clothing, funky jewelry, folk art from around the world, and reproductions of Art Deco accessories (☞ Vintage Fashion, Furniture, and Accessories, *below*). Used-book stores and used-record stores are another specialty.

Hayes Valley

Hayes Valley, just west of the Civic Center, is packed with art galleries and such unusual stores as **Worldware** (☞ Clothing for Men and Women, *below*), where everything from clothing to furniture to candles is made of organic materials.

Jackson Square

Gentrified Jackson Square is home to a dozen or so of San Francisco's finest retail antiques dealers, many of which occupy elegant Victorian-era buildings (☞ Antique Furniture and Accessories, *below*).

Japantown

Unlike the other ethnic enclaves of Chinatown, North Beach, and the Mission, the 5-acre **Japan Center** (⊠ between Laguna and Fillmore Sts. and Geary Blvd. and Post St.) is under one roof. The three-block complex includes an 800-car public garage and three shop-filled buildings. Especially worthwhile are the Kintetsu and Kinokuniya buildings, where shops and showrooms sell cameras, tapes and records, pearls, antique kimonos, *tansu* chests, paintings, and more.

The Marina District

Chestnut Street, one block north of Lombard Street and stretching from Fillmore to Broderick streets, caters to the shopping whims of Marina District residents, many of whom go for specialty foodstuffs.

The Mission

The diverse Mission District, home to large Latino and Asian populations, plus young artists and musicians of all nations, draws bargain hunters with its many used clothing, vintage furniture, and alternative bookstores. Shoppers can unwind with a cup of *café con leche* at one of a dozen or so cafés.

North Beach

Sometimes compared to New York City's Greenwich Village, North Beach is only a fraction of the size, clustered tightly around Washington Square and Columbus Avenue. Most of its businesses are small eateries, cafés, and shops selling clothing, antiques, and vintage wares. Once the center of the beat movement, North Beach still has a bohemian spirit that's especially apparent at **City Lights** (☞ Booksellers, *below*), where the beat poets live on.

Pacific Heights

Pacific Heights residents seeking practical services head straight for Fillmore Street between Post Street and Pacific Avenue, and Sacramento Street between Lyon and Maple streets, where private residences alternate with good bookstores, fine clothing and gift shops, thrift stores, and art galleries. A local favorite is the **Sue Fisher King Company**

(☞ Housewares and Accessories, *below*), whose quality home accessories fit right into this upscale neighborhood.

South of Market

The gritty warehouse and semi-industrial zone south of Market, often called SoMa, has the lowest prices. Dozens of **discount outlets,** most open daily, have sprung up along the streets and alleyways bordered by 2nd, Townsend, Howard, and 10th streets (☞ Outlets and Discount Stores, *below*). At the other end of the spectrum are the high-class gift shops of the **San Francisco Museum of Modern Art** and the **Center for the Arts Gift Shop** at Yerba Buena Gardens; both sell handmade jewelry and other great gift items (☞ Jewelry and Collectibles, *below*).

SoMa's South Park District, the so-called "Multimedia Gulch," is one of San Francisco's fastest-growing enclaves, home to much of the city's computer software industry, not to mention the 3rd Street offices of *Wired* magazine. Within the last few years the area has seen a proliferation of restaurants, designer boutiques, and specialty shops.

Union Square

Serious shoppers head straight to Union Square, San Francisco's main shopping area and the site of most department stores, including **Macy's, Neiman Marcus,** and **Saks Fifth Avenue** (☞ Department Stores, *above*). Also here are the **Virgin Megastore** (☞ Music, *below*), **F.A.O. Schwarz** and the **Disney Store** (☞ Toys and Gadgets, *below*), and **Borders Books and Music** (☞ Booksellers, *below*). Nearby are the pricey international boutiques of Emporio Armani, Versace, Hermès of Paris, Gucci, Alfred Dunhill, Louis Vuitton, and Cartier, plus a 50,000-square-ft Duty Free Shopping (DFS) Galleria. The streets around Union Square are currently enjoying a building boom, with such neighborhood newcomers as Levi's and Kenneth Cole, and heavyweight retailers Old Navy and Prada scheduled to open soon.

The **San Francisco Shopping Centre** (✉ 865 Market St., ☎ 415/495–5656), across from the cable car turnaround at Powell and Market streets, is distinguished by spiral escalators that wind up through the sunlit atrium. Inside are more than 35 retailers, including **Nordstrom** (☞ Department Stores, *above*), as well as a two-floor **Warner Bros.**

store (☎ 415/974–5254), with T-shirts, posters, and other mementos of the studio's past and present. At Post and Kearny streets, the **Crocker Galleria** (✉ 50 Post St., ☎ 415/393–1505) is a complex of 40 or so shops and restaurants that sit underneath a glass dome. The rooftop garden has dizzying views of the hectic streets and sidewalks below.

Union Street

Out-of-towners sometimes confuse Union Street—a popular stretch of shops and restaurants five blocks south of the Golden Gate National Recreation Area—with downtown's Union Square (☞ *above*). Union Street is a tiny, neighborhood version of Union Square. Nestled at the foot of a hill between Pacific Heights and the Marina District, the street is lined with high-end clothing, antiques, and jewelry shops, along with a few art galleries.

Outlets and Discount Stores

Christine Foley (✉ 430 9th St., ☎ 415/621–8126) offers discounts of up to 50% on sweaters for men, women, and children. In the small storefront showroom, pillows, stuffed animals, and assorted knickknacks sell at retail prices.

Cut Loose (✉ 690 Third St., ☎ 415/495–4581) specializes in loose, flowing casual clothing for women at discounted prices. Cotton and washable wool separates are between 20% and 40% off retail prices. Pick up a free outlet map to SoMa while you're there.

Esprit (✉ 499 Illinois St., at 16th St., south of China Basin, ☎ 415/957–2550), a San Francisco–based company, makes hip sportswear, shoes, and accessories, primarily for young women and children. Housed in a building as big as an airplane hangar, its bare-bones, glass-and-metallic interior feels somewhat sterile, but discounts of 30% to 70% keep customers happy.

Jeremy's New West (✉ 2 South Park Rd., ☎ 415/882–4929), at a very fashionable SoMa address, specializes in top-notch merchandise for both men and women, including Prada and Jil Sander, at drastic discounts—sometimes up to 50%.

Loehmann's (⊠ 222 Sutter St., near Union Sq., ☎ 415/982–3215), with its drastically reduced designer labels, is for fashion-conscious bargain hunters. This is not the place to learn who's who in the design world, as labels are often removed, but savvy shoppers will find astounding bargains.

Tower Records Outlet (⊠ 660 3rd St., ☎ 415/957–9660), the city's most prolific record chain, has found a ready-made market in the burgeoning SoMa neighborhood. Always crowded, the outlet has new and used CDs (mostly remainders), videotapes, and magazines at discount prices.

Specialty Stores

Antique Furniture and Accessories

The most obvious place to look for antiques is Jackson Square. Another option is the Design Center in Lower Potrero Hill, where a few retail showrooms are mixed in with those open only to the trade.

Asakichi Japanese Antiques (⊠ 1730 Geary Blvd., ☎ 415/921–2147) carries antique blue-and-white Imari porcelains and handsome *tansu* chests. Upstairs, **Shige Antique Kimonos** (⊠ 1730 Geary Blvd., on Webster St. Bridge between Kinokuniya and Kintetsu Bldgs., ☎ 415/346–5567) has antique hand-painted, silk-embroidered kimonos as well as cotton *yukatas* (lightweight summer kimonos), *obis* (sashes worn with kimonos), and other kimono accessories.

Dragon House (⊠ 455 Grant Ave., ☎ 415/781–2351; ⊠ 315 Grant Ave., ☎ 415/421–3693), unlike many other Chinatown stores that peddle cheap reproductions of Chinese art, sells genuine antiques and Asian fine arts. Its collection of ivory carvings, ceramics, and jewelry dates back 2,000 years and beyond—a fact that's especially evident in their prices.

Hunt Antiques (⊠ 478 Jackson St., ☎ 415/989–9531) feels like an English town house, with fine 17th- to 19th-century period English furniture, porcelains, Staffordshire pottery, and paintings. In the heart of Jackson Square, Hunt is surrounded by other worthwhile shops.

Origins (⊠ 680 8th St., ☎ 415/252–7089), in SoMa's Baker Hamilton Square complex, imports unusual collector's

items, Chinese furniture, porcelain, silk, and jade; antiques
here are up to 400 years old.

Telegraph Hill Antiques (✉ 580 Union St., ☎ 415/982–
7055), a tiny North Beach shop, stocks paintings and diverse objets d'art, including crystal, cut glass, Victoriana,
and bronzes. Among the store's collection of fine china is
a nice selection of Wedgwood pieces.

A Touch of Asia (✉ 1784 Union St., ☎ 415/474–3115) is
full of high-end 19th- and 20th-century Asian antiques,
mainly from Japan and Korea. Elm and cherrywood furniture, curio cabinets, and chests dominate. The store also carries Asian sculptures, prints and paintings, and antique vases.

Art Galleries

Art galleries are ubiquitous in San Francisco. While most
surround Union Square, Hayes Valley near the Civic Center has become another gallery enclave. Pick up a copy of
the free *San Francisco Arts Monthly* at the **TIX Bay Area**
booth in Union Square (✉ Stockton St., at Geary St., ☎
415/433–7827) for listings of galleries throughout the city.
For a quick overview, stop by **49 Geary Street,** which
houses three of the city's best galleries. Most galleries are
closed on Monday.

Art Options (✉ 372 Hayes St., ☎ 415/252–8334) specializes in contemporary glass crafts and one-of-a-kind non-
precious jewelry from local and nationally known artists.
A wide variety of affordable pieces are available.

Hespe Gallery (✉ 1764 Union St., ☎ 415/776–5918) is filled
with paintings and drawings by emerging Bay Area artists.
Styles include figurative, abstract, and realist. Owner Charles
Hespe is an instantly likable art enthusiast who equally de-
lights buyers and browsers.

San Francisco Women Artists Gallery (✉ 370 Hayes St., ☎
415/552–7392), a nonprofit organization, is run and staffed
by the women artists whose work is on display. In the tradition of the sketch clubs that began in the 1880s, in which
groups of artists shared and critiqued each other's work,
the SFWA displays sculptures, paintings, mixed-media
pieces, and video installations. All works are juried, and
prices are low.

Smile: A Gallery with Tongue in Chic (✉ 500 Sutter St., ☎ 415/362–3436) has a colorful collection of urban folk art, jewelry, mobiles, contemporary crafts, and wearable art.

Vorpal Gallery (✉ 393 Grove St., ☎ 415/397–9200), a nationally acclaimed gallery with a sister store in New York, carries old and new masters (Rembrandt and Picasso, for example), as well as Latin-American art and works by emerging artists.

Booksellers

All the major chains are represented in San Francisco. **Barnes & Noble** (✉ 2550 Taylor St., ☎ 415/292–6762) is near Fisherman's Wharf. The Union Square branch of **Borders Books and Music** (✉ 400 Post St., ☎ 415/399–1633) features four floors of books and magazines, topped off by a café where you can browse over a cappuccino. The **Virgin Megastore** (✉ 2 Stockton St., ☎ 415/397–4525) has a bookstore with a great selection of popular culture and travel books, as well as a large music department. Beyond the chains and blockbusters, countless small specialty bookstores delight bibliophiles.

Alexander Book Co. (✉ 50 2nd St., at Market St., ☎ 415/495–2992), with three floors of titles, is stocked with literature, poetry, and children's books, with a focus on hard-to-find works by men and women of color.

Booksmith (✉ 1644 Haight St., at Clayton St., ☎ 415/863–8688) is the place to shop for current releases, children's titles, international newspapers, and offbeat periodicals.

Bound Together Anarchist Book Collective (✉ 1369 Haight St., ☎ 415/431–8355), collectively run since 1976, is an old-school anarchist entity staffed entirely by volunteers, with profits contributed to anarchist projects. Books and magazines are divided into sections with such headings as Conspiracies, Drugs, Film & Media, Magick & Spirit, and Syndicalist Periodicals. There's also a small Spanish-language section.

City Lights (✉ 261 Columbus Ave., ☎ 415/362–8193), the city's most famous and historically interesting bookstore, is where the Beat renaissance of the 1950s was born, grew up, flourished, and then faltered. Poet Lawrence Ferlinghetti still remains active in the workings of his wooden three-story building in the heart of North Beach. Best known for poetry, contemporary literature and music, and translations of Third World literature, City Lights also carries books on nature, the outdoors, and travel.

A Clean Well-Lighted Place for Books (✉ 601 Van Ness Ave., ☎ 415/441–6670), in Opera Plaza, is a great place to while away the hours before or after a performance. Paperback literature and books on opera and San Francisco history are particularly well stocked.

A Different Light (✉ 489 Castro St., ☎ 415/431–0891), San Francisco's most extensive gay and lesbian bookstore, has books by, for, and about lesbians, gay men, bisexuals, and the transgendered. Subjects run the gamut from sci-fi and fantasy to religion and film criticism. There's also a large magazine section. A Different Light is the Castro's unofficial community center: Residents regularly phone for non-book information, and a rack in front is chock-full of flyers for local events.

Green Apple Books (✉ 506 Clement St., ☎ 415/387–2272), a local favorite since 1967, has one of the largest used-book departments in the city as well as new books in every field. Specialties are comic books, a history room, and a rare-books collection. Two doors down, at 520 Clement Street, you'll find a fiction annex which also sells CDs.

Kinokuniya Bookstore (✉ Kinokuniya Bldg., 1581 Webster St., 2nd Floor, ☎ 415/567–7625), in the heart of the Japan Center, may have the nation's finest selection of English-language books on Japanese subjects. A major attraction is the collection of beautifully produced graphics and art books.

Modern Times Bookstore (✉ 888 Valencia St., ☎ 415/282–9246), named after Charlie Chaplin's politically subversive film, carries quality literary fiction and nonfiction, much of it with a political bent. It also has a Spanish-language section and a wide variety of magazines. Author readings and public forums are held on a regular basis.

Rand McNally Map & Travel Store (✉ 595 Market St., ☎ 415/777–3131) will help you get from Tiburon to Tanzania, with an array of travel books and accessories, maps, and gift items. This is a great place to browse for topographical maps of California's national parks.

Stacey's (⊠ 581 Market St., ☎ 415/421–4687) has evolved from purely a professional-books specialist to include a large selection of general-interest books.

Children's Clothing

Dottie Doolittle (⊠ 3680 Sacramento St., ☎ 415/563–3244) is where Pacific Heights mothers buy Florence Eiseman dresses for their little women. Less pricey clothes for boys and girls, from infants to age 14, is also offered.

Mudpie (⊠ 1694 Union St., ☎ 415/771–9262; ⊠ 2220 Chestnut St., ☎ 415/474–8395) is filled with children's special-occasion wear, such as velvet dresses and handmade booties. Quilts, toys, and overstuffed child-size furniture make this a fun store for browsing. The Chestnut Street branch is geared toward tots two years old and younger.

Small Frys (⊠ 4066 24th St., ☎ 415/648–3954), in the heart of Noe Valley, carries a complete range of colorful cottons, mainly for infants but also for older children, including Oshkosh and many California labels.

Yountville (⊠ 2416 Fillmore St., ☎ 415/922–5050), an upscale store for children up to age eight, carries California and European designs.

Clothing for Men and Women

True to its reputation as the most European of American cities, San Francisco is sprinkled liberally with stores that feature traditional and trendy clothes by local designers. Shoppers eager to roam off the beaten track will find plenty of options.

Bella Donna (⊠ 539 Hayes St., ☎ 415/861–7182) offers more than just owner Justine Kaltenbach's self-designed hats. The oversize designer creations of New York's J. Morgan Puett, Los Angeles's Kevin Simon, and other top designers make this shop one of Hayes Valley's treasures. Don't miss the upstairs loft, which stocks only bridal garments.

Designers Club (⊠ 3899 24th St., ☎ 415/648–1057), in Noe Valley, specializes in local and national designers who use natural fibers and luxurious fabrics. In addition to clothing, there's a wide selection of hats and handbags.

Haseena (✉ 3024 Fillmore St., ☎ 415/775–6539; ✉ 526 Hayes St., ☎ 415/252–1104) is a fashionable boutique geared toward the urban-chic set. Both outlets sell clothing and accessories for women.

North Beach Leather (✉ 224 Grant Ave., ☎ 415/362–8300) is one of the city's best sources for high-quality leather garments—skirts, jackets, pants, dresses, and accessories.

Rolo (✉ 2351 Market St., ☎ 415/431–4545; ✉ 450 Castro St., ☎ 415/626–7171; ✉ 1301 Howard St., ☎ 415/861–1999; ✉ 25 Stockton St., ☎ 415/989–7656) is a San Francisco favorite, with men's and women's designer-brand denim, sportswear, shoes, and accessories that reveal a distinct European influence. The Howard Street location is Rolo's discount outlet.

Solo (✉ 1599 Haight St., ☎ 415/621–0342) is an opulent space with luxurious women's clothing, much of it designed in-house. One-of-a-kind pieces, custom work, and hard-to-fit sizes are offered along with jewelry, hats, and scarves.

Worldware (✉ 336 Hayes St., at Franklin St., ☎ 415/487–9030) is San Francisco's most ecologically correct store, featuring men's, women's, and children's clothing made from organic hemp, wool, and cotton. It also carries a potpourri of essential oils, skin care products, and aromatherapy candles.

Gourmet Food

Joseph Schmidt Confections (✉ 3489 16th St., ☎ 415/861–8682) may not be the city's most famous chocolatier (Ghirardelli wins that prize), but it *is* the classiest. Egg-shape truffles, which come in more than 30 flavors, are Schmidt's best-selling product. The store's real specialty is its stunning array of edible, often seasonal, sculptures—from chocolate windmills to life-size chocolate turkeys. Try the unique line of creme-filled chocolate rounds called slicks.

Just Desserts (✉ 248 Church St., ☎ 415/626–5774; ✉ 1000 Cole St., ☎ 415/664–8947; ✉ 3 Embarcadero Center,

☎ 415/421–1609; ✉ 836 Irving St., ☎ 415/681–1277; ✉ 3735 Buchanan St., ☎ 415/922–8675), a Bay Area favorite, carries chocolate velvet mousse cake, almond-flavored chocolate-chip blondies, and other deadly sins.

Lucca Delicatessen (✉ 2120 Chestnut St., ☎ 415/921–7873) is a bit of old Italy in the upscale Marina District. Take a number and wait your turn to choose from imported olive oils, homemade pastas and Italian sausages, and a wide selection of imported cheeses and prepared salads.

Molinari Delicatessen (✉ 373 Columbus Ave., ☎ 415/421–2337), billing itself as the oldest delicatessen west of the Rockies, has been making its own salami, sausages, and cold cuts since 1896. Other homemade specialties include meat and cheese ravioli, tortellini with prosciutto filling, tomato sauces, and fresh pastas.

Real Food Company (✉ 2140 Polk St., ☎ 415/673–7420; ✉ 1023 Stanyan St., ☎ 415/564–2800; ✉ 3939 24th St., ☎ 415/282–9500; ✉ 3060 Fillmore St., ☎ 415/567–6900), one of the city's most successful health food purveyors, offers some of the freshest produce outside the farmers' markets, as well as a full line of fresh fish, meat, and wines. The Polk Street branch has a small delicatessen.

Handicrafts and Folk Art

Small galleries throughout the city sell crafts, pottery, sculpture, and jewelry from countries around the world.

The Americas (✉ 1100 Folsom St., ☎ 415/864–4692) is a colorful SoMa outlet featuring such treasures as Pueblo and Navajo pottery, Day of the Dead artifacts, Zuni fetishes, brightly painted furniture, and wood carvings from Oaxaca.

Anokhi (✉ 1864 Union St., ☎ 415/922–4441), a small and inviting store, stocks clothing, home furnishings, and accessories from India, with fabrics block-printed by hand in Jaipur. You'll also find Indian tea caddies, scarves, and sarongs, as well as some locally made pottery.

Collage (✉ 1345 18th St., ☎ 415/282–4401) is a Potrero Hill studio-gallery that showcases the work of 80 Bay Area artists, including such handmade crafts as mosaic mirrors, earthquake-proof paper vessels, handblown glass objects, jewelry, and more.

Evolution (✉ 271 9th St., ☎ 415/861–6665; ✉ 805 University Ave., Berkeley, ☎ 510/540–1296) carries an unusual selection of furniture from Indonesia and, at its 9th Street store, pillows from Turkey. A wide range of Amish, Shaker, and Arts and Crafts reproduction furnishings can be found in its Berkeley location.

F. Dorian (✉ 388 Hayes St., ☎ 415/861–3191) has cards, jewelry, and crafts from Mexico, Japan, Italy, Peru, Indonesia, the Philippines, Africa, and Sri Lanka, as well as the glass and ceramic works of local craftspeople.

Folk Art International/Boretti Amber/Xanadu (✉ 140 Maiden La., ☎ 415/392–9999), three collections in one alluring space, offers a dazzling selection of Baltic amber jewelry, Latin-American folk art, Oaxacan wood carvings, and tribal art from Africa, Oceania, and Indonesia. Carved wood statues preside over a selection of utilitarian and ritual objects, including masks, sculptures, woven baskets, tapestries and textiles, tribal jewelry, and books on art and culture.

Global Exchange (✉ 4018 24th St., between Noe and Castro Sts., ☎ 415/648–8068; ✉ 2840 College St., Berkeley, ☎ 510/548–0370), a branch of the well-known nonprofit organization, sells handcrafted items from more than 40 countries. The staff works directly with village cooperatives and workshops: When you buy a Nepalese sweater, a South African wood carving, or a Pakistani cap, employees will explain the origin of your purchase.

Japonesque (✉ 824 Montgomery St., ☎ 415/391–8860), at Jackson Square, specializes in handcrafted wooden boxes, sculpture, paintings, and handmade glass from Japan and the United States.

Ma-Shi'-Ko Folk Craft (✉ Kinokuniya Bldg., 1581 Webster St., 2nd Floor, ☎ 415/346–0748) carries handcrafted pottery from Japan, including *mashiko,* the style that has been in production longer than any other. There are also masks and other antique and handcrafted goods, all from Japan.

Polanco (⊠ 393 Hayes St., ☎ 415/252–5753), a gallery that's devoted to showcasing the arts of Mexico, sells everything from antiques to traditional folk crafts to fine contemporary works. Brightly painted animal figures and a virtual village of Day of the Dead figures share space with religious statues and modern linocuts and paintings.

Soko Hardware (⊠ 1698 Post St., ☎ 415/931–5510), run by the Ashizawa family in Japantown since 1925, still specializes in beautifully crafted Japanese tools for gardening and carpentry.

Virginia Breier (⊠ 3091 Sacramento St., ☎ 415/929–7173), a colorful gallery of contemporary and traditional North American crafts, represents mostly emerging artists. Every piece in the store is one-of-a-kind, from jewelry to light fixtures to Japanese *tansus*.

Xela Imports (⊠ 3925 24th St., ☎ 415/695–1323), pronounced "Shay-La," carries merchandise from Africa, central Asia, and Bali, including jewelry, religious masks, fertility statuary, and decorative wall hangings. There are also textiles and jewelry from India.

Housewares and Accessories

Abitare (⊠ 522 Columbus Ave., ☎ 415/392–5800), a popular North Beach shop, has an eclectic mix of goods—soaps and bath supplies, candleholders, artsy picture frames, lamps, and one-of-a-kind furniture.

Biordi (⊠ 412 Columbus Ave., ☎ 415/392–8096), a family-run business for 50 years, imports hand-painted pottery directly from Italy—mainly Tuscany and Umbria—and ships it worldwide. Dishware sets can be ordered in any combination.

de Vera (⊠ 580 Sutter St., ☎ 415/989–0988; ⊠ 29 Maiden La., ☎ 415/788–0828) carries sleek decorative wares by owner and designer Federico de Vera. Both locations are brimming with household accessories and ephemera. The Sutter Street store also carries a line of de Vera's own furniture.

Fillamento (⊠ 2185 Fillmore St., ☎ 415/931–2224), a Pacific Heights favorite, has three floors of home furnishings—from dinnerware to bedding to bath and baby accessories—in addition to home office products. The eclectic mix of styles ranges from classic to contemporary.

Gordon Bennett (✉ 2102 Union St., ☎ 415/929–1172; ✉ Ghirardelli Sq., 900 N. Point St., ☎ 415/351–1172) carries housewares and ceramics made by local artists. The artfully designed wrought-iron garden sculptures and furniture, garden tools, and whimsical topiaries will tempt any homemaker.

Gump's (✉ 135 Post St., ☎ 415/982–1616), in business since 1861, is famous for its Christmas window displays and high-quality collectibles. One of the city's most popular stores for bridal registries, Gump's carries exclusive lines of dinnerware, flatware, and glassware, as well as Asian artifacts, antiques, and furniture.

Maison d'Etre (✉ 92 South Park, ☎ 415/357–1747), an up-scale shopping spot directly across from SoMa's popular Caffe Centro, carries eclectic luxury items for the home, including wrought-iron light fixtures, luxurious pillows, and ornate mirrors.

Only on Castro (✉ 518-A Castro St., ☎ 415/522–0122) showcases fine furnishings—mostly large pieces—with an international bent, including armoires, chests, and wrought-iron furniture from Malaysia and Indonesia.

Rayon Vert (✉ 3187 16th St., ☎ 415/861–3516), an artful boutique on the Mission's most stylish stretch of sidewalk, sells refurbished furniture and housewares with a unique rustic look. Items range from imposing armoires in metal and glass to such smaller items as antique candle holders and Christmas ornaments.

Scheuer Linen (✉ 340 Sutter St., ☎ 415/392–2813), a Union Square fixture since 1953, draws designers and everyday shoppers with luxurious linens for the bed, the bath, and the dinner table.

Sue Fisher King Company (✉ 3067 Sacramento St., ☎ 415/922–7276; ✉ 375 Sutter St., ☎ 415/398–2894) offers an assortment of decorative pillows and luxurious throws, Italian dinnerware, fine linens for the bedroom and kitchen, books on gardening and home decoration, and an aromatic mix of soaps, perfumes, and candles. Out back at the

Sacramento Street location is a small garden area chock-full of plants.

Terra Mia (✉ 2122 Union St., ☎ 415/351–2529; ✉ 4037 24th St., ☎ 415/642–9911) lets shoppers create ceramic pieces using their own designs and the store's art supplies and kiln. Teapots, mugs, goblets, and tiles are among the items that can be fired and ready to use within a week.

Used Rubber U.S.A. (✉ 597 Haight St., ☎ 415/626–7855; ✉ 2500 San Pablo Ave., Berkeley, ☎ 510/644–8339) uses recycled bicycle tubes to make handsome-looking handbags, wallets, and day planners. Other ecologically friendly wares include organic cotton clothing colored with natural dyes and housewares made from bicycle parts and computer circuit boards.

Z Gallerie (✉ 2071 Union St., ☎ 415/346–9000; ✉ 2154 Union St., ☎ 415/567–4891) carries modern home furnishings and trendy accessories: dinnerware, desks, chairs, lamps, and posters.

Jewelry and Collectibles

Center for the Arts Gift Shop (✉ 701 Mission St., ☎ 415/978–2710 ext. 168), in Yerba Buena Gardens, carries an outstanding line of handmade jewelry, ceramics, and crafts from both regional and national artists, as well as an unusual selection of glass tableware. Art publications, children's books, T-shirts, and cards top off the inventory.

Enchanted Crystal (✉ 1895 Union St., ☎ 415/885–1335) has a large collection of glass jewelry, ornaments, and other art pieces, many crafted by Bay Area artists. The store also has one of the largest natural quartz balls in the world—a full 12 inches in diameter.

Jade Empire (✉ 832 Grant Ave., ☎ 415/982–4498), one of the many fine jewelry stores in Chinatown, has uncut and pre-set jade, diamonds, and other gems as well as freshwater pearls, beads, porcelain dolls, and lanterns.

San Francisco Museum of Modern Art Gift Shop (✉ 151 3rd St., ☎ 415/357–4035) is famous for its exclusive line of watches and jewelry, as well as its artists' monographs, Picasso dishes, and other dinnerware. Posters, calendars, children's art-making sets and books, and art books for adults round out the offerings.

Shreve & Co. (⊠ 200 Post St., at Grant Ave., ☎ 415/421–2600), near Union Square, is one of the city's most elegant jewelers and the oldest retail store in San Francisco. Along with gems in dazzling settings, the store carries Baccarat crystal and Limoges porcelain figurines.

Union Street Goldsmith (⊠ 1909 Union St., ☎ 415/776–8048), a local favorite since 1976, prides itself on its wide selection of such rare gemstones as golden sapphires and violet tanzanite. You'll also find black Tahitian South Seas pearls. Three local jewelers work on the premises.

Wholesale Jewelers Exchange (⊠ 121 O'Farrell St., ☎ 415/788–2365), with 28 independent jewelers displaying their own merchandise, is the place to find gems and finished jewelry at less-than-retail prices.

ANTIQUE JEWELRY

Brand X (⊠ 570 Castro St., ☎ 415/626–8908) has vintage jewelry from the early part of the century, including a wide selection of estate jewelry and objets d'art.

Lang Antiques and Estate Jewelry (⊠ 323 Sutter St., ☎ 415/982–2213) carries vintage jewelry and small antique objects, including fine glass, amber, and silver.

Old and New Estates (⊠ 2181-A Union St., ☎ 415/346–7525) has antique and estate jewelry, crystal, objets d'art, antiques, and silver.

BEADS

The Bead Store (⊠ 417 Castro St., ☎ 415/861–7332) has a daunting collection—more than a thousand kinds of strung and unstrung beads, including such stones as lapis and carnelian, Czech and Venetian glass, African trade beads, Buddhist and Muslim prayer beads, and Catholic rosaries. Premade silver jewelry is another specialty, along with religious masks, figurines, and statuary from India and Nepal.

Yone (⊠ 478 Union St., ☎ 415/986–1424), in business since 1965, carries so many types of beads that the owner has lost track—somewhere between 5,000 and 10,000, he thinks. Individual beads, made of glass, wood, plastic, bone, sterling silver, and countless other materials, cost up to $100.

Music

Amoeba (✉ 1855 Haight St., ☎ 415/831–1200; ✉ 2455 Telegraph Ave., Berkeley, ☎ 510/549–1125), a longtime Berkeley favorite for new and used CDs, records, and cassettes at truly bargain prices, opened its doors to music-rich Haight Street in 1997. Both locations stock thousands of titles from punk and hip-hop to jazz and classical.

Aquarius Records (✉ 1055 Valencia St., ☎ 415/647–2272) began as *the* punk rock store in the 1970s. Owner Windy Chien carries on the tradition in the store's swank Mission District space, opened in 1996, which carries a large selection of dance music and experimental electronics.

Reckless Records (✉ 1401 Haight St., ☎ 415/431–3434) buys and sells rock and indie recordings, with a large section devoted to vinyl. Music-related magazines, T-shirts, and videos are also on sale.

Recycled Records (✉ 1377 Haight St., ☎ 415/626–4075), a Haight Street landmark, buys, sells, and trades a vast selection of used records, including obscure alternative bands and hard-to-find imports.

Streetlight Records (✉ 3979 24th St., ☎ 415/282–3550; ✉ 2350 Market St., ☎ 415/282–8000), a Noe Valley staple since 1973 with a branch on Market Street, buys and sells thousands of used CDs, with an emphasis on rock, jazz, soul, and R&B. There is plenty of vinyl for purists.

Virgin Megastore (✉ 2 Stockton St., ☎ 415/397–4525), the behemoth of Union Square, has hundreds of listening stations, a separate classical music room, and an extensive laser disc department, as well as a bookstore and a café overlooking Market Street.

Paper and Postcards

Kozo (✉ 1969 Union St., ☎ 415/351–2114) brings the art of papermaking to new levels. In addition to specialty papers made of materials like bark, papyrus, and bird's nest, Kozo imports hand-silk-screened papers directly from

Japan, Korea, and Italy. Also for sale are hand-bound photo albums and journals.

Quantity Postcard (⊠ 1441 Grant Ave., ☎ 415/986–8866) has a formidable collection of about 15,000 postcards, as well as autographed rock-concert posters by famed local artist Frank Kozik.

Sporting Goods

G & M Sales (⊠ 1667 Market St., ☎ 415/863–2855), a local institution since 1948, has one of the city's best selections of camping gear, with dozens of pitched tents on display, not to mention outerwear, hiking boots, ski goods, and fishing gear.

Lombardi's (⊠ 1600 Jackson St., ☎ 415/771–0600) has been serving its devoted clientele since 1948, with sports clothes and equipment, outerwear, camping goods, fitness equipment, and athletic footwear. Merchandise is discounted on a regular basis. Ski rentals are also available.

Niketown (⊠ 278 Post St., at Stockton St., ☎ 415/392–6453) is more a glitzy multimedia extravaganza than a sporting goods store, but it's still the best place in town to find anything and everything with that famous swoosh.

North Face (⊠ 180 Post St., ☎ 415/433–3223; ⊠ 1325 Howard St., ☎ 415/626–6444), a Bay Area–based company, is famous for its top-of-the-line tents, sleeping bags, backpacks, and outdoor apparel, including stylish Gore-Tex jackets and pants. The Howard Street store, an outlet, sells overstocked and discontinued items along with occasional seconds.

Patagonia (⊠ 770 N. Point St., near Fisherman's Wharf, ☎ 415/771–2050) specializes in technical wear for serious outdoors enthusiasts. Along with sportswear and casual clothing, the store carries body wear for backpacking, fly-fishing, kayaking, and the like.

Toys and Gadgets

The **Disney Store** (⊠ 400 Post St., ☎ 415/391–6866; ⊠ Pier 39, ☎ 415/391–4119), with its colorful walls and gargoyle-shape pillars, sells a potpourri of books, toys, clothing, and Disney collectibles. You'll also find Disney-oriented table- and glassware for sale.

F.A.O. Schwarz (⊠ 48 Stockton St., ☎ 415/394–8700), the San Francisco branch of the famed American institution, is every child's dream, with games, stuffed toys, motorized cars, model trains, and more.

Imaginarium (⊠ 3535 California St., ☎ 415/387–9885; ⊠ 3251 20th Ave., at the Stonestown Galleria, ☎ 415/566–4111), a California-based company, manufactures its own learning-oriented games and gadgets and imports European brands rarely found in larger stores.

Kitty Katty's (⊠ 3804 17th St., ☎ 415/864–6543) is where toy designer Flower Frankenstein works behind the counter to create wildly whimsical toys for "people old enough to know better." Thrill to the sight of an Elvis impersonator doll, squeeze a Squeaky Tiki Charm, and admire the changing displays of art and prints by local artists.

Sanrio (⊠ 39 Stockton St., ☎ 415/981–5568) is devoted to pop icon Hello Kitty and all her friends. You'll find a plethora of items ranging from lunch boxes to huge plush toys here.

Sharper Image (⊠ 532 Market St., ☎ 415/398–6472; ⊠ 680 Davis St., at Broadway, ☎ 415/445–6100; ⊠ Ghirardelli Sq., 900 N. Point St., ☎ 415/776–1443) carries high-end gadgets that bring out the child in everyone. Marvel over five-language translators, super-shock-absorbent tennis rackets, state-of-the-art speaker systems, Walkman-size computers, digital cameras, and more.

Uncle Mame (⊠ 2241 Market St., ☎ 415/626–1953) is a shrine to late 20th-century American pop culture. From cereal boxes to action figures, there's a collectible here for the kid inside every shopper.

Vintage Fashion, Furniture, and Accessories
FASHION

American Rag (⊠ 1305 Van Ness Ave., ☎ 415/474–5214) stocks a huge selection of new and used men's and women's clothes from the United States and Europe, all in excellent shape. They also carry shoes and such accessories as sunglasses, hats, belts, and scarves.

Buffalo Exchange (⊠ 1555 Haight St., ☎ 415/431–7733; ⊠ 1800 Polk St., ☎ 415/346–5726), part of a national chain, is one of the few stores where you can trade your used clothes for theirs. A wide selection of Levi's, leather jackets, sunglasses, and vintage lunch boxes are among the offerings. Some new clothes are available as well.

Crossroads Trading Company (⊠ 1901 Fillmore St., ☎ 415/775–8885; ⊠ 2231 Market St., ☎ 415/626–8989) buys, sells, and trades men's and women's new and used clothing, some of it vintage. Used contemporary sportswear is the specialty. Ties, belts, hats, and purses are also in stock.

Held Over (⊠ 1543 Haight St., ☎ 415/864–0818) carries an extensive collection of clothing, accessories, shoes, handbags, and jewelry from the 1940s, '50s, and '60s.

Rosalie's New Look (⊠ 782 Columbus Ave., ☎ 415/397–6246), in North Beach, has a huge selection of wigs and a full-service salon that specializes in '60s updos and extensions. The staff is friendly and happy to let shoppers try on as many wigs as they please.

FURNITURE AND ACCESSORIES

Another Time (⊠ 1586 Market St., ☎ 415/553–8900), an Art Deco–lover's delight, carries furniture and accessories by Heywood Wakefield and others. It's conveniently close to a host of other stores that stock vintage collectibles.

Cinema Shop (⊠ 606 Geary St., ☎ 415/885–6785), a tiny storefront, is jammed with more than 250,000 original posters, stills, lobby cards, and rare videotapes of Hollywood classics and schlock films.

Revival of the Fittest (⊠ 1701 Haight St., ☎ 415/751–8857) carries reproductions of such antique collectibles as clocks and vases along with cards, calendars, clothing, and jewelry.

San Francisco Rock Art and Collectibles (⊠ 1851 Powell St., ☎ 415/956–6749) takes you back to the 1960s with a huge selection of rock-and-roll memorabilia, including posters, handbills, and original art. Also available are posters from more recent shows—many at the legendary Fillmore Auditorium—with such musicians as George Clinton, Porno for Pyros, and Johnny Cash.

The Schlep Sisters (✉ 4327 18th St., near Castro St., ☎ 415/626–0581) stocks secondhand American dinnerware and glass, as well as such 1950s home accessories as cookie jars and salt-and-pepper shakers.

Zonal (✉ 568 Hayes St., ☎ 415/255–9307; ✉ 2139 Polk St., ☎ 415/563–2220), in the newly gentrified Hayes Valley, looks like an old garage, and the sign on the window reads ALWAYS REPAIR, NEVER RESTORE. The specialty here is Depression-era American country furniture—vintage porch gliders bump up against gardening equipment and old croquet sets. The Polk Street store specializes in larger furniture items, linens, and rugs.

Wine and Spirits

K&L Wine Merchants (✉ 766 Harrison St., ☎ 415/896–1734), a spacious, well-stocked, and reasonably priced showroom, has a friendly staff that promises not to sell what they don't taste themselves.

Mr. Liquor (✉ 250 Taraval St., ☎ 415/731–6222), in the city's Sunset District, is the only place to find well-known Bay Area importer Kermit Lynch's line of wines. It also has afternoon tastings: A sample of six to eight wines costs around $10.

PlumpJack Wines (✉ 3201 Fillmore St., ☎ 415/346–9870), a Marina favorite, has a well-priced, well-stocked array of hard-to-find California wines, along with a small selection of imported wines. You'll also find gift baskets here.

The **Wine Club** (✉ 953 Harrison St., ☎ 415/512–9086) is nothing much to look at, but it makes up for its barebones feel with a huge selection of wines at some of the best discount prices in the city. There's also a wide variety of wine paraphernalia, including glasses, books, openers, and decanters, along with caviar and cigars.

Wine House Limited (✉ 535 Bryant St., ☎ 415/495–8486) is a throwback to a different age: A highly informed and friendly sales staff is willing to help you find the perfect wine for any occasion. This SoMa store has especially good burgundy, Bordeaux, and Rhône selections and a small but well-chosen assortment of California wines, all at reasonable prices.

INDEX

A

A. P. Hotaling Company whiskey distillery, 21–22
Abitare (store), 161
Acquarello ✕, 84
Adelaide Inn ⌺, 101
Air travel, ix–x
Airport area lodging, 112–113
Airport transfers, x–xii
Alcatraz Island, 46–47
Alexander Book Co. (store), 155
Alta Plaza Restaurant & Bar, 130
American Conservatory Theater (ACT), 121
American/Contemporary restaurants, 63, 66, 67–68, 71, 72, 73–74, 75–76, 78–79, 80–81, 85, 87–88
American Indian Film Festival, 118
American Rag (store), 167
Americas (store), 159
Amoeba (store), 165
Angel Island, 47
Anokhi (store), 159
Another Time (store), 168
Ansel Adams Center for Photography, 16–17
Antiques, shopping for, 153–154
Apartment rentals, xx
Aqua ✕, 75
Aquariums, 56
Aquarius Records (store), 165
Aquatic Park, 140
Archbishops Mansion ⌺, 110
Art galleries, 38, 154–155
Art Options (gallery), 154
Asakichi Japanese Antiques (shop), 153
Asian American Film Festival, 118
Asian American Theatre, 122
Asian Art Museum, 55–56
Atherton House, 35
Automatic teller machines (ATMs), xxii

B

Baker Beach, 140
Balboa Cafe (singles bar), 125
Bank of America building, 23–24

Barbary Coast, 20–24. ☞ Also Financial District
Bars, 124–125, 127–130, 132–133, 135–138
Baseball, 145
Basketball, 145
Bay Area Rapid Transit (BART), xii
Beach Chalet ✕, 87
Beaches, 140–141
Bead Store, 164
Bed and Breakfast Inn ⌺, 109
Bed and-breakfasts, xx
Bella Donna (store), 157
Berkeley Repertory Theatre, 123
Berkeley Symphony Orchestra, 118–119
Bicycling, 141–142
Bijou ⌺, 100
Biordi (shop), 161
Bistro Aix ✕, 69
Bix ✕, 80, 135
Bizou ✕, 85–86
Black Cat ✕, 80–81
Blondies' Bar and No Grill, 127
Boat travel, xii
Boating and sailing, 141–142
Booksellers, 155–157
Booksmith (store), 155
Bottom of the Hill (nightclub), 133
Boulevard ✕, 72–73
Bound Together Anarchist Book Collective, 155
Box, The (lesbian bar), 127–128
Brand X (store), 164
Bridge (theater), 117
Broadway and Webster Street estates, 34
Brocklebank Apartments, 32
Bruno's (jazz club), 131
Buena Vista Café (bar), 135
Buena Vista Park, 44
Buffalo Exchange (store), 167–168
Bus travel, xii–xiii

C

Cabarets, 125–126
Cable Car Museum, 31

Cable car terminus, *10–11*
Cable car travel, *xiii*
Café, The (gay bar), *129*
Café de Young, *59*
Cafe du Nord (jazz club), *131*
Café Flore (gay bar), *129*
Café Marimba ✕, *70*
Cal Performances, *116, 119*
Calendar of events, *xxix–xxx*
California Academy of Sciences, *56, 58*
California Historical Society, *17*
California Palace of the Legion of Honor, *60*
California Shakespeare Festival, *123*
CalTrain, *xiii*
Campton Place ✕▣, *87, 92*
Cannery, the, *47*
Car rental, *xiii–xiv*
Car travel, *xiv–xv*
Carnelian Room (skyline bar), *23, 137*
Cartoon Art Museum, *17*
Cassis Bistro ✕, *69*
Castro District, *41–43*
Castro Theatre, *41–42, 117*
Center for the Arts, *17, 151, 163*
Cha Cha Cha ✕, *46*
Charanga ✕, *78*
Children, shopping for, *157, 166–167*
China Beach, *140*
Chinatown, *24–27*
Chinatown Gate, *25*
Chinese Culture Center, *25*
Chinese restaurants, *66–67, 73*
Christian Science church, *34–35*
Christine Foley (store), *152*
Cinch, The (gay bar), *129–130*
Cinema Shop, *168*
Cinematheque, *117*
City Hall, *37*
City Lights Bookstore, *28, 155–156*
Cityscape (skyline bar), *137*
Civic Center/Van Ness, *36–39*
Clarion, The ▣, *113*
Clay (theater), *117*
A Clean Well-Lighted Place for Books, *156*
Clift ▣, *93*
Climate, *xxix*
Climate Theatre, *122–123*
Clothing, shopping for, *157–158, 167–168*

Clothing for the trip, *xxii–xxiii*
Club Fugazi (cabaret), *121, 125–126*
Club Q (lesbian bar), *128*
Cobb's Comedy Club, *126*
CoCo Club (lesbian bar), *128*
Coit Tower, *28–29*
Coleman House, *35*
Collage (store), *159–160*
Comedy clubs, *126*
Commodore International ▣, *100*
Conservatory of Flowers, *58*
Consumer protection, *xv*
Cow Hollow. ☞ Marina/Cow Hollow
Credit cards, *xxii*
Crocker Galleria (stores), *152*
Crossroads Trading Company (store), *168*
Crown Room (skyline bar), *137*
Curran Theater, *121*
Customs and duties, *xv–xvii*
Cut Loose (store), *152*
Cypress Club ✕, *135*

D

DNA Lounge (nightclub), *127*
Dance, *115–116*
Dancers Group/Footwork, *116*
Dancing, *127*
Danilo Bakery, *28*
Department stores, *147–148*
Des Alpes ✕, *81*
Designers Club (store), *157–158*
de Vera (store), *161*
A Different Light (bookstore), *148, 156*
Discounts and deals, *xvii–xviii*
Disney Store, *166*
Dottie Doolittle (store), *157*
Dragon House (store), *153*
Dutch Windmill, *58–59*

E

Edinburgh Castle (bar), *135*
El Rio (dance club), *127*
Elbo Room (jazz club), *131*
Embarcadero, *15–20*
Embarcadero Center, *17–18, 149*
Embarcadero Center Cinemas, *117*
Embassy Suites San Francisco Airport–Burlingame ▣, *112*
Emergencies, *xviii*

Enchanted Crystal (store), *163*
Enrico's Sidewalk Café, *81, 131*
Eos Restaurant & Wine Bar ✕, *75–76*
Esprit (store), *152*
Esta Noche (gay bar), *130*
Ethnic Dance Festival, *116*
Evolution (store), *160*
Exit Theatre, *123*
Exploratorium (museum), *52*

F

F.A.O. Schwarz (toy store), *167*
F. Dorian (store), *160*
Fairmont Hotel, *31–32*
Farallon ✕, *89*
Fattoush ✕, *80*
Ferries, *xii, 47*
Ferry Building, *18*
Festivals and seasonal events, *xxix–xxx*
Fillamento (store), *161–162*
Fillmore (nightclub), *133*
Film, *116–118*
Film Arts Festival, *118*
Financial District, *20–24*
Finocchio's (cabaret), *126*
Fisherman's Wharf, *50*
Fishing, *142*
Fitness, *142–143*
Fleur de Lys ✕, *88*
Fog City Diner ✕, *71*
Folk Art International/Boretti Amber/Xanadu (gallery), *11, 160*
Food, shopping for, *158–159*
Football, *145*
Fort Mason Center, *52*
49 Geary Street (art galleries), *154*
42nd Street Moon Productions, *120*
42 Degrees ✕, *77–78*
450 Sutter Street, *11*
Franklin Street buildings, *34–35*
Freight and Salvage Coffee House, *133–134*
French restaurants, *69, 74, 78, 79–80, 81, 84, 85–86, 88*
Fringale ✕, *86*
Furniture, shopping for, *153–154, 168–169*

G

G & M Sales (store), *166*
G Spot (lesbian bar), *128*
Galleria Park 🖫, *97*
Gay and Lesbian Film Festival, *42, 118*
Gay and lesbian nightlife, *127–130*
Gay and lesbian travelers, *xviii–xix*
Gaylord's ✕, *83*
Geary Theater, *121*
George Coates Performance Works, *122*
Ghirardelli Square, *50*
Global Exchange (store), *160*
Globe ✕, *74*
Golden Gate Bridge, *53*
Golden Gate Fortune Cookies Co., *25–26*
Golden Gate Park, *54–56, 58–61*
Golden Gate Theater, *121*
Golf, *143*
Gordon Bennett (store), *162*
Gordon Biersch Brewery and Restaurant (singles bar), *125*
Grace Cathedral, *32*
Grant Avenue, *29*
Grant Plaza Hotel 🖫, *101*
Grateful Dead house, *44–45*
Great American Music Hall, *134*
Great China Herb Co. (store), *149*
Great Eastern ✕, *66*
Green Apple Books, *156*
Greens ✕, *71*
Gump's (store), *162*

H

Haas-Lilienthal House, *35*
Haight, The, *43–46*
Haight-Ashbury intersection, *45*
Hallidie Building, *11*
Handicrafts and folk art, shopping for, *159–161*
Harbor Court 🖫, *103*
Hard Rock Cafe, *125*
Harrington's (bar), *135–136*
Harris' ✕, *85*
Harry Denton's ✕, *72, 125*
Harry Denton's Starlight Room (skyline bar), *137*
Harvey Milk Plaza, *42–43*
Haseena (store), *158*

Hawthorne Lane ✕, 85
Hayes and Vine (wine bar), 138
Hayes Street Grill ✕, 68
Hayes Valley, shopping in, 149
Health concerns, xix
Held Over (store), 168
Herbst Theatre, 38
Hespe Gallery, 154
Hockey, 145
Hollywood Billiards, 128
Home exchanges, xx
Hostels, xx–xxi
Hotel Bohème 🏨, 107
Hotel Del Sol 🏨, 109
Hotel Diva 🏨, 99
Hotel Majestic 🏨, 111
Hotel Monaco 🏨, 93
Hotel Rex 🏨, 97
Hotel Sofitel–San Francisco Bay 🏨, 112
Hotel Triton 🏨, 97–98
Hotels, xxi–xxii
House of Shields (bar), 136
Housewares and accessories, shopping for, 161–163
Hunt Antiques (store), 153
Huntington 🏨, 104–105
Hyde Street Pier, 50
Hyatt Regency San Francisco Airport 🏨, 113

I

Il Fornaio ✕, 71–72
Imaginarium (store), 167
In-line skating, 143–144
Ina Coolbrith Park, 32–33
Indian restaurants, 83
Inn at the Opera 🏨, 111–112
Inn at Union Square 🏨, 98–99
Insurance, xix, xxiii
Intersection for the Arts, 122
Italian restaurants, 68, 69, 71–72, 77, 78, 81–82, 84, 88
Itinerary recommendations, 6–7
Izzy's Steak House & Chop House ✕, 70

J

Jackson Square, 21–22
shopping, 149–150
Jade Empire (store), 163

Japan Center, 150
Japanese restaurants, 75, 76
Japanese Tea Garden, 59
Japantown, 36, 76, 150
Japonesque (store), 160
Jardinière ✕, 67
Jazz, 131–132
Jazz at Pearl's, 131–132
Jeremy's New West (store), 152
Jewelry and collectibles, shopping for, 163–165
Jewish Film Festival, 118
Jewish Museum, 18
John Lee Hooker's Boom Boom Room (nightclub), 134
Joseph Schmidt Confections (store), 158
Julius' Castle ✕, 29
Just Desserts (store), 158–159

K

K & L Wine Merchants (store), 169
Kay Cheung Seafood Restaurant 🏨, 26
Kimball's East (jazz club), 132
Kimo's (gay bar), 130
Kinokuniya (bookstore), 156
Kitty Katty's (store), 167
Kong Chow Temple, 26
Kozo (store), 165–166
Kronos Quartet, 119
Kyo-ya ✕, 75

L

La Folie ✕, 84
La Taqueria ✕, 79
Laghi ✕, 77
Laguna Street Victorian houses, 35
Lamplighters Opera, 120–121
Lang Antiques and Estate Jewelry, 164
Laserium, 58
Last Day Saloon (nightclub), 134
Latin American restaurants, 78, 86
Latino Film Festival, 118
Lawrence Pech Dance Company, 116
Le Central ✕, 74
Lesbian bars, 127–128
Lexington Club (lesbian bar), 128
Lincoln Park and the Western Shoreline, 60–61

Lines Contemporary Ballet, *116*
Lion Pub (gay bar), *130*
Loehmann's (store), *153*
Lombard Street, *33*
Lombardi's (store), *166*
London Wine Bar, *138*
Lorraine Hansberry Theatre, *122*
L'Osteria del Forno ✕, *82*
Louise M. Davies Symphony Hall, *37–38*
Lou's Pier 47 (nightclub), *134*
Lucca Delicatessen, *159*
Luggage, rules for checking, *xxiii*
LuLu ✕, *86*
Lumière (theater), *117*

M

M. H. de Young Memorial Museum, *59*
Macy's (store), *147*
Magic Theatre, *121*
Maiden Lane, *11*
Maison d'Etre (store), *162*
Make-A-Circus, *122*
Mandarin Oriental ⊡, *102*
Margaret Jenkins Dance Company, *116*
Marina District/Cow Hollow, *51–54*
Marine Mammal Store & Interpretive Center, *51*
Marines Memorial Theatre, *121*
Mark Hopkins Inter-Continental Hotel, *33*, *105*
Marsh (theater), *122, 126*
Ma-Shi'-Ko Folk Craft (store), *160–161*
Masa's ✕, *88*
Masons (piano bar), *132*
Maykadeh ✕, *83*
McBean Gallery, *34*
McCormick & Kuleto's ✕, *83*
Mecca ✕, *63, 66*
Mediterranean restaurants, *68, 70, 82–83, 86*
Metro (gay bar), *129*
Metronome Ballroom (dance club), *127*
Mexican Museum, *52*
Mexican restaurants, *70, 79*
Middle Eastern restaurants, *80, 83*
Midnight Sun (gay bar), *129*
Mifune ✕, *76*

Mill Valley Film Festival, *117*
Mission District, *39–41*
Mission Dolores, *40–41*
Mr. Liquor (store), *169*
Modern Times Bookstore, *156*
Molinari Delicatessen, *159*
Money, *xxii*
Moose's ✕, *82–83, 132*
Morrison Planetarium, *58*
Motherlode (gay bar), *130*
Mudpie (store), *157*
Municipal Railway System (MUNI), *xii–xiii*
Murphy Windmill, *59*
Museo Italo-Americano, *52–53*
Museum of the City of San Francisco, *47*
Music, *118–120*
shopping for, *165*
venues, *133–135*

N

N Touch (gay bar), *130*
Names Project, *43*
National parks, *xxii, 51*
Natural History Museum, *56*
Neiman Marcus (store), *147*
New Asia ✕, *26*
New Conservatory Theatre, *122*
New Orleans Room (cabaret), *126*
New Pickle Circus, *122*
Niketown (store), *166*
Nob Hill, *30–34*
Nob Hill Lambourne ⊡, *106*
Noe Valley, *80, 148*
Nordstrom (store), *148*
North Beach, *27–30*
North Beach Leather (store), *158*
North Face (store), *166*
Northern Waterfront, *46–47, 50–51*

O

ODC/San Francisco (dance company), *116*
Ocean Beach, *140–141*
Old and New Estates (store), *164*
Old First Concerts, *119*
140 Maiden Lane, *11*
One Market ✕, *73*
Only on Castro (store), *162*
Opera, *120–121*

Opera Plaza Cinemas, *117*
Origins (store), *153–154*
Orpheum Theater, *121*
Outlets and discount stores, *152–153*
Ovation (piano bar), *132–133*

P

Pacific Film Archive, *117*
Pacific Heights, *34–36*
Pacific Stock Exchange, *22*
Packing for the trip, *xxii–xxiii*
Palace Hotel ⊠, *18–19, 102*
Palace of Fine Arts, *53–54*
Pan Pacific ⊠, *93, 96*
Panetti's (store), *148*
Paper and postcards, shopping for, *165–166*
Paradise Lounge (nightclub), *134*
Paramount Theatre, *117*
Park Hyatt ⊠, *103*
Passports and visas, *xxiii–xxiv*
Patagonia (store), *166*
Perry's ✕, *68–69, 125*
Petite Auberge ⊠, *100–101*
Philharmonia Baroque, *119*
Piano bars, *132–133*
Pier 39, *50–51*
Planetarium, *58*
Plouf ✕, *74–75*
PlumpJack Café ✕, *70*
PlumpJack Wines (store), *169*
Pocket Opera, *120*
Polanco (store), *161*
Polk Street, nightlife on, *124, 129–130*
Pops concerts, *119*
Portsmouth Square, *26–27*
Postrio ✕, *87–88*
Prescott Hotel ⊠, *96*
Presidio, *54*
Presidio Museum, *54*
Price charts
dining, 63
lodging, 92
Punch Line (comedy club), *126*

Q

Quantity Postcard (store), *166*
Queen Wilhelmina Tulip Garden, *59*

R

R & G Lounge ✕, *66–67*
Radisson Miyako Hotel ⊠, *110–111*
Rail travel, *xii, xiii*
Rand McNally Map and Travel Store, *156–157*
Randall Museum, *43*
Rayon Vert (store), *162*
Real Food Company (store), *159*
Reckless Records (store), *165*
Recycled Records (store), *165*
Red Devil Lounge (nightclub), *134*
Red Roof Inn ⊠, *113*
Red Vic Movie House, *117*
Red Victorian Peace Center bed & Breakfast ⊠, *45*
Redwood Room (piano bar), *133*
Revival of the Fittest (store), *168*
Rincon Center, *19*
Ripley's Believe It or Not, *50*
Ritz-Carlton Dining Room and Terrace ✕, *79–80*
Ritz-Carlton, San Francisco ⊠, *105–106, 133*
Robert Henry Johnson Dance Company, *116*
Rolo (store), *158*
Rosalie's New Look (store), *168*
Rose Pistola ✕, *81*
Rose's Café ✕, *69*
Roxie Cinema, *117*
Rubicon ✕, *73–74*
Running, *141*
Russian Hill, *30–34*

S

Safety, *xxiv*
Saints Peter and Paul (church), *29*
Saks Fifth Avenue (store), *148*
Saloon, The (nightclub), *134*
San Francisco African-American Historical and Cultural Center, *53*
San Francisco Art Institute, *33–34, 117*
San Francisco Arts Commission Gallery, *38*
San Francisco Ballet, *115–116*
San Francisco Brewing Company (pub), *22–23*
San Francisco Craft and Folk Art Museum, *53*

San Francisco International Film Festival, *117*

San Francisco International Jazz Festival, *118*

San Francisco Jewish Film Festival, *118*

San Francisco Lesbian and Gay International Film Festival, *118*

San Francisco Mime Troupe, *122*

San Francisco Museum of Modern Art (SFMOMA), *19, 53, 151, 163–164*

San Francisco Opera, *120*

San Francisco Performances, *115, 119*

San Francisco Performing Arts and Library, *38*

San Francisco Public Library, *38*

San Francisco Residence Club ☒, *106*

San Francisco Rock Art and Collectibles (store), *168*

San Francisco Shakespeare Festival, *122*

San Francisco Shopping Center, *151–152*

San Francisco Symphony, *118*

San Francisco Visitors Information Center, *14*

San Francisco Women Artists Gallery, *154*

San Francisco Zoo, *60–61*

San Remo ☒, *107–108*

Sanppo ✕, *76*

Sanrio (store), *167*

Scala's Bistro ✕, *88*

Schlep Sisters (store), *169*

Scheuer Linen (store), *162*

Seafood restaurants, *68, 72, 75, 83, 89*

SF-Eagle (gay bar), *128–129*

Shannon Court Hotel ☒, *99*

Sharper Image (store), *167*

Sherman House ☒, *108*

Shige Antique Kimonos (store), *153*

Shopping, *147–169*

Shreve & Co. (store), *164*

Sightseeing tours, *xxv*

Sir Francis Drake ☒, *98*

Skyline bars, *136–137*

Slanted Door ✕, *79*

Slim's (nightclub), *134–135*

Small Frys (store), *157*

Smile: A Gallery with Tongue in Chic (store), *155*

Smoking, *xxv*

Soko Hardware (store), *161*

Solo (store), *158*

Solo Mio Festival, *123*

South of Market (SoMa), *15–20*

Spanish restaurants, *84*

Specialty stores, *153–169*

Spec's (bar), *136*

Spectator sports, *145*

Sporting goods, shopping for, *166*

Spreckels Mansion, *35–36*

Stacey's (store), *157*

Stage Door Theater, *121–122*

Stars ✕, *67*

Steak houses, *70, 85*

Steinhart Aquarium, *56*

Stern Grove (concerts), *120*

Stow Lake, *60*

Streetlight Records (store), *165*

Strybing Arboretum & Botanical Gardens, *60*

Stud (gay bar), *129*

Sue Fisher King Company (store), *150–151, 162–163*

Sunset District, dining in, *87*

Swallow, The (gay bar), *130*

T

Tavolino ✕, *82*

Taxes, *xxv*

Taxis, *xxv–xxvi*

Telegraph Hill, *29-30*

Telegraph Hill Antiques (store), *154*

Telephones, *xxvi*

Tennis, *144–145*

Terra Mia (store), *163*

Thai restaurant, *76*

Theater, *121–123*

Theater Artaud, *122*

Theatre on the Square, *122*

Theatre Rhinoceros, *122*

Thep Phanom ✕, *76*

Thirstybear ✕, *86*

330 Ritch Street (jazz club), *132*

Ti Couz ✕, *78*

Tickets, *115*

Timing the visit, *xxviii–xxix*

Tipping, *xxvi*

TIX Bay Area, *14*

Tonga Room (bar), *32, 136*

Top of the Mark (skyline bar), *33, 137*

Tosca Café (bar), *136*

A Touch of Asia (store), *154*
Tours and packages, *xxvi–xxvii*
Tower Records Outlet, *153*
Town House Motel 🏨, *109–110*
Toys and gadgets, shopping for, *166–167*
Transamerica Pyramid, *23*
Travel agencies, *xxvii–xxviii*
A Traveling Jewish Theatre, *122*
Tuscan Inn 🏨, *107*
2223 ✕, *66*

U

Uncle Mame (store), *167*
Under One Roof (store), *148*
Underwater World, *51*
Union Square/Downtown, *10–11, 14–15*
Union Street, *124, 152*
Union Street Goldsmith (store), *164*
Union Street Inn 🏨, *108–109*
Up and Down Club (jazz club), *132*
Used Rubber U.S.A. (store), *163*
USS *Pampanito* (World War II submarine), *50*

V

Vegetarian restaurants, *71*
Venetian Carousel, *51*
Vesuvio Cafe (bar), *136*
Veterans Building, *38*
Victorian houses (Pacific Heights), *35*
Vietnamese restaurants, *79*
View Lounge (skyline bar), *137*
Vineria ✕, *78*
Vintage fashion, furniture, and accessories, shopping for, *167–169*
Virginia Breier (store), *161*
Virgin Megastore, *165*
Visitor information, *xxviii, 14, 51, 91*
Vivande Porta Via ✕, *77*
Vivande Ristorante ✕, *68*
Vorpal Gallery, *155*

W

W San Francisco 🏨, *104*
War Memorial Opera House, *38–39*
Warfield (rock club), *135*
Warner Bros. (store), *151–152*
Washington Square, *30*
Washington Square Bar & Grill, *133*
Waterfront Restaurant ✕, *72*
Wax Museum, *50*
Web sites, *xxviii*
Wells Fargo Bank History Museum, *23*
Westin St. Francis Hotel 🏨, *15, 96–97*
White Swan Inn 🏨, *99–100*
Whittier Mansion, *36*
Wholesale Jewelers Exchange, *164*
Wine and spirits, shopping for, *169*
Wine bars, *137–138*
Wine Club (store), *169*
Wine House Limited (store), *169*
Worldware (store), *149, 158*

X

Xela Imports (store), *161*

Y

Yank Sing ✕, *73*
Yerba Buena Gardens, *19–20*
Yerba Buena Center for the Arts, *117, 122*
Yone (store), *164–165*
Yoshi's (jazz club), *132*
Yountville (store), *157*

Z

Z Gallerie (store), *163*
Zarzuela ✕, *84*
Zonal (store), *169*
Zoo, *60–61*
Zuni Café & Grill ✕, *68*

Fodor's

Looking for a different kind of vacation?

Fodor's makes it easy with a full line of specialty guidebooks to suit a variety of interests—from adventure to romance to language help.

Fodor's. For the world of ways you travel.